POLITICAL TRADITIONS IN FOREIGN POLICY SERIES
Kenneth W. Thompson, Editor

The values, traditions, and assumptions undergirding approaches to foreign policy are often crucial in determining the course of a nation's history. Yet, the interconnections between ideas and policy for landmark periods in our foreign relations remain largely unexamined. The intent of this series is to encourage a marriage between political theory and foreign policy. A secondary objective is to identify theorists with a continuing interest in political thought and international relations, both younger scholars and the small group of established thinkers. Only occasionally have scholarly centers and university presses sought to nurture studies in this area. In the 1950s and 1960s the University of Chicago Center for the Study of American Foreign Policy gave emphasis to such inquiries. Since then the subject has not been the focus of any major intellectual center. The Louisiana State University Press and the series editor, from a base at the Miller Center of Public Affairs at the University of Virginia, have organized this series to meet a need that has remained largely unfulfilled since the mid-1960s.

EISENHOWER AND THE SUEZ CRISIS OF 1956

3 August 2000
West Point

Hal and Peggy Dawson,

Thank you for joining me on an exciting voyage through American history. I hope you will enjoy reading this book as much as I enjoyed writing it.

Cole C. Kingseed
Colonel, Infantry
U. S. Army

EISENHOWER AND
THE SUEZ CRISIS OF 1956

COLE C. KINGSEED

LOUISIANA STATE UNIVERSITY PRESS
Baton Rouge and London

Copyright © 1995 by Louisiana State University Press
All rights reserved
Manufactured in the United States of America
First printing
04 03 02 01 00 99 98 97 96 95   5 4 3 2 1

Designer: Amanda McDonald Key
Typeface: Sabon
Typesetter: Moran Printing, Inc.
Printer and binder: Thomson-Shore, Inc.

Library of Congress Cataloging-in-Publication Data
Kingseed, Cole C. (Cole Christian), 1949–
    Eisenhower and the Suez Crisis of 1956   /   Cole C. Kingseed.
       p.   cm. — (Political traditions in foreign policy series)
    Includes bibliographical references (p.   ) and index.
    ISBN 0-8071-1987-3 (alk. paper)
    1. Eisenhower, Dwight D. (Dwight David), 1890–1956.   2. Egypt—
    History— Intervention, 1956—Case studies.   3. United States—
    Foreign relations—1953–1961—Decision making—Case studies.
    I. Title.   II. Series.
    E836.K55   1995
    327.72056'09'045—dc20   95-1104
                                                                  CIP

For
my parents
William and Marilyn Kingseed
who instilled in me a sense of honor and patriotism
and
my family
Leslie, John, and Maura
who remain a constant source of happiness and inspiration

CONTENTS

ACKNOWLEDGMENTS

As in any project of this nature, there are contributions of many persons to acknowledge. First and foremost, I wish to thank Colonel Paul L. Miles (U.S. Army, Retired), who initially conceived this project in conjunction with a United States Military Academy symposium on the conduct of national security policy during the Truman and Eisenhower administrations. Professor Allan R. Millett, my dissertation adviser from The Ohio State University, patiently guided my initial research and served as a trusted friend, colleague, and mentor. In 1992 while on duty at the United States Naval War College in Newport, Rhode Island, I had the good fortune to work under the tutelage of Professor John Hattendorf, holder of the Ernest J. King Chair of Maritime History, and Dr. Robert S. Wood, holder of the Chester W. Nimitz Chair of National Security and Foreign Affairs. In completing an advanced research project on the Eisenhower presidency, I benefited from my professional association with Professor Richard Megargee, who generously served as my project adviser and offered many recommendations to assist me in focusing my research. So also did Professor George Baer, chairman of the Department of Strategy and Policy at the Naval War College and current holder of the Alfred Thayer Mahan Chair of Maritime Strategy. Although he was working on his own book on maritime history, Professor Baer critiqued my preliminary draft and suggested novel approaches to address the complex nature of crisis management and international relations. Special kudos also belong to Professor Ira Gruber of Rice University, who reviewed the entire manuscript with a trained historian's eye. Like Gruber, Colonel Robert A. Doughty, professor and head of the Department of History at the Military Academy at West Point, challenged me to look beyond the growing body of postrevisionist scholarship in exploring Eisenhower's leadership. More than one anonymous reviewer offered candid assessments of my work and offered constructive criticisms, the majority of which I readily followed. Many thanks go to Tom Branigar of the Dwight D. Eisenhower Library for his assistance on two visits to Eisenhower's boyhood home in Abilene, Kansas.

In addition to the Eisenhower Library, where I conducted the vast majority of my research, I used many other libraries: the Seeley G. Mudd Manuscript Library at Princeton University; the National Archives and the Library of Congress in Washington, D.C.; the Operational Naval Archives and the United States Marine Corps Historical Center at the Washington Navy Yard; and the United States Military Academy Library at West Point, New York. All the staffs gave freely of their time and assistance.

Among the contributors to the book, several individuals merit special mention. Andrew J. Goodpaster and Stephen Ambrose were kind enough to read preliminary drafts of this manuscript and to offer valuable suggestions to improve my analysis and methodology. It was Goodpaster's unwavering encouragement that brought this project to fruition. The superintendent of the United States Military Academy at West Point and the chairman of the Atlantic Council of the United States do not really have time to grant interviews and answer letters from brash, inquisitive scholars, but Goodpaster somehow found time from his busy schedule to do just that. In both capacities, he went out of his way to discuss his role as staff secretary and outlined the differences between daily operations and long-range planning. For his assistance and insights, I am particularly grateful. The same is true of Ambrose, whose biography of the thirty-fourth president serves as an inspiration to every student of the Eisenhower era. General Maxwell D. Taylor and Admiral Arleigh A. Burke (U.S. Navy, Retired) also donated their precious time to discuss the role of the Joint Chiefs of Staff during the Eisenhower years. C. Douglas Dillon, former American ambassador to France, did likewise and spent an afternoon providing an insider's perspective on American-European foreign relations at the time of the Suez crisis. The staff at the Louisiana State University Press was friendly, extraordinarily cooperative, and extremely helpful.

Last, and surely not least, my heartfelt thanks to my wife Leslie, who first encouraged me to write, and to my children, John and Maura, to whom this book is partially dedicated.

To those named above, and to all others whom I may have unintentionally omitted, I express my gratitude and thanks.

I alone am responsible for any errors that appear in this narrative. Such deficiencies are sins of omission rather than commission.

ABBREVIATIONS

DDE   Dwight D. Eisenhower

EP   Eisenhower Papers

EL   Eisenhower Library

RG   Record Group

EISENHOWER AND THE SUEZ CRISIS OF 1956

INTRODUCTION

During the last quarter century, American historians have produced an avalanche of monographs and literature on the Eisenhower presidency. The majority of contemporary authors viewed Eisenhower as an aging hero who seldom controlled the daily operations of the White House. Since the mid-1970s, however, there has been a steady rise in Eisenhower revisionism. At a four-day conference commemorating the centennial of Eisenhower's birth held at Gettysburg College in October 1990, historians, lecturers, and statesmen portrayed Eisenhower as a skilled practitioner of presidential politics who dominated the decision-making process. Indeed, the majority of scholars now concede that Eisenhower was a far more active chief executive than originally envisioned, although there remains considerable skepticism as to his effectiveness as president and crisis manager.

Some of the renewed interest stems from the fact that Eisenhower was unique in successfully maintaining the image of a popular chief executive throughout two terms as president.[1] Only Franklin Roosevelt matched Eisenhower's popularity at the end of his respective administration. So popular was the thirty-fourth president that for only two months in eight years did Eisenhower's support dip below 50 percent. Eisenhower also held the distinction of being the only president in the post–World War II era to depart office with greater popularity than when he entered it. Even Ronald Reagan, the self-styled "Great Communicator" and the only other two-term president since the passage of the twenty-second amendment, failed to match Eisenhower's popularity over the same period.

1. For a comprehensive analysis of Eisenhower's popularity, see John E. Mueller, "Presidential Popularity from Truman to Johnson," *American Political Science Review,* LXIV (March, 1970), 18–34. Concluding his presidential survey, Mueller states that if a president intended to leave office a popular chief executive, he would either have to be Dwight D. Eisenhower or resign the day after the inauguration. The Gallup polls for the decade consistently place Eisenhower as the most admired man in the United States during the period 1952–1960 inclusive. See George Gallup, *The Gallup Poll: Public Opinion, 1935–1971* (New York, 1972), II, 1462, 1486, 1536, 1584. See also Stephen Ambrose, "The Ike Age," *New Republic,* May 9, 1981, p. 26.

Another explanation for Eisenhower's immense popularity originated in what Fred I. Greenstein termed "the nostalgia for the alleged placid, uncomplicated nature of the 1950s."[2] Despite increased Cold War tension during his administration, Eisenhower presided over eight years of peace, prosperity, low inflation, and modest unemployment. Closely aligned with Greenstein was Arthur Schlesinger, Jr., who offered perhaps the best explanation of Eisenhower's refurbished reputation. Although the 1950s seemed somewhat stressful and bland at the time, the Eisenhower age appears in nostalgic retrospect a blessed decade of peace and harmony. Moreover, the successive faults of Eisenhower's successors—what Schlesinger termed Kennedy's activism, Johnson's obsessions, Nixon's crookedness, Ford's mediocrity, Carter's blah, and Reagan's stringent ideology—have given Eisenhower's virtues new value.[3] Of far greater significance to Eisenhower's reputation than presidential popularity or a yearning for simpler times, however, has been the recent declassification of federal archives previously closed by security classification or donor restriction. This availability of primary documents has generated a total reappraisal of Eisenhower, both as chief executive and as crisis manager, and has prompted renewed interest in Eisenhower's ability to manage the international crises that occurred during his administration.

The Suez crisis of 1956 is a valuable case for the examination of presidential decision making and crisis management. The president himself felt that no region of the world received as much of his close attention and that of his colleagues as did the Middle East. There against a background of new nations emerging from colonialism, in the thrusts of new Communist imperialism and complicated by the old implacable hatred between Israeli and Arab, the world faced a series of crises. These crises posed a constant test to United States' will, principle, patience, and resolve.[4] Suez was the most important Middle East crisis Eisenhower faced during his first administration. Between July and mid-December 1956, Eisenhower remained locked in a fierce diplomatic confrontation that pitted Egyptian nationalism against European imperialism. Caught in the middle was the American president, who pursued his own policies aimed at preventing the expanding influence of the Soviet Union into one of the world's most volatile regions. The Middle East crisis was cer-

2. Fred I. Greenstein, "Eisenhower as an Activist President: A Look at New Evidence," *Political Science Quarterly*, XCIV (Winter, 1979–80), 575.

3. See Arthur M. Schlesinger, Jr., *The Cycles of American History*, (Boston, 1986), 387–90, 392–95, 398–405, as quoted in Thomas G. Paterson, ed., *Major Problems in American Foreign Policy*, Volume II: *Since 1914* (Lexington, Mass., 1989), 470.

4. Dwight D. Eisenhower, *Waging Peace* (Garden City, 1965), 20.

tainly one of the most threatening during Eisenhower's two terms and was important and complex enough to engage the president in a full test of his ability as a crisis manager. In adopting a strategy that not only resulted in an awkward arrangement by which the Soviet Union supported the American position against armed aggression, but also brought the United States into direct confrontation with its traditional allies, Eisenhower faced strong opposition within both the executive and legislative branches in the execution of his policy. Throughout the crisis, he ensured that his judgments and decisions prevailed amid dissenting allies, contentious military chiefs, and political opposition in a presidential election year. The crisis also illuminated the president's perceptions of United States interests, the Soviet threat, Arab nationalism, and other international variables, such as the solidarity of the NATO alliance and America's "special relationship" with Israel. How Eisenhower managed the Suez problem, articulated a national policy, and developed a strategy to achieve his policy objectives is the focus of this study.

In developing a viable foreign policy toward the Middle East, Eisenhower remained convinced that he was pursuing a coherent policy founded on traditional American values of anticolonialism, self-determination, and resistance to tyrannical totalitarian regimes. In my opinion, he made many correct decisions during Suez, but he also made some significant mistakes. His policy achieved his short-term goal of halting foreign aggression against Egypt, but he failed to obtain his ultimate objective of lasting regional stability to prevent the conditions that were conducive to Soviet incursions into the Middle East. Whether his ultimate political objective was frustrated by events beyond his control is highly questionable, but his primary goal of ending hostilities was clearly within his power. I believe Eisenhower was certainly correct in opposing the use of force to settle the dispute; he was right in taking the lead in submitting the dispute to the United Nations; and he was correct in applying the full measure of American diplomatic and economic pressure against the aggressor states until they complied with the United Nations resolutions. At the same time, his own mistrust of Soviet intentions too frequently produced rigidity and aggression in pursuing Cold War objectives in regions where the United States confronted emerging Third World nationalism and Soviet opportunism. By focusing the American response to the Suez crisis through the lens of the Cold War magnifying glass, Eisenhower failed to identify accurately the competing forces that vied for supremacy in Egypt and the Middle East in 1956—emerging Egyptian nationalism and pan-Arabism against Western imperialism and colonialism. He also failed to inform his European allies of the extent to which he would oppose their use of armed force to resolve the crisis.

My own prejudices aside, I have attempted to avoid using late twentieth-century hindsight in making an assessment as to the correctness of Eisenhower's actions during the Suez crisis, for such attempts, to paraphrase Eisenhower biographer Stephen Ambrose, inevitably reveal more about the person doing the assessing than they do about Eisenhower.[5] Rather, I have sought to explain the Suez crisis as a study in presidential leadership, concentrating on what Eisenhower did and how and why he did it. My principal focus then, is on the president as a decision maker and director of foreign policy, not the crisis itself. Suez forms the backdrop for an analysis of how effectively Eisenhower dominated the decision-making apparatus of the federal government.

Where possible, I have relied on the president's own diary, his private letters and memoranda, and his official correspondence to give the reader Eisenhower's perspective of the events as they unfolded in the summer of 1956. Of immeasurable value to my research were the official Department of State records, the minutes of the National Security Council and cabinet meetings, presidential secretary Ann C. Whitman's diary and journals, and the written records and personal correspondence of Staff Secretary Andrew J. Goodpaster, whose staff memoranda are the *sine qua non* of any study on the Eisenhower presidency. Of complementary importance was the wide array of oral histories now on file at the Eisenhower Library in Abilene, Kansas. The combination of these records portrays the Suez crisis from the president's perspective far more accurately than the wealth of secondary literature and personal memoirs written in the immediate decades after the event and prior to the declassification of the primary documentation of the Eisenhower administration. By their nature, political memoirs, including those of the principal protagonists during the Middle East crisis of 1956, too frequently seek self-justification rather than objective analysis.

A brief word about organization. This study initially describes the broad outlines of Eisenhower's domestic and foreign policy, principally the New Look and its associated themes. The monograph next examines the team Eisenhower selected to implement his policies, as well as his orchestration of the executive departments of the federal government. A major premise of this analysis is that the manner in which a president organizes and supervises the decision-making apparatus has a profound impact on the successful attainment of political goals. Consequently, I have provided the reader a short synopsis of the Eisenhower White House, the leading statesmen of the period, their relationship with the president,

5. Stephen Ambrose, *Eisenhower: The President* (New York, 1984), 618.

as well as the formal and informal advisory agencies that Eisenhower employed in his management of the Suez crisis. Succeeding chapters examine the effectiveness of his managerial style in directing foreign policy, with particular emphasis on the Middle East crisis.

I also have frequently referred to the foreign leaders whose actions affected Eisenhower's policies, principally Prime Minister Anthony Eden of Great Britain and Premier Guy Mollet of France. Throughout the crisis, their actions were constant sources of anxiety and frustration to Eisenhower as he directed American foreign policy. In my opinion, this perspective complements, rather than detracts from, my analysis of the president as a decision maker and crisis manager, because Eisenhower firmly believed that America's future lay in maintaining close political ties with Western Europe. Additionally, references to events in London and Paris, as well as how European leaders viewed Eisenhower's actions, not only provide the essential background to the Suez crisis, but also afford the reader valuable insight into the complete spectrum of presidential involvement in foreign policy.

The purpose of this book is to examine presidential activism and crisis management. How did Eisenhower make decisions in times of crisis? With whom did he consult? Did he borrow from his military experience a fully articulated managerial design from which he seldom departed, or was he more flexible in his decision making? What was the purpose of the National Security Council, the Departments of State and Defense, the Central Intelligence Agency? Did Eisenhower really take the lead in formulating American foreign policy or did he subordinate himself to Secretary of State John Foster Dulles? What can we say about his effectiveness in dealing with allies and adversaries? How successful was the president in achieving a high degree of bipartisan support from the legislative branch during the critical months of 1956? In short, who was actually in charge and how were decisions made in the Eisenhower White House in times of crisis?

My examination of the primary documentation reinforces the revisionist view that Eisenhower did not delegate major foreign policy decisions to his subordinates. Though he could not always control his secretary of state's expressed sympathy for Great Britain's diplomatic position during the crisis, Eisenhower maintained tight control of the decision-making process by organizing the security departments within the federal government in such a manner that it was only at the presidential level that all aspects of strategy and policy coalesced. Eisenhower was at the center of events. As president, he made the important foreign policy decisions during the Suez crisis, not the secretary of state; as president, he directed economic and military strategy, not the director of the Office of Defense Mobilization or the secretary of defense. Throughout the crisis, Eisenhower personally articulated policy goals to cabinet and executive departmental leaders. He did not share his decision-making responsibility with subordinates in times of crises. The primary evidence clearly suggests that Eisenhower was not the passive chief executive his contemporaries labeled him, but an extraordinarily active president who utilized a unique style of leadership to achieve his political objectives.

1

ORGANIZING THE WHITE HOUSE

Leadership is a word and a concept that has been more argued than almost any other I know. I am not one of the desk-pounding type that likes to stick out his jaw and look like he is bossing the show. I would far rather get behind and, recognizing the frailties and the requirements of human nature, I would rather try to persuade a man to go along—because once I have persuaded him, he will stick.

—Dwight D. Eisenhower, *Managing the Presidency*

How actively and effectively a chief executive manages crises often determines the relative success of his presidency. With the inauguration of Dwight D. Eisenhower in January 1953, the country acquired a president who justifiably perceived himself an expert in national security affairs and crisis management. The nation also acquired a chief executive who was no stranger to decision making. Since his arrival on the national scene in 1941, Eisenhower had been at the center of global events for the most tumultuous decade in the twentieth century. As supreme commander of the Allied Expeditionary Forces that liberated Western Europe, Eisenhower refined his managerial and diplomatic skills, dealing effectively with a diverse group of war leaders, ranging from notoriously egocentric leaders like Churchill and Roosevelt to such temperamental subordinates as Patton and Montgomery. His success as supreme commander lay in large part in his skilled selection of subordinates and his uncanny ability to interject himself in the decision-making process at the decisive moment to make the critical decision. His wartime experience also witnessed his successful response to a number of unexpected crises during the campaign in Europe, the most serious of which was the German Ardennes offensive, which was totally unexpected and demanded immediate and decisive intervention on the part of the supreme commander. Not surprisingly, the same principles of crisis management and executive decision making that characterized Supreme Allied Headquarters in 1944 accompanied Eisenhower to the White House in 1953 and served him well during the Suez crisis.

Foremost of Eisenhower's concerns about long-term policy was his reluctance to approve any obligational expenditure for the Department of Defense that exceeded an amount that the president felt the country could support. Accordingly, Eisenhower directed his efforts at limiting defense spending and holding the line on taxes. The 1955 defense budget became the pacing factor of Eisenhower's strategic programs, since it had to be complete by December 1953. From his desire to curtail the cost of an adequate, but not extravagant, defense establishment, the president championed a "new look" at defense policy.

Enunciated in NSC 162/2 on October 30, 1953, Eisenhower defined the New Look as "first, a reallocation of resources among the five categories of forces, and second, the placing of greater emphasis than formerly on the deterrent and destructive power of improved nuclear weapons, better means of delivery, and effective air defense units."[1] The five categories of forces were (1) nuclear retaliatory air and land-based weapons systems; (2) land forces and tactical air forces stationed overseas; (3) naval and marine forces in the Atlantic and the Pacific, charged with keeping the sea lanes open; (4) continental air defense units; and (5) strategic reserve forces in the United States. The increased reliance on nuclear weapons became the crux of the "massive retaliation" strategy and was a significant departure from the prior administration's greater reliance on a huge conventional force to contain the Communist threat. The New Look quickly evolved into the basic defense policy of the Eisenhower administration and served as the foundation for crisis management and the containment of the Soviet threat.

The basic structure of the New Look was an expanded strategic air force and a reduced conventional force on land and sea. Convinced that atomic bombs had made conventional warfare of the World War II nature obsolete, the president remained firm against attempts by the service chiefs to expand the conventional force. Responding to Ed Folliard of the Washington *Post,* Eisenhower asserted that he was maintaining a one-million-man army, the largest peacetime army in American history, and he regarded calls for an even larger force as totally irresponsible. The New Look was designed to prevent a sudden Pearl Harbor–type attack on the United States.[2] In January 1954, Eisenhower presented this program to Congress in a series of addresses in which he explained the necessity of curbing defense spending and obtaining "more bang for the buck."[3]

1. Dwight D. Eisenhower, *Mandate for Change, 1953–1956* (New York, 1963), 451. For the complete text of NSC 162/2, see Report to the National Security Council by the Executive Secretary, found in *Foreign Relations of the United States, 1952–1954,* Volume II: *National Security Affairs* (Washington, D.C., 1984), 577–97.

2. Ambrose, *Eisenhower: The President,* 171.

3. The president addressed Congress in the State of the Union Address (January 7),

Increased emphasis on the possible use of nuclear retaliatory forces was not the only tenet of Eisenhower's strategic program. Since NSC 162/2 did not include a particular year of maximum enemy threat, the president sought to strengthen national security by constructing formal alliances beyond the traditional zones of interest of the United States. Eisenhower's desire to pursue containment as a strategic policy led to his active involvement in Middle East politics. The decade of the 1950s witnessed the apogee of alliance formation. In addition to establishing mutual security treaties with Japan and the Republic of Korea, the United States formed alliances with Australia and New Zealand (ANZUS), various countries in Southeast Asia (SEATO), and moderate Middle Eastern nations (CENTO), and expanded the membership in NATO. None of the Asian alliances, however, had the same force as NATO, which called for immediate defense and a centralized command system. In his zeal to strengthen American ties to the Third World and prevent the extension of communism, Eisenhower had, in effect, extended containment from a European to a global policy.

To implement the New Look and related policies, Eisenhower developed comprehensive theories of executive leadership and crisis management that affected his selection of an organized White House staff and the efficient use of the personalities of that staff.[4] By the time of the Suez crisis, Eisenhower had organized a most effective bureaucratic system for handling long-term policy and international crises. His theories of executive management followed a noticeable pattern of making a division between policy development (including long-range planning) and operations that required his personal involvement. He expected most operations to be executed at departmental level within the guidelines of policy. Consequently, the newly elected chief executive carefully organized the White House to reflect his personal style of leadership and his assessment of the nation's needs.

---

the annual Budget Message (January 21), and the Economic Report (January 28). See *Public Papers of the President: 1956* (Washington D.C., 1958), 6, 79, 215, respectively. Other phrases that proponents of the New Look used to sell their program included "security through solvency," "massive retalition," and "the long haul."

4. For superb analyses of presidential management, see Phillip G. Henderson, *Managing the Presidency* (Boulder, 1988), and Douglas Kinnard, *President Eisenhower And Strategy Management* (Lexington, Ky., 1988). Whereas Kinnard focuses solely on the Eisenhower administration, Henderson examines Eisenhower's legacy of presidential management from Kennedy to Reagan. Henderson concludes that Eisenhower extended the scope of the presidency beyond any one man and his greatest legacy may well rest with his ability to shape the presidential office into a vital extension of the president's reach.

Within this framework, the president permitted a high degree of latitude for individual subordinates. Delegation of authority had its roots in Eisenhower's military experience. Reflecting on his analysis of staff cooperation, Eisenhower noted, "Principal subordinates must have confidence that they and their positions are widely respected, and the chief must do his part in assuring that is so."[5] The president's theory sounded better in dialogue than practice. He was willing to delegate authority, but he was unwilling to delegate responsibility. Although he often relied heavily on his advisers, Eisenhower was very clear and emphatic about reserving the power of decision to himself.[6]

The key to understanding Eisenhower's style of leadership and management lay in its covert character. The author of a biography of Ike's wartime chief of staff identified five techniques by which Eisenhower concealed the direct, personal aspects of his leadership style: (1) the selective delegation of authority to subordinates, allowing them considerable freedom while simultaneously using them as foils to deflect criticism from himself; (2) the insightful evaluation of friends and antagonists and the careful calculation of the help or damage they might render in any situation; (3) the apparent avoidance of making unilateral decisions, insisting upon multiple advocacy for any major policy shift; (4) the refusal to engage in personality clashes; and (5) the intentional use of evasiveness and ambiguity to screen his actions and unbalance his critics. Indeed, the secret to Eisenhower's effectiveness was deliberate ambiguity and deception.[7] Variations of this analysis were visible in virtually all of the revisionist literature and certainly in the president's active involvement in foreign policy during the Suez crisis in 1956.

Foremost of his advisers of cabinet status was Secretary of State John Foster Dulles. Dulles remains an enigma today just as he was during the Eisenhower presidency. As secretary of state for most of the Eisenhower administration, Dulles attracted his share of admirers and detractors, foremost of whom were Michael Guhin and Townsend Hoopes, respectively. Guhin sympathized with Dulles' efforts to construct a realis-

5. Eisenhower to Henry Luce, August 8, 1960, as quoted in Ambrose, *Eisenhower: The President,* 345.

6. See the Andrew Goodpaster Papers, Recollections and Reflections: Oral History conducted by Colonel William Johnson and Lieutenant Colonel James Ferguson, February 25, 1976. A transcript of the interview is on file at the U.S. Army Military History Institute, Carlisle Barracks, Pennsylvania (hereinafter cited as Goodpaster Papers). For a comprehensive examination of Eisenhower's decision-making process, see Fred I. Greenstein, *The Hidden-hand Presidency* (New York, 1982), 101–51.

7. D. K. R. Crosswell, *The Chief of Staff: The Military Career of General Walter Bedell Smith* (Westport, 1991), 295. Ambrose also discusses Eisenhower's emphasis on flexibility and ambiguity in *Eisenhower: The President,* 245.

tic foreign policy and portrayed him as a man responsive to his times, a reflection of the image that characterized the United States during the 1950s.[8] Hoopes, the most comprehensive critic of Dulles, presented an appraisal of the excessively moralistic Dulles, whom he charged with widening and institutionalizing the attitudes and structure of the Cold War in American life.[9] The truth lay somewhere between the two, but probably closer to Hoopes. Far more intransigent than the president in dealing with world leaders, Dulles lacked his chief's talent for compromise and reconciliation in the pursuit of common political goals. Dulles probably infuriated and antagonized more foreign leaders than was prudent in his role as the president's primary adviser in foreign affairs. They, in turn, disliked the secretary and resented his manner as well as their inability to move him in his views, but they were not his boss. As long as Eisenhower remained pleased—which was almost all the time—others' opinions of the secretary of state were irrelevant.

Eisenhower's selection of Dulles as secretary of state was neither a surprise nor a foregone conclusion.[10] Dulles had vast experience in foreign affairs. Born in Watertown, New York, in 1888, he was the eldest of five children. Greatly influenced by his maternal grandfather, John W. Foster, who served as secretary of state during the last eight months of Benjamin Harrison's administration, John Foster Dulles was also the nephew of Robert Lansing, secretary of state under Woodrow Wilson. Graduating from Princeton shortly after the turn of the century, Dulles first achieved diplomatic renown as a legal consultant to Bernard Baruch, the United States representative to the Reparations Committee at the Versailles Conference in 1919. Following the war, Dulles joined the law firm of Sullivan and Cromwell. In 1939 he wrote *War, Peace and Change,* which was characterized by its high-minded impracticality. Beginning in 1944, Dulles served as Thomas Dewey's principal adviser on foreign policy, and by the late 1940s he emerged as the unofficial spokesman of the international wing of the Republican party. His most notable achievement prior to 1953 was writing the Japanese Peace Treaty, on which he worked as a diplomatic consultant to the Truman

8. Michael Guhin, *John Foster Dulles: A Statesman and His Times* (New York, 1972), 10. The most laudatory biographer of Dulles is Leonard Mosely, who examines the Dulles family network in *Dulles* (New York, 1978).

9. Townsend Hoopes, *The Devil and John Foster Dulles* (Toronto, 1973), 487.

10. Walter Isaacson and Evan Thomas state that the president had misgivings about choosing Dulles as his secretary of state and that Eisenhower actually preferred John McCloy. See Isaacson and Thomas, *The Wise Men: Six Friends and the World They Made* (New York, 1986), 570. Most scholars of the period, however, agree that Dulles was the natural selection for the top diplomatic post.

administration. What appealed most to the President-elect in late 1952 was Dulles' commitment to internationalism. Nominated by Eisenhower to be his chief diplomatic adviser, Dulles reached the pinnacle of a career marked by extensive service and grooming for his nomination as secretary of state. With his analytical mind, he was able to synthesize conflicting viewpoints and present the best recommendation for a given diplomatic problem. Indeed, it was Dulles who had so eloquently enunciated the "massive retaliation" formula in a speech that he delivered to the Council of Foreign Relations on January 12, 1954.

Eisenhower had first met Dulles at Supreme Headquarters, Allied Powers Europe (SHAPE) in April 1952. Dulles had also been instrumental in the formation of the foreign policy plank of the Republican party for the November election. Although the president often regretted Dulles' more bellicose statements, such as those dealing with "rolling-back" communism, "liberating" Eastern Europe, and "massive retaliation," he appreciated Dulles' commitment to NATO, foreign aid, and internationalism. Impressed with Dulles' knowledge of global affairs, Eisenhower later told speech-writer Emmet Hughes, "There's only one man I know who has seen more of the world and talked with more people and knows more than he does—and that's me."[11]

A theorist more than an executive, Dulles was not overly popular in diplomatic circles, due primarily to his abrasive character and imprecise language. Biographer Hoopes characterized Dulles as possessing titanic energy, iron determination, and a tactical guile that he did not hesitate to use in order to mislead and manipulate his allies. To Winston Churchill, Dulles was not a smart man. Churchill once remarked that Dulles was the only case he knew of a bull carrying his china shop with him. Anthony Eden often referred to Dulles as "that terrible man."[12] One American critic stated that Dulles was driven by the need to satisfy the right wing of the Republican party, by his enormous ego, by an insatiable desire to go down in history as a greater secretary of state than his immediate predecessor, Dean Acheson, and finally by an unnatural craving to create an image of forceful, successful leadership.[13]

11. Ambrose, *Eisenhower: The President,* 21.

12. According to Ambassador to the Court of St. James Winthrop Aldrich, Churchill never referred to the secretary of state as Dulles, but as "Dullith," hissing through his teeth. When informed that Allen Dulles was Director of Central Intelligence, Churchill reportedly said: "They tell me there's another Dullith. Is that possible?" See Aldrich Oral History (OH 250) October 16, 1972, pp. 18–19, on file at the Eisenhower Library. Eden's assessment of Dulles is found in Roscoe Drummond, *Duel at the Brink* (New York, 1960), 162.

13. For a very critical view of the Eisenhower era, see Norman Graebner, *The New Isolationism: A Study in Politics and Foreign Policy Since 1950* (New York, 1956).

For his part, Eisenhower respected his secretary of state, but he was certainly not in awe of him. Four months after the inauguration, the president analyzed the performance of each of his associates. Of Dulles, he wrote:

I still think of him, as I always have, as an intensive student of foreign affairs. He is well informed and, in this subject at least, is deserving, I think, of his reputation as a "wise" man. Moreover, he is a dedicated and tireless individual—he passionately believes in the United States, in the dignity of man, and in moral values.

He is not particularly persuasive in presentation and, at times, seems to have a curious lack of understanding as to how his works and manner may affect another personality. Personally, I like and admire him; my only doubts concerning him lie in the general field of personality, not in his capacity as a student of foreign affairs.[14]

The Eisenhower-Dulles relationship warmed considerably as both men grew more accustomed to the strengths and weaknesses of the other. Dulles emerged as Eisenhower's most influential cabinet member and maintained the president's confidence throughout his tenure due to their mutual view of the United States' role as leader in global affairs, Eisenhower's recognition of the secretary's political and diplomatic skill, and Dulles' respect for the president's political acumen.[15]

Unlike the secretary of state, the office of secretary of defense was not as firmly established. Having undergone modification in both 1949 (1949 Amendments to the National Security Act) and 1953 (Reorganization Plan Number 6), the position was still in the transitional phase. Eisenhower's choice for secretary of defense was Charles E. Wilson, former president of General Motors. Arriving in Washington with little knowledge of foreign affairs, Wilson did not mature in his position as much as Eisenhower desired.[16] Eisenhower noted in May 1953 that Wilson was prone to lecture, rather than to answer, when asked a specific question. This not only annoyed members of Congress, but gave them

14. Dwight D. Eisenhower Diary, May 14, 1953, in DDE Diary Series, Box 9, folder marked "Diaries Miscellaneous," EP, EL; Ann Whitman File. See also Robert H. Ferrell, ed., *The Eisenhower Diaries* (New York, 1981), 237.

15. Herbert S. Parmet, *Eisenhower and the American Crusades* (New York, 1972), 185. On the occasion of Dulles' fiftieth anniversary in foreign affairs (June 15, 1957), Ike wrote, "My personal appreciation of your extraordinary ability in the field of international relations has constantly grown since you became Secretary of State in 1953." See folder marked "J. F. D," Box 944, President's Personal File, White House Central Files, EP, EL.

16. For the most comprehensive analysis of the office, see Douglas Kinnard's *The Secretary of Defense* (Lexington, Ky., 1980). For a description of Wilson's background and shortcomings, see p. 48.

unlooked for opportunities to discover flaws in reasoning and argument.[17] Moreover, Wilson's refusal to delegate authority to subordinates in the field of legislative coordination consumed far too much of the secretary's time.

To exacerbate matters, Wilson's blunt use of words had caused considerable embarrassment during his confirmation hearings when the appointee implied that what was good for General Motors was good for the country. Such remarks bordered on a major conflict of interest with his former job and did not endear him to either the president or the members of the executive and legislative branches. On March 10, 1955, Eisenhower counseled Wilson about the casual statements he was constantly making in press conferences and elsewhere about the conduct of foreign affairs. Eisenhower regretted that, although Wilson considered himself a master of public relations, he seemed to have no comprehension at all of what embarrassment his remarks caused the president and secretary of state in their efforts to keep the tangled international situation [Quemoy-Matsu crisis] from becoming completely impossible.[18]

Another aspect of Wilson's style that tended to alienate the president dealt with the sessions between the two men in which Wilson tended to bore the president by discussing the intricacies of operating the Department of Defense. It was exactly the sort of thing that Eisenhower detested and found tedious. He had chosen Wilson due to the latter's bureaucratic and managerial skill. It was the president's intent that Wilson supervise the administrative operation of the Department of Defense, while he, as chief executive, concentrated on the larger, more complex military and budgetary matters. At one point, Eisenhower chastised his defense chief, telling him, "Charlie, you run Defense. We both can't do it, and I won't do it. I was elected to worry about a lot of other things than the day-to-day operations of a department."[19]

The president was not the only official who found Wilson burdensome. Colonel Andrew J. Goodpaster, defense liaison officer and staff secretary to the president, echoed Eisenhower's increasing dissatisfaction with Wilson and informed the secretary of defense that his organization was weak and deficient.[20] According to Goodpaster, there was doubt in Eisenhower's mind whether the secretary could control the individual services under his jurisdiction. This was particularly true during the Suez crisis when presidential dissatisfaction peaked over security

17. As quoted in Ferrell, ed., *Eisenhower Diaries*, 237.

18. *Ibid.*, 296.

19. Bruce E. Geelhoed, *Charles E. Wilson and the Controversy at the Pentagon, 1953–1957* (Detroit, 1979), 19.

20. Goodpaster Papers, 48–49.

leaks from the Department of Defense. In no uncertain terms, the president informed Wilson that comments by Department of Defense representatives on matters of political significance should be avoided and that comments on military actions should be carefully restricted to avoid disclosure of matters that should remain classified.[21] As a result of these problems and his occasional inflammatory remarks to the press and Congress, Wilson's influence gradually diminished during Eisenhower's first administration.

Aside from the problems with Wilson, there were several other reasons why the secretary of defense failed to play a decisive role in strategy management. Eisenhower regarded the secretary of defense as a business manager of Pentagon activities. Because of his own extensive expertise in international relations, the president reserved long-range policy decisions relating to national defense to himself. Actually, Eisenhower operated as his own defense secretary, thereby relegating Wilson to a purely administrative role. Additionally, the close rapport the president enjoyed with Admiral Arthur W. Radford, the chairman of the Joint Chiefs of Staff, complicated what would ordinarily have been Wilson's senior role in the administration.

Like the Department of Defense, the Joint Chiefs of Staff (JCS) was a relatively new organization. Formally created in legislation by the National Security Act of 1947, the Joint Chiefs of Staff lacked direction and coordination until Congress authorized the position of chairman of the Joint Chiefs of Staff in 1949.[22] By law, the chairman's responsibilities included the coordination of the activities of the organization and the rendering of advice to the president and other agencies of the executive department on matters affecting national security. During the Suez crisis, the Joint Chiefs included Radford; Admiral Arleigh A. Burke, Chief of Naval Operations; General Maxwell D. Taylor, chief of staff of the Army; General Nathan Twining, chief of staff of the Air Force; and on matters relating to the Marine Corps, General Randolph McC. Pate, commandant of the Marine Corps.

Radford was Secretary Wilson's personal choice as chairman of the Joint Chiefs. Both Wilson and Eisenhower had first met Radford, then the commander of the American Pacific Fleet, on the president-elect's

21. See L. Arthur Minnich Series, Office of the Staff Secretary, Box 8, folder marked "Actions by the President, November 12, 1956," in White House Office Files, EP, EL.

22. For the history of the Joint Chiefs of Staff, see Lawrence Korb, *The Joint Chiefs of Staff* (Bloomington, 1976). See also the Historical Division of the Joint Secretariat of the Joint Chiefs of Staff's publication *Joint Chiefs of Staff: Special Historical Study* (Washington, D.C., 1980). Today's chairman has considerably more power than did Radford as a result of the recent Goldwater-Nichols Act.

visit to Korea in November 1952. Radford favorably impressed the president's entourage with his articulation and grasp of the strategic situation in the Far East. In addition, Radford possessed the credentials that satisfied the Republican conservative element. He was the Navy's leading advocate of air power and supported the formation of a "positive" policy toward Nationalist China. What convinced Eisenhower to select Radford, however, was the latter's commitment to new strategic technology and his sympathy with the president's budgetary and strategic policies.[23] Radford fully supported the president's military concepts and became one of the New Look's most vocal advocates.

Maxwell Taylor succeeded General Matthew Ridgway as Army chief of staff on June 30, 1955. Ridgway had never been a strong proponent of Eisenhower's defense policies, and he emerged as one of the leading military critics of the diminished role of the Army under the New Look. By early 1955, Wilson summoned Taylor from his position as commander of American military forces in the Far East to discuss Taylor's qualifications for the Army's highest post. Questioned by both Wilson and Eisenhower, Taylor indicated a complete acceptance of the president's views on national security. Once in the job, however, Taylor, like Ridgway before him, questioned the basic assumptions on which the president based his national security policies. Never in complete accord with the New Look, Taylor began advocating a new defense policy that called for a more "flexible response" to the country's military problems.[24] Taylor admired the president, but sometimes found it troublesome that Eisenhower was so unsympathetic to his efforts, which were frequently seconded by the Navy and the Marine Corps, to give more support to the conventional forces.[25]

General Nathan Twining was Eisenhower's appointee for chief of staff of the Air Force. His selection did not surprise anyone in military circles. Twining was a strong supporter of the New Look, because the strategy strongly enhanced the role and the mission of the Air Force. Moreover, Twining had somewhat of an advantage over his colleagues in that Eisenhower's emphasis on a strong deterrent force coincided with increased

23. Geelhoed, *Wilson and the Controversy at the Pentagon*, 65–66; Kinnard, *Secretary of Defense*, 49.

24. See Maxwell Taylor, *The Uncertain Trumpet* (New York, 1959) for Taylor's views on massive retaliation and flexible response.

25. Taylor interview by the author, June 17, 1981. In Taylor's view, Eisenhower felt that he (the president) knew more about the Army than did the chief of staff. This resulted in frequent clashes over priorities and defense allocations. Nathan Twining confirms Taylor's assessment in his own oral history conducted by John T. Mason, Jr., August 17, 1967. See Oral History 274, pp. 223–24, on file at EL.

monetary expenditures for the nation's air forces. A leading advocate of massive retaliation, Twining remained immensely popular with the president and eventually succeeded Radford as chairman of the Joint Chiefs in 1957.

The most surprising selection to the Joint Chiefs was the appointment of Arleigh Burke as Chief of Naval Operations. Burke was a relatively junior admiral in 1955 when Eisenhower advanced him over ninety senior officers to the Navy's highest office. Like his colleagues on the Joint Chiefs, Burke had to confirm his support for the administration's defense policies before receiving his appointment.[26] An exceptional officer who fully enjoyed the president's confidence, Burke remained Chief of Naval Operations for the remainder of Eisenhower's presidency and the initial years of the Kennedy administration.

In selecting officers to serve as members of the Joint Chiefs, Eisenhower preferred men who would view their duties as members of the nation's highest military council as more important than their command of their respective services. On February 10, 1956, the president met with the Joint Chiefs and emphasized the necessity of their working as a corporate body. The president verbalized his anger the following month when he regretted that the chiefs of staff were not "big enough" to look at the whole picture, the whole sweep of the country's economy in conjunction with their particular problems.[27] It was the president's feeling that the Joint Chiefs formed the union between the military establishment and the government. Their greatest asset was as an institution charged with the development of doctrine in its overall terms, not in minute details of tactics and operational procedures. The president desired unanimity from the organization, not proposals based on the requirements of the individual services. Eisenhower felt that the Vice or Deputy Joint Chiefs, all of whom were four-star rank and who worked directly for their respective heads of the individual services, could

26. Like Taylor, Burke felt his hands were often tied by the presence of a senior officer from his service in the defense establishment. According to Burke, his biggest fights and quarrels were the result of Radford's agreement on something pertaining to the Navy. Burke once confronted Radford and told him, "Now listen, I'm the representative of the Navy, not you." When Radford replied that he knew about the maritime service since he had been in the Navy for a while, Burke retorted, "I know you do, Admiral, but you don't have the responsibilities for that now." Despite such differences, Burke always retained a professional respect for Radford that transcended a normal senior-subordinate relationship. Burke interview by the author, June 18, 1981.

27. See Memorandum for Record, Conference of the President and the Joint Chiefs of Staff, February 10, 1956, Office of the Staff Secretary, Department of Defense Subseries, White House Office Files, EP, EL. See also folder marked "Mar 56 Diary-acw (2)", Box 8, Ann Whitman Diary Series, Ann Whitman File, EP, EL.

handle the daily operations of their services while the Joint Chiefs concentrated on their roles as principal military advisers to the president and secretary of defense. Despite his efforts to instill this concept in the Joint Chiefs, Eisenhower made little or no progress in developing real corporate thinking.

Eisenhower's quest for unanimity did not please the individual Joint Chiefs, particularly Burke. Although the president informed him that his principal task was not to run the Navy, but to serve as a member of the Joint Chiefs, Burke disagreed with the principle that the Joint Chiefs should render corporate advice. According to Burke, it was totally nonproductive to demand forced agreement, because the minority had very legitimate reasons for believing the way they did. The commander in chief needed to know the opposing opinions of the dissenting members.[28] Burke also believed that the president should meet with the entire Joint Chiefs of Staff, not just the chairman, on a regular basis. This was necessary not so much for Eisenhower to hear the views of the individual chiefs as much as for the chiefs to hear the president's views.

Taylor echoed Burke's dissent concerning corporate advice.[29] He believed that Eisenhower's desire for unanimity was totally unrealistic. Taylor knew that the defense budget was the "pay-off." One could weave all sorts of theories about the New Look and massive retaliation in an academic context, but it was real business when someone translated strategic theory into dollars needed to produce forces compatible with it. Despite the disagreement with the president over the budget and the role of the Joint Chiefs of Staff as an institution, Taylor, as well as Burke, personally admired Eisenhower.

Only in the chairman of the Joint Chiefs of Staff did Eisenhower find the team player he desired. "Strangely enough," he wrote his friend Everett "Swede" Hazlett, "the one man who sees this [the breadth of understanding and devotion of country over individual service] is a Navy man who at one time was an uncompromising exponent of Naval power and its superiority over any other kind of strength."[30] Unfortunately,

28. Burke interview by the author, June 18, 1981.

29. For Taylor's view of the Joint Chiefs of Staff, see his autobiography, *Swords and Plowshares* (New York, 1972), 164–78.

30. Eisenhower, *Mandate for Change*, 455. See also Dwight D. Eisenhower to "Swede" Hazlett, August 20, 1956, quoted in Robert W. Griffith, ed., *Ike's Letters to a Friend, 1941–1958* (Lawrence, Kan., 1984), 169. At times, the president even became frustrated with Radford, commenting in March, 1956, that he (Eisenhower) had made a "mistake" in keeping Radford as chairman for an additional two years. Eisenhower contemplated summoning General Alfred Gruenther from NATO to replace Radford because Radford was "too slow for the job he had." See folder marked "Mar '56 Diary-acw (1)", Box 8, Ann Whitman Diary Series, Ann Whitman File, EP, EL.

Radford was unable to bring the individual chiefs to his way of thinking, and the internal differences among the military leaders tended to neutralize the advisory capacity they might have enjoyed as a body. However, the president met frequently with Radford, as he wanted to continue the arrangement he had had with General Omar Bradley, Radford's predecessor, with whom he met every Monday morning when both were in Washington.[31]

Relations between the Joint Chiefs and the Department of State remained amicable throughout the Eisenhower presidency. Deputy Secretary of State Robert Murphy met weekly with the Joint Chiefs, and no major friction existed between the Joint Chiefs and Secretary Dulles. All the Chiefs maintained a healthy respect for Dulles, although individual members did not always approve of the secretary's methods.[32]

Another institution of increasing importance in the Eisenhower decision-making process was the National Security Council (NSC).[33] The National Security Act of 1947 formally created the National Security Council to "advise the President with respect to the integration of domestic, foreign, and military policies relating to the national security." Although Truman utilized the NSC as a small advisory board, Eisenhower transformed the body into a highly structured staff system under a special assistant to the president for national security affairs. The president appointed Robert Cutler, a Harvard-trained attorney and Boston banker, to the post. Cutler and his successors, Dillon Anderson, William Jackson, and Gordon Gray, organized and administered a system of comprehensive policy planning that evolved into a highly efficient advisory body consisting of the NSC Planning Board and the Operations Coordinating Board. Through these mechanisms, Eisenhower "institutionalized the NSC and gave it clear lines of responsibility and authority."[34] The NSC Planning Board had the responsibility of developing comprehensive "basic national security policy," area policies, and functional policies. After the president analyzed and approved the Planning Board's recommendations, the Operations Coordinating

31. Stephen Jurika, ed., *From Pearl Harbor to Vietnam: The Memoirs of Admiral Arthur R. Radford* (Stanford, 1978), 323. For the frequency of his meetings with the president, see Radford's personal log, on file at the Operational Naval Archives, Washington Navy Yard, Washington, D.C.

32. See Burke interview by the author, June 18, 1981.

33. For a reappraisal of the Eisenhower National Security Council, see Henderson, *Managing the Presidency,* 69–90. For an insider's view of the NSC, see Robert Cutler, *No Time for Rest* (Boston, 1965). See also Ambrose, *Eisenhower: The President,* 25.

34. R. Gordon Hoxie, "The National Security Council," *Presidential Studies Quarterly,* XII, (Winter, 1982), 109. See also Henderson, *Managing the Presidency,* 74.

Board had the task of supervising policy implementation and interagency coordination.

Theoretically, the NSC was responsible for long-term policy guidance and identification of long-term policy objectives. Defense Liaison Officer Goodpaster stated that Eisenhower often used the council as a forum within which the president would have the benefits of the comments of those cabinet members who commanded the departments with national security responsibilities. During the eight years of the Eisenhower presidency, the NSC met 346 times. Two and one-half hours was the typical duration, and Eisenhower presided over 329 of these meetings—approximately 90 percent of the time.[35] Statutory members of the NSC included the president, the vice-president, the secretary of defense and the secretary of state, but the legislation identified a number of "advisers" to assist the president in formulating policy. Participants of the NSC during the Suez crisis included Eisenhower, Vice-President Nixon, Dulles, Wilson, Secretary of the Treasury George Humphrey, Radford, Director of Central Intelligence Allen Dulles, Lewis L. Strauss of the Atomic Energy Commission, and Cutler.[36] Also in attendance when Eisenhower presided were Adams, who acted as the president's unofficial chief of staff, and Goodpaster, who kept meticulous memoranda of conversations for the president.

Eisenhower remained adamant about keeping the number of attendees to a minimum. When Cutler informed him that several officials, including the service secretaries and the individual members of the Joint Chiefs of Staff, thought they needed to attend the NSC meetings in order to be "kept abreast," Eisenhower stated, "Bobby [Cutler], I won't have people sitting around just for a free ride. The Council is a place for workers with a significant interest."[37] In the words of military bureaucracy with which the president was quite familiar, the NSC was a place for those who had "a need to know, not a nice to know requirement." Although Eisenhower convened the NSC more regularly than his successors, he reserved making policy decisions for himself. According to Special Assistant Dillon Anderson, "While he [Eisenhower] welcomed the use of the NSC mechanism, as an advisory body, or a sort of a superstaff for him in the delineation of our national security policy, he nev-

35. See Index to NSC, Ann Whitman File, EP, EL. See also Henderson, *Managing the Presidency,* 81. Henderson also gives a detailed breakdown of the membership of the National Security Council on pp. 187–88.

36. All positions are at the time of the Suez crisis.

37. Cutler, *No Time for Rest,* 403. The service secretaries' authority had begun to erode as early as 1949 when they lost their cabinet status as a result of the 1949 amendments to the National Security Act of 1947.

ertheless felt that the onus and responsibility for decision lay exclusively with him."[38]

Despite the theoretical role that the NSC played or the actual prestige the institution enjoyed in subsequent administrations, it seldom was a forum that executed policy decisions in the Eisenhower era. Indeed, the president often found the sessions burdensome, as evidenced by a letter in which his private secretary remarked that the NSC meetings seemed to be the president's most time-consuming task and "he [Eisenhower] himself complains that he knows every word of the presentations as they are made. However, he feels that to maintain the interest and attention of every member of the NSC, he must sit through every meeting—despite the fact that he knows the presentations so well."[39] More and more he used the forum to announce his operational decisions, not to explore long-range policy possibilities.[40] Still, the meetings were part of an important information-gathering process that gave the president the benefit of advice from most of his key political advisers in formulating long-term policy.

There were two other individuals who played important roles within the executive branch: Allen Dulles and Andrew Goodpaster. Dulles, who was the secretary of state's brother, served Eisenhower as Director of Central Intelligence; Goodpaster performed the dual duties of staff secretary and defense liaison officer. Dulles was particularly important during the NSC sessions, as he generally opened each meeting with an assessment of the particular topic of discussion. A former Department of State employee, Dulles had earned his reputation as a highly successful officer for the Office of Strategic Services, the forerunner of the Central Intelligence Agency (CIA), during World War II. Following the war, he was instrumental in the creation of the CIA, which the National Security Act of 1947 formally established.

The CIA was an independent intelligence-gathering agency, responsible to the National Security Council (thus, ultimately to the president),

38. Dillon Anderson, Oral History Interview, (OH 101), EL.

39. Ann C. Whitman to Milton Eisenhower, August 28, 1956, Ann Whitman Name Series, Box 8, Folder marked "August, 1956 (2)," Ann Whitman File, EP, EL. See also Ambrose, *Eisenhower: The President*, 345. Following a relatively short NSC meeting in mid-July, 1956, Eisenhower announced that it had been the "shortest and sweetest" NSC meeting during his three years in office. See folder marked "291st Meeting of NSC, July 19, 1956," Box 8, National Security Council Series, Ann Whitman File, EP, EL.

40. Cutler, *No Time for Rest*, 403. See also Ambrose, *Eisenhower: The President*, 509. During the Suez crisis the National Security Council convened sixteen times and conducted a special session on November 21, 1956, during which the council focused more on economic measures than political or military solutions to the crisis.

not the Department of Defense. The CIA had five general functions as outlined by the National Security Act of 1947: (1) to advise the National Security Council on matters relating to national security, (2) to make recommendations to the NSC regarding the coordination of intelligence, (3) to correlate and evaluate intelligence and provide for its appropriate dissemination, (4) to carry out "service of common concern," and (5) to "perform such other functions and duties related to intelligence affecting national security as the NSC will from time to time direct."[41]

The last function grew from a deep concern over the inroads the Soviet Union was making in Western Europe after World War II. Alarmed that Soviet-inspired Communists were attempting to control the political, social, and economic aspects of life in destitute France and Italy, the Truman administration thought it should have some facility for covert operations to counter the Communists. Two years later, Congress passed the Central Intelligence Agency Act of 1949, which exempted the CIA from all federal laws requiring disclosure of personnel employed by the agency and permitted the director to account for any expenditures solely by signing a certificate of expenditure. No additional financial records were necessary.

Upon the resignation of Walter Bedell Smith as Director of Central Intelligence (DCI), Eisenhower promptly nominated Allen Dulles as the agency's new director. Dulles previously served as Smith's deputy director and was a strong believer in covert operations. When Smith resigned, Dulles was the logical choice to replace him. The Senate immediately confirmed the appointment. Although the relationship between Eisenhower and Dulles was never particularly close, the highly unusual arrangement of having two brothers serving in key positions within the administration ensured a close relationship between the CIA and the Department of State. Dulles remained Director of Central Intelligence for the entire Eisenhower presidency.

Unlike the visible role Dulles played, Goodpaster often worked behind the scenes. Staff secretary was Goodpaster's formal title, but he spent the bulk of his time as Eisenhower's principal liaison officer to the intelligence and national security departments. McGeorge Bundy, Kennedy's national security adviser, described Goodpaster and his role as "tending the door and handling urgent messages silently—a wise and good man."[42] A 1939 graduate from the United States Military Acad-

41. Stephen Ambrose, *Ike's Spies* (Garden City, 1981), 165–66.
42. I. M. Destler, "A Lost Legacy" (Paper delivered at the USMA History Symposium on the Theory and Practice of American National Security, West Point, New York, April 23, 1982), 13.

emy at West Point, Goodpaster had already acquired a distinguished combat record in World War II and was recognized by Eisenhower as an Army officer of exceptional ability. Succeeding Brigadier General Paul T. "Pete" Carroll as staff secretary in 1954, Goodpaster was constantly at the president's side, and quickly emerged as one of Eisenhower's most trusted advisers and confidants. Rapidly establishing links to all the senior departmental and White House officials, he became an effective conduit through whom all important information reached the president. Analogous to the military rank of command sergeant major, the senior enlisted noncommissioned officer and adviser to a commander, Goodpaster earned the respect of the commander in chief and served as a focal point who handled the flow of material and information pertaining to those daily operations in the international arena in which the president was personally involved. The accent was on day-to-day operations. In that capacity, Goodpaster briefed the president on intelligence every morning and coordinated the *ad hoc* meetings demanded by Eisenhower.[43]

Eisenhower also brought clear ideas of cabinet government to the White House in 1953, borne largely from his military experience that spanned three decades. Like the National Security Council meetings, cabinet sessions proved a burden on the president's time. Still, the meetings had an important function for Eisenhower, who once characterized his feelings toward cabinet government in this manner: "One of the big purposes that I wanted to achieve was to make sure that everybody was informed on the workings of the Administration, so that no matter whether you were before Congress, making a speech, or anywhere, we would not be working at opposite ends of the spectrum."[44]

As Bradley Patterson, assistant to the cabinet secretary under Eisenhower, noted:

> Cabinet members are beset from every side by congressional pressures, by the pressures of special constituencies, by the pressures of their bureaucracies, by the pressures of the press, by the pressures of foreign nations, heaven knows what other sources—all of these pressures tending to grind special axes and sort of turn their heads away from the President who put them in office, and to whom they're responsible. And it actually takes some special effort to remind them that they are the President's men. The President needs to take all the occasions he can to remind them of what his views are. So the Cabinet meeting is the time when he does that.[45]

43. For Eisenhower's relationship with Goodpaster, see Ambrose, *Eisenhower: The President,* 217.

44. Dwight D. Eisenhower, Oral History Interview by Philip A. Crowl (OH 14), EL.

45. Bradley H. Patterson, Jr., Oral History Interview by Paul L. Hopper, September 19, 1968 (OH 225), 7, EL.

Consequently, Eisenhower frequently met with the cabinet to provide presidential direction to policy development. During his administration, Eisenhower's cabinet met a total of 227 times, with Eisenhower presiding over 205 of these meetings.[46] During the Suez crisis, Eisenhower met with the cabinet only six times. The crisis was never a principal topic of discussion except on November 16, 1956, when the cabinet requested an update.

In addition to managing the executive agencies in the federal government, the president spent considerable effort in cultivating congressional support. In the first off-year election (1954), Eisenhower traveled over ten thousand miles and made over fifty speeches in support of his fellow Republicans. Unfortunately for Eisenhower, the Republicans lost control of both houses to the Democrats. In spite of these losses, Eisenhower continued to pursue the goal of budgetary restraints in the period 1955–56. Throughout his administration, he made it his practice to meet every Monday with congressional leaders of both parties. Additionally, he instructed each cabinet member to establish contacts with the members of every congressional committee with which he had dealings.[47] Lastly, the president established a staff section under General Wilton B. Persons with the mission of maintaining effective liaison with Congress. For the most part, the Eighty-fourth Congress and the administration worked together harmoniously, due mainly to the cordial relations with House Speaker Sam Rayburn and Senate Majority Leader Lyndon Johnson.[48] Even though bipartisanship did not exist in the exercise of foreign policy on all issues, Eisenhower averted major disputes with members of Congress by avoiding confrontational rhetoric and urging the need for unity in the face of Cold War dangers.

Although Eisenhower relied heavily on his legislative liaison staff to foster a good working relationship with Congress, the president was hardly a passive observer. During his first year in office, he invited every member of Congress to a series of luncheons at the White House.

46. Vice-President Nixon chaired the remaining twenty-two meetings when Eisenhower was not present. See Henderson, *Managing the Presidency,* 51–59, for a superb analysis of Eisenhower and cabinet government. Henderson outlines Eisenhower's creation of the first cabinet secretariat in American history, when on October 19, 1954, the president appointed Maxwell Rabb to serve as secretary of the cabinet. Rabb was assisted in his work by Bradley Patterson, Jr., a career civil servant. For cabinet minutes and agenda during the Suez crisis, see Boxes 7 and 8, Cabinet Series, Ann Whitman File, EP, EL.

47. Eisenhower, *Mandate For Change,* 194.

48. For an excellent study of Eisenhower's relationship with Congress, see the following works by Gary W. Reichard: *The Reaffirmation of Republicanism* (Knoxville, 1975); and "Divisions & Dissent: Democrats and Foreign Policy," *Political Science Quarterly,* XCIII (Spring, 1978), 51–72.

More than once, he chastised his cabinet members for their inflexible approach in dealing with congressional leaders. His reprimand of Secretary of Agriculture Ezra Benson, in 1958, illustrates Eisenhower's acute sensitivity to legislative politics to a greater degree than most contemporaries realized. The president chastised the secretary in relatively harsh language: "All I want to say here is that I believe it is not good Congressional politics to fail to listen seriously to the recommendations of our own congressional leaders. Charlie Halleck, Les Arends, Joe Martin and Bill Hill from the House, as well as Bill Knowland, Everett Dirksen and others from the Senate, will find it difficult to keep their cohorts solidly together in critical moments unless we are ready to make what they consider are some necessary concessions from time to time."[49]

In summation, the office of the presidency, and that institution alone, was the coordinating agency of the Eisenhower era. On complex matters relating to strategic policy, the president drew together the people who had competence and responsibility in those areas, who then had the analytical preparatory work completed, and finally who deliberated on those matters. During his collaboration with his subordinates, Eisenhower relied directly on his agency chiefs to take responsibility and exercise their authority within their respective areas. On matters of operations that required his direct participation, of which the Suez affair was a prime example, he assembled a close group of personal advisers to his office for consultation. In the final analysis, however, the power of decision rested not on any committee, but squarely on Eisenhower. By dealing actively with his departmental chiefs on policy and an inner circle of advisers for operational matters, Eisenhower ensured that it was only at the presidential level that all aspects of strategic management coalesced. Thus, the president met the Suez crisis with a clearly established leadership role, capable subordinates, a definite policy framework, and an efficient system for responding to foreign policy problems.

49. Eisenhower to Ezra Taft Benson, March 20, 1958, in folder marked "DDE Diary: March 1958," Box 31, DDE Diary Series, Ann Whitman File, EP, EL; also quoted in Henderson, *Managing the Presidency,* 43.

2

BACKGROUND TO SUEZ:
THE ASWAN DAM PROBLEM

When Washington sheds every decent principle on which foreign relations are based and broadcasts the lie, smear, and delusion that Egypt's economy is unsound, then I look them in the face and say: Drop dead of your fury for you will never be able to dictate to Egypt.

—Gamal Nasser

The Suez crisis was not the first attempt by Eisenhower to develop a consistent, comprehensive policy toward the Middle East. Indeed, the crisis had its roots in the context of Republican foreign policy and the president's personal desire to exclude Soviet influence from the Middle East. Containment of the Soviet Union remained the dominant foreign policy of the United States during the decade of the 1950s, and American strategic planners formulated policy to counter expected Soviet expansion into the volatile Middle East. As late as November 4, 1958, NSC 5820/1 stated that the primary policy objective was the denial of the region to Soviet domination. Consequently, Eisenhower and Dulles initiated a number of diplomatic forays to achieve American policy objectives, chief of which was the desire to keep the Middle East independent of Communist domination and oriented toward the West.[1]

To support the policy of containment and to enhance American prestige in the Middle East, Eisenhower developed a number of policy goals to guide strategists and policy formulation. These goals reflected the president's own cold war ideology and included promoting regional stability, guaranteeing the free flow of Middle Eastern oil to Western Europe, supporting Arab nationalism and Israeli independence, improving relations with the Arab states, hastening the decline of European colonial empires, maintaining the solidarity of the Western alliance, and avoiding an arms race between Israel and its Arab

1. See File CCS 381-EMMEA, Section 35, Records of the United States Joint Chiefs of Staff, Record Group 218, National Archives of the United States, Washington, D.C. (hereinafter cited as Records of the Joint Chiefs of Staff, RG 218).

neighbors, with the United States and Russia the principal arms suppliers.[2]

Unfortunately, these goals contained a number of inherent contradictions that made the formulation of a coherent foreign policy in the region difficult to achieve. The American president often found it difficult to distinguish between emerging Egyptian nationalism and pan-Arabism, with Gamal Nasser as its principal spokesman. This was particularly true during the Suez crisis when Eisenhower found himself confronted with support of European colonialism on one hand and the nationalistic aspirations of Nasser's Egypt on the other. This conflict of interest was best summed up in a conversation between Eisenhower and Treasury Secretary George Humphrey during the president's first administration. When Humphrey opined that the United States should not support emerging Third World nations, but the colonial powers instead, because the Europeans would run the countries more efficiently and thus improve living conditions faster, an incredulous Eisenhower immediately responded, "It is my personal conviction that almost any one of the newborn states of the world would far rather embrace Communism or any other form of dictatorship than to acknowledge the political domination of another government, even though that brought to each citizen a far higher standard of living."[3] It seemed ironic that Eisenhower, who was an avowed anticolonialist, was willing to accept Great Britain as the principal guardian of Western interest in the Middle East until 1956 and to use American power to support British actions.[4]

Further complicating the administration's attempts to construct a viable Middle Eastern policy was Eisenhower's acute sensitivity to the Soviet Union's efforts to foster revolution in the already unstable Arab states. In that respect, he did not perceive the Soviet Union's challenge to be fundamentally military. Rather, Eisenhower saw a greater challenge in its subversive activities and its techniques of installing totalitarian governments, communist-dominated, by use of force or revolution. By 1955 the Soviet bloc had technicians operating in fourteen

2. Eisenhower's biographer focuses on Eisenhower's desire to be friends with all parties, improvement of American relations with the Saudis, and avoiding an arms race in the Middle East as the fundamental tenets of Eisenhower's policy in Ambrose, *Eisenhower: The President*, 328–29.

3. Stephen Ambrose, *The Wisdom of Dwight D. Eisenhower: Quotations from Ike's Speeches and Writings, 1939–1969* (New Orleans, 1990), 19.

4. See William Roger Louis and Roger Owen, eds., *Suez 1956: The Crisis and Its Consequences* (Oxford, 1989), 395, for a detailed analysis of the special relationship between the United States and Great Britain with respect to foreign policy prior to 1956.

countries in the Middle East and Southwest Asia. In addition, the Soviet Union extended financial credit amounting to $600 million to the Arab states, a considerable increase over the previous year.[5] From Eisenhower's perspective, emerging nationalism in the developing world and encroaching Soviet opportunism combined to convince most administration officials that the Soviet Union fostered much of the political instability in the Middle East. With the benefit of twenty-twenty hindsight, that was probably not the case, but when viewed from the perspective of an American president in the midst of the cold war, such perceived Soviet adventurism was a challenge that Eisenhower was determined to confront to deter the Soviets from extending their influence throughout the Third World.

In addition to the perceived Soviet threat, several external factors complicated American efforts to promote regional stability. Rivalry among the Arab states forced difficult decisions upon policy-makers. Any demonstration of support for Iraq, for example, might antagonize Egypt, whose president viewed his country as the dominant Arab state. Secondly, support of Israel created a seemingly insurmountable problem. The United States had been the first state to recognize Israel as a sovereign nation in 1948. Because the Arab nations were bent on the destruction of Israel, any lasting American treaty of friendship between the United States and the Arab world was virtually impossible. What the Arabs desired most—the elimination of Israel as an independent Zionist state—was beyond Eisenhower's ability to grant, even had he so been inclined. Eisenhower's answer to this diplomatic morass was to be friends with all sides. In a telephone conversation on April 7, 1956, with Dulles about the Middle East, Eisenhower said, "We can't do any one of these things in a vacuum—[we] have to look at the rounded picture—everybody has got to have something."[6]

In an early attempt to prevent the instability that might result in radical revolutions, the United States had joined Great Britain and France in signing the Tripartite Declaration of May 25, 1950, in which the United States set forth its deep interest in promoting the establishment and maintenance of peace and stability in the Middle East.[7] The declaration, to

5. Burton I. Kaufamn, *Trade and Aid: Eisenhower's Foreign Economic Policy, 1953–1961* (Baltimore, 1982), 58.

6. Telephone conversation between Eisenhower and John Foster Dulles, April 7, 1956, as quoted in Ambrose, *Eisenhower: The President*, 328.

7. See Department of State *Bulletin*, No. 869 (February 20, 1956), 285–86. A copy of the Tripartite Declaration is also located in 091 Palestine, Records of the Joint Chiefs of Staff, RG 218.

which none of the Middle East states was a party, was an attempt by the Western powers to regulate the supply of arms, supplied primarily by the Western states, in such a manner to make another Middle East war unlikely. The chief provisions of the declaration recognized the necessity for Middle Eastern countries to maintain adequate armed forces for national defense, as opposed to an arms race among the states in the region, and asserted the West's unalterable opposition to the use of armed force in the Middle East to settle regional disputes. In a separate part of the declaration, the three external powers undertook to take immediate action "both within and outside the United Nations" to stop any threatened action to violate frontiers or armistice lines.[8]

Prior to 1955, however, Eisenhower's focus remained on Europe and East Asia, and the president seemed reluctant to make a major diplomatic foray in the Middle East. He believed that Great Britain and France had far more experience in dealing with the troublesome Arabs. Eisenhower's only significant involvement in the area occurred in 1953, when he confronted the ardent Iranian nationalist Mohammed Mossedeq. Mossedeq had created economic chaos by nationalizing the oil fields and refineries of the Anglo-Persian Oil Company in 1951. Unable to counter Mossedeq's increasing popularity and support from the Iranian masses, the British appealed to Eisenhower for assistance. Hoping to remain neutral, Eisenhower refused to support his European ally until Mossedeq forced the pro–British Shah to abdicate for "reasons of health." When the Iranian Prime Minister courted the Communist Tudeh Party in 1953, Eisenhower reasoned that the time had come to remove Mossedeq and restore Mohammed Reza Shah Pahlavi to power. By use of the president's "good offices" and a Central Intelligence Agency–sponsored coup, code-named AJAX, the United States succeeded in placing the Shah back on Iran's peacock throne.[9]

For the remainder of his presidency, relations between the United States and the government of Iran remained cordial. Washington continued to support the Shah financially, although never to the Shah's com-

8. See Keith Kyle, "Britian and the Crisis, 1955–1956," as quoted in Louis and Owen, eds., *Suez 1956*, 105.

9. For a complete account of the CIA involvement, see Ambrose, *Ike's Spies*, 189–214. AJAX was actually a cooperative effort between the United States and Great Britian. In August 1954, Kermit Roosevelt of the CIA and a five-man team entered Iran clandestinely to organize special military units and armed mobs to remove Mossedeq from office. Financed by $1 million in Iranian currency, Roosevelt succeeded in removing Mossedeq. On August 22, Mohammed Reza Shah Pahlevi returned in triumph to Teheran. Loy Henderson examines the Iranian crisis in great detail in his oral history on file at the Eisenhower Library. See OH 191, by Don North, December 14, 1970, pp. 9–22.

plete satisfaction. Additionally, Eisenhower promised assistance in the event of a Soviet attack, and the administration generally attempted to encourage the Shah to initiate programs for economic and social reforms. Only through such programs could domestic tranquillity prevail. In the interim, the United States avoided provoking the Soviet Union into harassing the country.[10]

Eisenhower viewed his role in resolving the Iranian crisis among the achievements of his first administration. Although the morality of his intervention in the domestic affairs of a sovereign nation was highly questionable, Eisenhower sacrificed morality for political expediency. Fearing that the chaotic political and economic situation in Iran might lead to increased Soviet opportunism, he acted resolutely to prevent domestic anarchy and to deter the expansion of Soviet influence into one of the world's most important economic regions. Although the Soviet threat during the Mossedeq crisis was dubious at best,[11] Eisenhower remained convinced that he had saved Iran from communism and overthrown Mossedeq's "Communist-dominated regime." His decision to interfere in Iran, however, became the foundation on which future generations of Iranian nationalists based their strong anti-American sentiment.

Eisenhower's first venture into the Middle East also reflected much about the manner in which he would conduct foreign policy and manage crises during his tenure as president. Purposely excluding himself from the details of the plot, Eisenhower took no part in the meetings that coordinated AJAX. Yet once he convinced himself that Mossedeq had adopted a pro-Communist stance, Eisenhower gave CIA official Kermit Roosevelt the approval to proceed. The decision to intervene was the president's and his alone. He never regretted it. The ends fully justified the means.[12] Three years later, the president would act in a similar fashion during the Suez crisis. During both crises, Eisenhower initially assessed the threat, weighed the alternatives, decided on a course of action that would achieve his policy objective, and then acted without worrying about the consequences.

Having prevented the Soviet Union from benefiting from the economic crisis in Iran in 1954, Eisenhower made a determined effort the following year to enhance American influence in the Middle East. His objectives were twofold: first, to bolster containment by constructing a Middle East Treaty Organization comparable to NATO and SEATO;

10. Barry Rubin, *Paved with Good Intentions: The American Experience in Iran* (New York, 1980), 91–98.

11. Richard Cottam, *Nationalism in Iran* (Pittsburgh, 1979), 230.

12. For a summary of Eisenhower's crisis management in the Mossedeq affair, see Ambrose, *Eisenhower: The President,* 109–13, 129–30.

second, to settle the Arab-Israeli dispute. Complicating any United States diplomatic initiative in the area, however, was President Gamal Nasser of Egypt. An extreme pan-Arabist and Egyptian nationalist who viewed himself as the dynamic leader of the Arab community, Nasser possessed ambition that transcended his position as president of Egypt.[13]

In response to Nasser's emerging nationalism and Soviet expansionism, Iraq and Turkey concluded an agreement in 1955 that was aimed at extending cooperation "to ensure the internal stability and security of the Middle East."[14] With the urging of the United States, several other nations joined the newly constructed Baghdad Pact; these included Great Britain (April 5, 1955), Pakistan (July 1, 1955), and Iran (October 9, 1955). The official American reaction to the formation of the "northern tier" was somewhat peculiar. On October 13, the Department of State welcomed the Iranian decision to join the pact as further evidence of the desire and ability of nations of the Middle East to develop regional arrangements for collective self-defense. In spite of the priority that the United States attached to the formation of the Baghdad Pact, Eisenhower balked at formal membership. This stance somewhat mystified the British, who had heartily endorsed the project. In response to repeated British appeals to join the pact, Dulles dispatched the ambassador to Iraq, Waldemar Gallman, as an observer to the Baghdad Pact. According to the secretary of state, the United States would join "if and when it seemed in doing so, it would be a contribution to the general stability of the area."[15]

Behind the American refusal to join the Baghdad Pact was Eisenhower's and Dulles' desire to maintain their diplomatic options. Neither Eisenhower nor Dulles could see why the United States should alienate both Egypt and Israel by joining a pact whose avowed goal was to halt Soviet expansion, but whose real purpose, according to Nasser, was to preserve British colonial power in the Middle East. Nasser's rhetoric aside, the Egyptian president's opposition to the pact reflected his own disapproval of any organization that might hinder his own personal influence among the Arab states. For its part, Israel viewed the pact as an attempt to form a unified Arab front against the Jewish state.[16]

13. There are numerous books on the significance of Nasser's role in Egypt and the Arab Middle East. For an insider's view, see Mohammed Heikal, *The Cairo Documents* (New York, 1973) and his *Cutting the Lion's Tail: Suez Through Egyptian Eyes* (New York, 1987). As a Cairo newspaper editor and personal friend of the Egyptian president, Heikal is decidedly pro-Nasser in his outlook. R. Hrair Dekmejian analyzes Nasser's charismatic appeal in *Egypt Under Nasir* (Albany, 1971). Raymond Baker explores Egypt's changing political and economic conditions in *Egypt's Uncertain Revolution* (Cambridge, 1978).

14. See Section 381 EMMEA SCC 27, Records of the Joint Chiefs of Staff, RG 218.

15. Department of State *Bulletin* No. 865 (January 23, 1956), 121.

16. Ambrose, *Eisenhower: The President,* 316. M. Perlman examines Nasser's op-

The American military establishment's view of the Baghdad Pact mirrored that of Dulles. The Joint Chiefs did not support adherence to the organization because formal membership would affect American influence in bringing about a reduction in Arab-Israeli tensions and constitute a new commitment, implying a willingness to provide a substantial increase in military and economic aid. In any event, the United States remained "sympathetic" toward the organization, but refused outright membership, while maintaining continuous liaison with the Baghdad Pact through Loy Henderson, deputy secretary of state.

Unfortunately, the United States, in its tacit acceptance of the formation of the Baghdad Pact, misjudged the actual temperament of the Arab Middle East. In 1956 the dominant figure in Arab politics was Nasser, and Nasser's strong nationalistic policies angered American policy-makers. Initially, Eisenhower and Dulles sought to sway Nasser to join the Western bloc. Indeed, Dulles had been instrumental in persuading Great Britain to sign the Anglo-Egyptian accord of 1954, in which Great Britain agreed to withdraw its troops from the Suez Canal zone by 1956. However, Nasser became increasingly bellicose in Dulles' eyes.

On February 28, 1955, an Israeli raid into the Gaza strip left twenty-eight slain Egyptians. The attack had a marked impact on Nasser, who considered the strike as a signal that Israel had revived its policy of large-scale reprisals to force Egypt to negotiate a peace settlement with Israel. Shocked by the carnage, and vowing that the attackers would not get away unpunished, Nasser appealed to the United States for a shipment of arms to counter Israel's growing military power and apparent willingness to use its army as an instrument of policy. When Nasser's effort failed because of Eisenhower's desire to preserve the status quo and because of domestic political pressure from the Jewish lobby, the Egyptian president made secret overtures to the Soviet Union to obtain the necessary arms to redress the military balance in the Middle East.

To the United States, Nasser's flirtation with the Soviet Union was the first solid evidence of Soviet penetration into the unstable Middle East since the Iranian crisis of 1953. Eisenhower immediately dispatched George V. Allen, assistant secretary of state for Near Eastern, South Asian, and African affairs, to the region to discourage the proposed arms deal, but Allen was unsuccessful. On September 27, 1955, Nasser announced that he had concluded an arms agreement with Czechoslova-

position to the Baghdad Pact in "Egypt Versus the Baghdad Pact," *Middle Eastern Affairs,* VII (March, 1956), 95–101.

kia in which Egypt would exchange its domestic cotton production for Soviet arms. Nasser's announcement caused an immediate furor within the Western community of nations.[17] With its cold war mentality, the Eisenhower administration was alarmed about the incursion of the Soviet Union, albeit by proxy, into the Middle East. Moreover, the influx of Soviet arms not only would disrupt the military balance of power previously existing in one of the most important regions in the world, but also would allow the Soviet Union to leap over the bridge of northern tier states included in the Baghdad Pact.[18] This fear highlighted Eisenhower's growing concern that Nasser's pan-Arab movement would ally itself with the Soviet Union and jeopardize the flow of oil to Western Europe.

The Czech arms deal, coupled with Nasser's continued vociferous verbal attacks on the Baghdad Pact, convinced Eisenhower that Nasser was untrustworthy and unpredictable. Never fully comprehending the urgency of Nasser's concerns about Egypt's national security, Eisenhower interpreted his Egyptian counterpart's actions as "Communist-inspired" and detrimental to the regional balance of power. Nasser's actions, of course, were perfectly understandable from Egypt's perspective. At a dinner with Egyptian ambassador Ahmen Hussein, Chief of Naval Operations Burke expressed concern about Nasser's alleged ties with the Soviets, which had the appearance of being much stronger than the Egyptians claimed.[19] Hussein stated that his country had to obtain arms to protect itself and because the United States had been unwilling to supply the necessary munitions, Egypt had gone to the only other country willing to provide arms. These assurances did not assuage American fears, but an alternative to secure Nasser's friendship and hopefully block further Soviet influence was at hand.

For several years, Nasser had contemplated the construction of a high dam at Aswan that would increase the arable land of Egypt by one quarter. Visualized as a reservoir of 23,000 million cubic meters of water over

17. Amin Hewedy, a lieutenant colonel and vice-director of the Planning Section, Operational Department, General Staff of the Egyptian Armed Forces in 1956, views the Czech arms deal as the spark that ignited the Suez Canal crisis of 1956 and the sensitive juncture between peace and war in the region. See his essay "Nasser and the Crisis of 1956," in Louis and Owen, eds., *Suez 1956*, 161–72.

18. Egypt received 530 armored vehicles (230 tanks, 200 armored troop carriers, and 100 self-propelled guns), some 500 artillery peices, and nearly 200 combat aircraft. Figures are reported by Israeli intelligence, as quoted in Chaim Herzog, "The Suez-Sinai Campaign: Background," in Selwyn Ilan Troen and Moshe Shemesh, eds., *The Suez-Sinai Crisis, 1956* (New York, 1990), 4.

19. See Memorandum for Record, March 24, 1956, CJCS 091 Palestine, in Records of the Joint Chiefs of Staff, RG 218.

an area of 739 square miles, the project was of primary importance to Nasser's economic program. If Nasser was the key to cordial relations with Egypt, the dam was the key to Nasser's good will.[20] The problems involved in building the project, however, were immense and resulted in another confrontation between the superpowers, which led to the deterioration of relations between Egypt and the Western states.

The chief obstacle involved in the construction of the dam was the immense cost of the project, estimated at $1.3 billion, a sum far exceeding Egypt's resources, thereby necessitating outside assistance. Eugene Black, the president of the International Bank of Reconstruction and Development (World Bank), was extremely optimistic about the project and had visited Egypt early in 1953 to examine the feasibility of jointly financing the dam. On November 21, 1955, negotiations to secure Western aid for construction began in Washington with Black, American Under Secretary of State Herbert Hoover, Jr., British Ambassador Sir Roger Makins, and the Egyptian financial minister, Abdel Kaissouni. By December 16 the quartet had reached a tentative agreement in which they decided that, after an initial allocation of funds by the United States and Great Britain, the Western nations would consider supporting the later stages of the development "subject to legislative authority."[21] By terms of the agreement, the World Bank planned to lend Egypt $200 million, and the United States and Great Britain would make initial grants of $54 million and $14 million, respectively. Cairo would provide the remaining $900 million in local currency. Nasser's immediate reaction to this phased economic support was not encouraging, but following Black's sojourn to Cairo in January, Nasser accepted the negotiated settlement.

Nasser's initial reluctance to accept the Western offer seemed to confirm Eisenhower's suspicions that Nasser was courting the Soviet Union and playing one side against the other. The president's diary of March 1956 was filled with growing apprehension that Nasser was becoming more difficult to control and influence. On March 8, Eisenhower wrote, "We have reached the point where it looks as if Egypt, under Nasser, is going to make no move whatsoever to meet the Israelites in an effort to settle outstanding differences. Moreover, the Arabs, absorbing major consignments of arms from the Soviets, are daily growing more arrogant and disregarding the interests of Western Europe and of the United States in the Middle East region."[22] One week later, Eisenhower stated that

20. Heikal, *The Cairo Documents*, 58–59.

21. Ralph H. Magnus, ed., *Documents on the Middle East* (Washington, D.C., 1969), 102. See also Parmet, *Eisenhower and the American Crusades*, 479, and *Congressional Record*, 84th Cong. 2nd Sess., 12208, for discussions of jointly financing the dam.

22. Ferrell, ed., *Eisenhower Diaries*, 318–19.

Nasser proved to be a complete stumbling block toward regional stability. On March 28, the president met with Dulles, Radford, and Wilson to revise American policy toward Egypt. Extremely concerned about Nasser's insatiable ambition and his links to the Soviet Union, Eisenhower directed that Dulles prepare a memorandum designed to let "Colonel Nasser realize that he cannot cooperate as he is doing with the Soviet Union and at the same time enjoy most-favored-nation treatment by the United States."[23]

Throughout the spring, there was a general shift in American policy from accommodation with Nasser to pressure tactics designed to induce Nasser to cooperate in the settlement of the Arab-Israeli dispute and to moderate his criticism of the Western governments. To Eisenhower's chagrin, Nasser refused to be intimidated, and on May 16 the Egyptian president committed the unpardonable sin of officially recognizing the People's Republic of China. For a cold warrior like Eisenhower, this action was the final straw and served to confirm Nasser's pro-Communist tendencies. Any lines differentiating Egyptian nationalism and communism vanished.

Nasser's continued verbal attacks on the Western powers should have prompted Eisenhower to withdraw the formal American financial offer to support the Aswan project, but the administration procrastinated throughout the late spring and early summer. By July, congressional support for the Aswan Dam was lukewarm at best. As early as the preceding December, Dulles had approached Senate Majority Leader Lyndon Johnson, an avowed anti-Nasserite, and informed him that the Department of State "placed special emphasis on the economic aspects of foreign policy, particularly in view of the stepped-up Soviet campaign in this field."[24] Dulles' insistence on supporting the project did not persuade many congressional leaders, and support from Capitol Hill remained less than enthusiastic. Democratic leaders expressed dissatisfaction with the magnitude of the loan and the long-term (10–14 years) aid authorization. Richard Russell, chairman of the Senate Armed Services Committee, complained that the Department of State was "so sterile of ideas that the only answer they have to the Russians is to ask for more money

23. *Ibid.*, 323. See also Memorandum for the President, March 28, 1956, in folder marked "Near Eastern Policies," Box 5, Dulles-Herter Series, Ann Whitman File, EP, EL; Memorandum of Conversation, in folder marked "March 1956 (1), Misc.," Box 13, DDE Diary Series, Ann Whitman File, EP, EL; Ambrose, *Eisenhower: The President,* 318; and Louis and Owen, eds., *Suez 1956,* 191.

24. Department of State *Bulletin,* No. 861 (December 26, 1955), 1049. Loy Henderson confirms the economic emphasis of foreign policy and the House of Representatives' reluctance to finance the Aswan Dam in transcript of his oral history (OH 191), 41, EL.

[to finance the Aswan Dam]."[25] Louisiana Representative Otto Passman, chairman of the House Appropriations Subcommittee that handled foreign aid, bitterly denounced the package as "unwarranted by the facts."[26] In the Senate, both Oregon senators, Wayne Morse and Richard Neuberger, attacked the administration, stating that they would not support Eisenhower unless the president supported their efforts to build a dam on the Snake River in their home state.[27] Additionally, senators from the southern cotton states were generally disinclined to support a project that would inevitably lead to greater cotton production by one of their chief economic competitors. The Washington *Post* reported that Passman's and his colleagues' opposition seemed to signal a Democratic drive to cut the foreign assistance program for Egypt.[28]

To complicate the administration's early efforts at obtaining congressional support for the Aswan project, many legislators had written off Egypt as a result of the Czechoslovakian arms agreement. House Majority Leader John McCormick wanted "to throw the fear of America into Nasser to dissuade him from buying more Soviet weapons." Senator Estes Kefauver of Tennessee viewed the arms deal as a turning point in the Middle East because it brought the cold war into the region, and Nasser's chief aim was the destruction of Israel. Fellow Democratic Senator Hubert Humphery expressed dismay as to why the administration was not contemplating increasing arms shipments to Israel to counter Nasser's recent acquisitions.[29] Soon congressional opposition to the Aswan Dam project was coming from both sides of the aisle as Senate Minority Leader William Knowland put himself on record as opposing any long-term aid commitment.[30] Despite strong pressure by the president and the secretary of state, Congress refused to yield and by mid-July, the Senate Appropriations Committee recommended that no further aid be extended to Egypt for construction of the Aswan Dam without prior approval of the committee.[31]

Mounting congressional opposition and pressure from the strong Israeli lobby convinced Eisenhower to abandon the project, but the United States did not immediately withdraw its offer. According to Mohammed

25. San Francisco *Chronicle*, February 28, 1956.

26. William Klingaman, "Congress and American Foreign Policy for the Middle East" (Ph.D. dissertation, University of Virginia, 1978) 10.

27. *Congressional Record*, 84th Cong., 2nd Sess., 1443–45.

28. Washington *Post*, January 4, 5, and 8, 1956.

29. *Congressional Record*, 84th Cong., 2nd Sess., 195, 1817, and 2671.

30. *Ibid.*, 195.

31. *Congressional Quarterly Weekly Report*, XIV, No. 29 (Washington, D.C., 1956), 883 (hereinafter cited as *CQ Weekly Report*).

Heikal, Nasser's most intimate counselor, the Egyptian president came to the conclusion that the United States was serious for possibly one month at the beginning of 1956 about helping to finance the High Dam.[32] Although Nasser failed to comprehend the difficulties Eisenhower encountered in his efforts to propel unpopular legislation through a recalcitrant Congress, he was probably correct in his conviction that the administration's enthusiasm for the project had cooled markedly by the spring. Still, Eisenhower felt obligated to help finance the construction of the dam, and on June 20, 1956, Eugene Black returned to Cairo to brief Nasser on a final Western offer. When Nasser countered with proposals that were unacceptable to the United States, Great Britain, and the World Bank, Eisenhower considered the matter dead for all practical purposes.[33]

Nasser's action should have prompted Eisenhower and Dulles to terminate the financial arrangement, but the administration hesitated to take what many congressional leaders felt was the next logical step. By that time, Anthony Eden, prime minister of Great Britain, began expressing serious doubts about the wisdom of upholding the British end of the financial package.[34] Following King Hussein of Jordan's abrupt dismissal of Sir John Bagot Glubb, commander of Jordan's Arab Legion—an action that Eden wrongly attributed to Nasser's influence—the prime minister decided that "the world was not big enough to hold him and Nasser."[35] For Eden and his British colleagues, this was the final straw. In their eyes, Nasser was reminiscent of Hitler and Mussolini, and Eden was intent on avoiding any policy of appeasement. Reinforcing his distaste for the Egyptian president were reports that Egypt was diverting funds earmarked for the dam's construction to additional arms from the Soviets. Gradually Eden and Foreign Secretary Selwyn Lloyd decided they "could not go on with a project likely to become increasingly onerous in finance and unsatisfactory practice."[36] In other words, Great Britain was looking for an escape from a difficult diplomatic situation, much of which was its own design.

As Eden and Eisenhower sought to revise their policies toward Egypt, both leaders had become increasingly doubtful of the wisdom of Anglo-American participation in the Aswan project. The deterioration of re-

32. Heikal, *Cairo Documents,* 61.
33. Eisenhower, *Waging Peace,* 30–31.
34. Anthony Eden, *Full Circle* (Boston, 1960), 468–69.
35. Hoopes, *The Devil and John Foster Dulles,* 335. See also Robert R. Bowie, "Eisenhower, Dulles, and the Suez Crisis," in Louis and Owen, eds., *Suez 1956,* 190–91.
36. Hugh Thomas, *Suez* (New York, 1967), 22. See also Selwyn Lloyd, *Suez 1956* (New York, 1978), 66–70.

lations between the United States and Egypt was most obvious in Nasser's vehement criticism of Western attitudes toward the Arab-Israeli dispute. These denunciations, coupled with Egyptian objections directed against Great Britain for its encouragement of Jordan to join the Baghdad Pact, finally convinced Eisenhower and Dulles to terminate the pledge of financial support.[37] Throughout July, Dulles and the British ambassador reviewed together most of the reasons for not proceeding. In addition to their growing dissatisfaction with Nasser, the Western statesmen doubted Egypt's ability to devote the domestic resources needed to complete the High Dam. Dulles also ascertained that the Aswan project might prove an economic liability for foreigners involved in carrying it through, to say nothing of congressional opposition and other complaints that Egypt was getting more assistance by blackmail than it was by cooperation.[38]

Consequently, Dulles prepared a single page draft of the official cancellation of the American offer and submitted it to the president for approval on July 19, 1956. Eisenhower, who had recently returned from Gettysburg where he had been recovering from a brief illness, made a few editorial revisions and approved the draft, which he returned to the secretary of state. At noon of the same day, Dulles met with Egyptian Ambassador Hussein and formally withdrew American support. The Egyptian minister appeared incredulous, as he had just agreed to all the formerly announced American restrictions on the aid package. Unfortunately, he indicated to Dulles that if American assistance was not forthcoming, he had a Russian offer in his pocket. That indiscretion gave the secretary of state the opportunity he needed. Stating that the United States was not subject to international blackmail, Dulles addressed Hussein in abrupt terms, to which Hussein justifiably took personal affront. In explaining the American position, Dulles stated, "Developments within the succeeding seven months [since December when the initial offer of support was negotiated] have not been favorable to the success of the project, and the United States had concluded that it is not feasible in present circumstances to participate in the project. Agreement by the ripar-

37. Eugene Black, the president of the International Bank of Reconstruction and Development, attributes the change of Dulles' attitude toward financing the dam to congressional dissatisfaction, Nasser's recognition of the People's Republic of China, Nasser's alleged support of Algerian rebels, and the dismissal of Glubb from Jordan. For his general views on Nasser, Dulles, and the Aswan Dam project, see his oral history transcript (OH 341) at the Eisenhower Library and on file at the Dulles Oral History Project at Princeton University.

38. Bowie, "Eisenhower, Dulles, and the Suez Crisis," in Louis and Owen, eds., Suez 1956, 194–95.

ian states has not been achieved, and the ability of Egypt to devote adequate resources to assure the project's success has become more uncertain than at the time the offer was made."[39]

For his part, Eisenhower never doubted the wisdom of withdrawing the offer of financial support, but he was concerned about the manner in which Dulles had handled the negotiations. In a total lack of diplomatic etiquette, the secretary of state had released the news of the American withdrawal to the American newspapers prior to Hussein having the opportunity to inform Nasser. As a result of this indiscretion, Eisenhower wrote Dulles and asked him if the withdrawal of American assistance had been "abrupt." Dulles replied:

There had for some time been mounting Congressional opposition. The Senate Appropriations Committee had already passed a resolution directing that there should be no support for the Aswan Dam without the approval of the Committee—an action which, while it was probably not constitutional, indicated a Congressional attitude, in the face of which it would have been impossible to finance the Dam. If I had not announced our withdrawal when I did, the Congress would certainly have imposed it on us, almost unanimously. As it was, we retained some flexibility.

Of course Egypt, with its flirtations with the Soviet Union, had itself consciously jeopardized our sharing in this project, and they had tried to bluff us by pretending to accept Soviet "offers." The outcome was not in fact anything in the nature of a "shock" or "surprise" to the Egyptians.[40]

Dulles never addressed the discourtesy of releasing the information prematurely to the press.

By withdrawing the American offer, Eisenhower took the step that Congress had urged since February. Senator Mike Mansfield noted there was little opposition to the secretary's action. According to Mansfield, "I believe that Secretary Dulles did the right thing in finally turning down the Aswan Dam proposal, with it would have meant the creating . . . of a moral commitment to the tune of hundreds of millions of United States dollars to build the project."[41]

Mansfield's comments were representative of both the Senate and the

39. Department of State Press Release 401, July 19, 1956, in Department of State *Bulletin*, No. 892 (July 30, 1956), 188. See also Magnus, ed., *Documents on the Middle East*, 103. The complete text outlining the American withdrawal of financial support is in the New York *Times*, July 20, 1956. Ambrose states that Eisenhower's actions were an attempt to "weaken Nasser." Ambrose, *Eisenhower: The President*, 330.

40. See Ann Whitman's comments and notation in folder marked "Sept '56 Diary-acw," Box 8, Ann Whitman Diary Series, Ann Whitman File, EP, EL. For text of Dulles' reply, see Eisenhower, *Waging Peace*, 33.

41. *Congressional Record*, 84th Cong., 2nd Sess., 15571.

House of Representatives. By July, there was virtually no support in Congress for the Aswan Dam. Minnesota Republican Senator Edward Thye stated, "It is not feasible for us to participate in the project," and Democrat Daniel Flood of Pennsylvania lauded Dulles' action: "The Secretary of State . . . is to be complimented on this point."[42] George Mahan, a Texas Democrat on the House Appropriations Committee, declared that Dulles "deserves to be complimented for assuming this position." Summarizing the attitude of his committee, Mahan concluded, "I am willing for our government to help other people when such efforts also promote our welfare and defense. But we have no business undertaking to underwrite even in part the proposed gigantic Aswan Dam in Egypt."[43]

In spite of what Dulles said publicly, there were other reasons the United States withdrew its offer of financial support. Nineteen fifty-six was a presidential election year, and pro-Israeli lobbyists had been exerting pressure on the executive and legislative leaders in the federal government. Additionally, the administration was reluctant to alienate southern congressmen representing the cotton-producing states, who were fearful of supporting the huge financial package to a potential competitor in the textile market.[44] Moreover, many leaders were still irritated over Nasser's recognition of the People's Republic of China. Still others viewed Egypt's so-called neutralist stance as an invitation to the Soviet Union to enter the Middle East. The *Times* of London echoed these concerns as it reported that Dulles had taken a "calculated risk" that might drive the Arab states farther into the Communist camp.[45]

With the withdrawal of American financial support, Great Britain quickly followed suit. Eden claimed he had been informed about Dulles' action beforehand, but had not been consulted. Therefore, he had no prior opportunity to comment on the matter. The British Cabinet met on July 20 and decided to join the United States in withdrawing from the project because "both Governments had come to doubt Egypt's capacity to meet the cost of so grandiose a scheme."[46] According to Foreign Secretary Lloyd, the decision was made on strictly economic grounds, principally the perception that Egyptian industrialization and arms expenditures prevented the degree of priority necessary to ensure the dam's success.[47]

42. *Ibid.*, 13086, 14179. See also Klingaman, "Congress and American Foreign Policy for the Middle East," 62–71.

43. *Congressional Record*, 84th Cong., 2nd Sess., 15571.

44. George Allen, assistant secretary of state for the Near East and Africa, places the southern senators at the heart of the opposition to financial aid to Egypt in his oral history on file at the Dulles Oral History Project at Princeton University, p. 30.

45. *Times* (London), July 23, 1956.

46. *Ibid.*, July 21, 1956.

47. Lloyd, *Suez 1956*, 71. Both Eden and Lloyd are a bit duplicitous in their respec-

As predictable as was the British reaction, the Egyptian response was totally unexpected. The New York *Times* reported that a "gasp of surprise and anger swept the city of Cairo at the news that the United States and Britain had withdrawn their offers to aid in the project."[48] As Hussein hurried to call Nasser and Egyptian Foreign Minister Fawzi in Cairo, he learned that Fawzi already knew of the American action, due to the leak to the American press. For his part, Nasser was extremely angry and claimed that Dulles and Eden had been deceiving him all the time.[49]

On July 23 Nasser met with members of Egypt's Revolutionary Command Council and proposed nationalization of the Suez Canal to offset the lost Anglo-American revenues. The following day he delivered a vitriolic attack against the United States for violating every decent principle of foreign relations. Two days later, July 26, Nasser addressed a throng estimated at a quarter of a million people in the Mancia Square in Alexandria. In a three-hour speech that delighted the crowd, the Egyptian president proclaimed the nationalization of the Suez Canal Company.[50] Even as he was speaking, Egyptian forces occupied the various company installations.

Had Eisenhower forced Nasser's hand by withdrawing the offer of financial support? Maybe, but the Egyptian president had long decided on a policy to remove all vestiges of Egypt's colonial heritage. Eisenhower had simply provided him an opportunity. Still, Eisenhower must share some of the responsibility for the events that initiated the Suez crisis. Fully aware of Eden's animosity toward the Egyptian president and Dulles' own anti-Nasser sentiments, Eisenhower had weighed the diplomatic alternatives and approved the withdrawal of American financial support. Once he equated Egyptian nationalism, as personified by the Egyptian president, with Soviet expansionism, Eisenhower had in fact eliminated many of the diplomatic options that he so cherished in conducting foreign policy. He now faced an additional crisis of how to deal effectively with an Egyptian nationalist, who in one momentous step had defied the West and had seized the Middle East's foremost public waterway.

---

tive memoirs. Neither was fond of Nasser, and both welcomed the American initiative as an excellent opportunity to weaken their principal nemesis in the Middle East.

48. New York *Times,* July 21, 1956.

49. For Nasser's reaction, see Heikal, *Cairo Documents,* 85, and *Cutting the Lion's Tail,* xiii–xiv. Recent accounts cast doubt as to the extent that Nasser was surprised by Dulles' withdrawal of financial support. See Bowie, "Eisenhower, Dulles, and the Suez Crisis," in Louis and Owen, eds., *Suez 1956,* 196.

50. Dekmejian states that Nasser's actions were dictated by political and psychological reasons, the latter being inherent in revolutionary systems. See Dekmejian, *Egypt Under Nasir,* 45. For the complete text of the nationalization order, see Magnus, ed., *Documents on the Middle East,* 167–69, or CCS 092 Egypt SCC.1, Appendix C, JCS 2105/38, Records of the Joint Chiefs of Staff, RG 218.

3

THE CRISIS INTENSIFIES

Crisis management, particularly at the opening stages of diplomatic crises, is laden with dangerous escalatory potential.
—Alexander L. George

The Western governments greeted Nasser's unilateral expropriation of the Suez Canal with incredulity and astonishment. Neither Eisenhower nor Eden had any advance warning from their respective intelligence agencies of the Egyptian president's plan. Eden received the news of the seizure on the evening of July 26 when he was entertaining King Faisal of Iraq and Prime Minister Nuri-es-Said. Interrupted by a private secretary, Eden immediately adjourned the dinner and withdrew to a private study with Selwyn Lloyd, Lord Salisbury, who was Lord President of Council and acting secretary of state for foreign affairs, and Lord Home, the minister for Commonwealth Relations. Shortly thereafter, the British Lord Chancellor Viscount David Patrick Kilmuir and the British Chiefs of Staff joined them, quickly followed by French Ambassador Chauvel and American chargé d'affaires Andrew B. Foster, whom Eden summoned because Ambassador Winthrop Aldrich was in the United States for a short vacation.[1]

Getting underway at midnight, the meeting lasted two hours as Eden contemplated Great Britain's response. Clearly infuriated by an act that he termed international piracy, Eden demanded immediate and strong action. Speaking in vitriolic terms, he directed his attention to Foster and charged that the "Egyptian has his thumb on our windpipe. Tell Mr. Dulles I can not allow that."[2] A legal adviser then informed Eden that Nasser's action had certain precedence in law, but this did not diminish the prime minister's ire.

1. For accounts of this meeting, see Eden, *Full Circle*, 472–73, and Winthrop W. Aldrich, "The Suez Crisis: A Footnote to History," *Foreign Affairs*, LXX (April, 1967), 541. See also Hoopes, *The Devil and John Foster Dulles*, 347, and Lloyd, *Suez 1956*, 82.

2. Terrence Robertson, *Crisis: The Inside Story of the Suez Conspiracy* (New York, 1965), 73.

Long determined upon a policy to weaken and possibly topple Nasser, Eden directed the military chiefs to work through the evening and prepare plans to seize the Suez Canal. According to Lord Louis Mountbatten, First Sea Lord of the Admiralty, Eden had become "very fierce" and insisted on immediate military operations to retake the canal.[3] Such insistence failed to comprehend the logistics and training necessary to initiate complex military operations. Only when all three military leaders, including Chief of the Imperial General Staff Sir Gerald Templer and Chief of the Air Staff Sir Edward Boyle, in addition to Mountbatten, threatened to resign did Eden come to his senses. The following morning, July 27, Eden released a statement, "The unilateral decision of the Egyptian Government to expropriate the Suez Canal Company, without notice and in breach of the concession agreements, affects the right and interests of many nations. Her Majesty's Government is consulting other Governments immediately concerned with regard to the serious situation thus created; both in respect of the effect of the decision upon the operation of the Suez Canal and also of the wider questions raised by this arbitrary action."[4] Hugh Gaitskell, leader of the Labor opposition, joined Eden in condemning Nasser's action.

The conservative British press, like Her Majesty's Government, sharply protested the seizure of the Suez Canal. The *Times* of London called Nasser's act "international brigandage" and "the biggest blow so far dealt against the West by a so-called neutralist country." The conservative *Daily Mail* gave Nasser the sobriquet "Hitler of the Nile" and insisted that British troops should reoccupy the Suez Canal. The conservative *Daily Telegraph* likened Nasser to Hitler and Mussolini. Winston Churchill best summarized the national sentiment in stating, "We can't have that malicious swine sitting across our communications."[5]

France and Great Britain were aghast at the seizure of the waterway and reacted with expected militancy. The French government was decidedly anti-Nasser, since it attributed its problems in Algeria to Nasser's influence. Foreign Minister Christian Pineau was due in London on July

3. See Donald Neff, *Warriors at Suez* (New York, 1981), 276.

4. For parliamentary debates during the Suez Crisis, see *Parliamentary Debates (Hansard's)*, 5th Series, Vols. 556–62, House of Commons (hereinafter cited as *Hansard's Parliamentary Debates*). Copy of Eden's July 27 statement is quoted in Eden *Full Circle*, 473, and Department of State, *Foreign Relations of the United States, 1955–1957*, Volume XVI: *Suez Crisis, July 26–December 31, 1956* (Washington, D.C., 1990), 5 (hereinafter cited as Department of State, *Suez Crisis*).

5. *Times* (London), July 28, 1956, and New York *Times*, July 28, 1956, carried accounts of newspaper commentary. For Churchill's reaction, see Neff, *Warriors at Suez*, 277.

29 to discuss diplomatic options, but rumors were already rampant that the French preferred immediate military action to resolve the crisis. As early as July 30, French sources disclosed that French staff officers had arrived in London and indicated that France was prepared to commit two divisions in any action against Egypt. Pineau believed that any other action, such as debate by the United Nations or the International Court of Justice, would be too slow and detrimental to the immediate solution of the problem.

The official condemnation of Nasser by French officials was remarkably similar to that of Great Britain. Premier Guy Mollet chastised Egypt's "would be dictator who addressed the Western democracies in insulting terms."[6] With the support of the French Assembly, which had urged an energetic and severe riposte by a vote of 416–150, Mollet and Pineau advocated the immediate use of force to seize the Suez Canal and topple the Nasser regime. Within hours, American Ambassador Douglas Dillon cabled the Department of State with news of possible Anglo-French military action and Pineau's intention to send twenty-four *Mystere* aircraft to Israel.

In short, the British and French attitudes did not relate solely to the Suez Canal issue itself. Both nations were seeking a solution to their problems with the Egyptian president. The French viewed Nasser as the instigator of Algerian resistance, and the British considered Nasser's action as a threat to their vital national interests in the Middle East. Neither government fully comprehended the twin concepts of Arab nationalism and pan-Arabism, nor was either willing to relinquish the last vestiges of their colonial empires. Eden and Mollet then turned to the United States to determine the extent to which the United States would go in supporting and participating in firm action vis-à-vis Nasser in terms of economic sanctions and, beyond that, if necessary, military action.

Eisenhower's response to Nasser's unilateral proclamation was in sharp contrast to that of Great Britain and France. Unlike his NATO allies, Eisenhower's surprise was much more controlled and certainly less bellicose. Having received Foster's cable outlining the somber British cabinet meeting on July 26, Eisenhower contemplated his courses of action. Even at its incipient stage, the Suez Canal crisis had the potential of a major international dispute with traditional American allies. Confronting Eisenhower was a problem that, if not taken seriously or evaluated carefully, might disrupt the foundation of American foreign policy in the Middle East. Since the beginning of his administration, the president had sought to preserve tranquillity in the region lest the Soviet

6. As quoted in New York *Times,* August 1, 1956.

Union take advantage of a chaotic situation. It was the containment dimension of foreign policy, much more than public solidarity with the British, that bothered Eisenhower. As early as April 6, 1956, the president had written Eden to highlight his growing apprehension with the expansion of Soviet influence in the Middle East. Stated Eisenhower, "We should not be acquiescent in any measure which would give the Bear's claws a grip on production or transportation of oil which is so vital to the defense and economy of the Western world."[7] Now America's principal allies were contemplating the use of military force to restore the privileged position they had long enjoyed in the Middle East. In opposing Great Britain and France, Eisenhower realized he risked alienating his European partners, for such action might damage the solidarity of the Western alliance. If he sought to placate Great Britain and France and condemn Nasser, the United States might forfeit any credibility it had among the Arab states.

How to react? With whom to consult? The requirements of prudent foreign policy dictated a reasonable course that achieved near-term goals without sacrificing long-term political objectives. In responding to the emerging Suez crisis, Eisenhower followed a procedure with which he was familiar from his military career. As supreme commander during the invasion of Western Europe in World War II, Eisenhower had carefully assessed his mission, developed several courses of action to accomplish his goal of landing the Allied Expeditionary Forces on the beaches of Normandy, and finally selected the option that would best achieve that objective. He based his final decision on his analysis of his mission and available resources, as well as those of his adversary. His methodology for making critical decisions in response to the Suez crisis was virtually identical to any number of his military campaigns. Loosely translated to his current role as president, Eisenhower considered his nation's interests and national power and the interest and power of his potential adversaries and allies. Throughout the planning cycle for Operation OVERLORD, he had repeatedly consulted with various senior advisers in order to obtain the best advice available, but the decision to launch the invasion rested on his shoulders alone. He did not abrogate that responsibility in 1944, nor did he in 1956.

As was his custom when confronted with any major domestic or international dilemma that required his personal involvement, Eisenhower summoned a small group of trusted advisers to the White House for consultation. Since Dulles was in Lima, Peru, on the last leg of a Latin American tour and Admiral Radford was in East Asia, the president met with

7. Elizabeth D. Sherwood, *Allies in Crisis* (New Haven, 1990), 68.

Acting Secretary of State Herbert Hoover, Jr., Allen Dulles, and Staff Secretary Goodpaster.[8] In the discussion that followed, Eisenhower expressed his grave concern over the situation and instructed Hoover to address Nasser's invectives. Next, the president charged Hoover with the responsibility of supervising all press releases on the topic of Suez since the subject was so delicate. The acting secretary then turned the discussion to NATO, whereupon Eisenhower stated that the nationalization of the vital waterway should be a matter of immediate discussion among the NATO membership. Before terminating the meeting, Eisenhower directed Hoover to prepare an official statement outlining his personal concern with the deteriorating situation in the Suez Canal region, the shorter the better, discuss it with the secretary of state, and then bring it to him [president] for approval. The statement was in terms of "viewing with grave concern," but to give no hint of what the United States was likely to do.[9] In addition, Eisenhower directed Hoover to challenge the inaccuracies included in Nasser's public speech and convey the president's dissatisfaction to the Egyptian ambassador.

Eisenhower's use of the *ad hoc* meeting with a small group of intimate advisors was the principal forum in which he made key operational decisions. Not content with summoning the National Security Council or the cabinet, both of which he frequently found burdensome and time-consuming, Eisenhower used informal sessions to provide presidential direction and personal guidance to his "top lieutenants," as he called his primary advisers. Not only did this process allow the president to solicit advice from his principal aides, but the sessions permitted him to maximize his own influence on the decision-making apparatus, particularly from the outset of any crisis. Only after this original group of informal advisors had done its work did the president turn to the official bodies, such as the NSC or JCS. The meeting on July 27 to discuss Nasser's nationalization of the Suez Canal Company was quite typical of the manner in which the president conducted foreign policy and crisis manage-

8. As staff secretary, Goodpaster prepared detailed memoranda outlining his *ad hoc* meetings with the president. The July memoranda are located in a folder marked "July '56 Diary Staff Memos," in Box 16, DDE Diary Series, Ann Whitman File, EP, EL. For accounts of the July 27 meeting, see Ann Whitman Diary Series, July 27, 1956, Ann Whitman File, and DDE Diary Series, July 27, 1956, Ann Whitman File, both in EP, EL.

9. At noon on July 27, the Department of State issued press release No. 413, which read: "The announcement by the Egyptian government on July 26 with respect to the seizure of the installations of the Suez Canal Company carries far-reaching implications. It affects the nations whose economies depend upon the products which move through this international waterway and the maritime countries as well as the owners of the Company itself. The United States Government is consulting urgently with other governments concerned." U.S. Department of State *Bulletin* (August 6, 1956), 221–22.

ment. Prior to convening the session, Eisenhower already had Foster's cable outlining Eden's tentative response in his possession. He also had cable communications with Secretary Dulles. During the meeting, the president solicited advice and recommendations from the acting secretary of state and the Director of Central Intelligence. Had Radford been available, he would have provided military options for Eisenhower's consideration. Goodpaster's memoranda clearly demonstrated that Eisenhower directed the discussions and gave his subordinates detailed instructions and outlined specific parameters in which they would operate. For the duration of the Suez crisis, the president repeatedly convened small groups of advisers to receive his personal direction to ensure that the United States met its political objectives.

Shortly after the White House meeting, Eisenhower received an urgent telegram from Eden in which the prime minister called for a firm stand on the part of the Western democracies against Nasser. Eden stated:

We are all agreed that we cannot afford to allow Nasser to seize control of the Canal in this way, in defiance of international agreements. If we take a firm stand over this now, we shall have the support of all the maritime powers. If we do not, our influence and yours throughout the Middle East will, we are convinced, be irretrievably undermined. . . . As we see it we are unlikely to attain our objective by economic pressures alone. I gather that Egypt is not due to receive any further aid from you. . . . We ought in the first instance to bring the maximum political pressure to bear on Egypt. For this, apart from our own action, we should invoke the support of all the interested powers. My colleagues and I are convinced that we must be ready, in the last resort, to use force to bring Nasser to his senses. For our part we are prepared to do so. I have this morning instructed our Chiefs of Staff to prepare a military plan accordingly.[10]

The bellicose tone of Eden's message startled the president, but he was somewhat assuaged when the prime minister urged a tripartite conference in London to discuss the issue and to determine a coordinated response.

Upon receipt of the cable, Eisenhower directed Goodpaster to summon Hoover for another meeting to discuss the ramifications of Eden's dispatch. With respect to the London meeting, there was mutual agreement. Eisenhower decided to notify Eden that Deputy Under Secretary of State Robert Murphy would go to London immediately. Regarding the possible use of force, unless the United States limited itself

10. For copies of all correspondence from Eden to Eisenhower during the crisis, see folders marked "Eden (1–6)," in Box 19, International Series, Ann Whitman File, EP, EL. From July 27 until November 7, Eden sent seventeen dispatches to Eisenhower, all but four of which dealt exclusively with the Middle East crisis.

to providing arms, Eisenhower felt he would have to call Congress back into session. When Hoover stated that it was his feeling that the United States must move strongly in the Middle East lest the whole Western position be quickly challenged, Eisenhower said he doubted whether he would authorize military force unless Nasser attacked American citizens. The president then directed Hoover to bring the Joint Chiefs of Staff up to date on the matter. Eisenhower then dictated a brief note to Eden, which Goodpaster phoned to the Department of State for transmission. The response to Eden read as follows:

> Your cable just received. To meet immediate situation we are sending Robert Murphy to London to arrive there Sunday [July 29]. . . . I shall not take time in this cable to outline for you the trend of our own thinking. While we agree with much that you have to say, we rather think there are one or two additional steps that you and we might profitably consider. Murphy will be prepared to talk these over with Selwyn Lloyd. We are of the earnest opinion that the maximum number of maritime nations affected by the Nasser action should be consulted quickly in the hope of obtaining an agreed basis of understanding.[11]

Early the next morning, Eisenhower summoned Hoover and Murphy to the White House for another meeting to outline the American position for Murphy to take to London. The president stressed the importance of keeping clear of any precipitate action with the French and the British, which might later tie his hands. He also warned Murphy to keep the French from tying the Suez Canal issue to the Arab-Israeli question. Moreover, he stated it was not desirable to take any action strictly on a tripartite basis—he thought action should be with all of the maritime powers affected. Murphy's mission was simply to proceed to London and "see what it's all about and to hold the fort."[12] As was his custom, Eisenhower preferred to keep his diplomatic options open, using military force only as the final resort.

In the interim between Murphy's departure and the commencement of the tripartite negotiations, Hoover informed the embassy in London that the United States favored the holding of a tripartite meeting initially and a wider meeting later, the latter conceivably by the NATO countries. Insofar as the actual seizure of the Suez Canal Company was concerned,

11. Goodpaster's memorandum of the conference with the president is in folder marked "July, 1956 (1) Misc.," Box 16, DDE Diary Series, Ann Whitman File, EP, El. The memorandum is also outlined in full in Department of State, *Suez Crisis,* 11–12. The message was transmitted in telegram 545 to London on July 27.

12. Robert Murphy, *Diplomat Among Warriors* (New York, 1964), 379. The Memorandum of the Conversation with the President, White House, July 28, 1956, which outlines the executive meeting, is found in folder marked "July 1956 (1) Misc.," Box 16, DDE Diary Series, Ann Whitman File, EP, EL.

the Department of State's preliminary view was that it was very different from the expropriation of an institution such as an oil company and that possibly Nasser had a legal foundation for his action. The American chargé reported these points in a meeting with Lloyd and French Ambassador Jean Chauvel on July 27. Dillon stated the American position to Mollet in identical terms the following day. Murphy's mission was simply to buy time to allow British and French tempers to cool.

Keenly aware of European dependence on the Suez Canal as a conduit for oil shipments, Eisenhower could, nevertheless, afford to take a more relaxed attitude than his allied partners, since only a small percentage of American shipping used the waterway. In addition, American investments in the Suez Canal Company were negligible. Clearly, the Suez Canal was not as vital a national interest from the American standpoint as it was from the European perspective. This was not to say that Eisenhower did not view the Suez situation as gravely serious, but he considered the problem serious only insofar as it affected American interests of promoting regional stability and denying the region to Soviet incursions. As a result, the president handled the situation as a routine diplomatic matter and did not recall Dulles from his Latin American tour. Nor did he reconvene Congress, which had just adjourned for its summer recess. In the absence of his principal diplomatic and military advisers, Eisenhower relied on Staff Secretary Goodpaster and an inner circle of consultants to implement presidential directives.

Whether or not Eisenhower regarded the seizure of the Suez Canal Company as detrimental to the regional interests of the United States, his national security apparatus immediately went into action. At its center, directing the action, was the president. In addition to his White House meetings with Hoover, Allen Dulles, and Goodpaster, Eisenhower instructed Vice-President Nixon to keep congressional leaders informed of all diplomatic actions on-going in London. Eisenhower then summoned Dulles, who returned to Washington on July 29, to the White House for lengthy consultation. Reviewing British and French dispatches, both leaders felt that the British and the French were anxious to start a war and get the United States involved.[13] The president expressed his concern that the Russians might seize the opportunity to increase their influence in the area, and Dulles concurred that there was a definite possibility that this might occur. In any event, the United States should prepare for such an emergency.

13. See Telephone Conversation to Richard Nixon, July 30, 1956, in Telephone Conversation Memoranda, 1956, in Box 5, John Foster Dulles Papers, Seeley G. Mudd Manuscript Library, Princeton University.

Turning his attention to the Joint Chiefs of Staff, Eisenhower directed them to study the situation and explore a wide range of alternative strategies to implement presidential policy. Consequently, the Joint Chiefs directed the Joint Strategic Plans Committee (JSPC) to prepare a study detailing the arguments for and against the following courses of action: (1) participation by U.S. forces with British forces in direct military action to seize control of the Suez Canal, (2) U.S. support of British military action without direct participation by American forces, and (3) U.S. support of British military action limited to diplomatic and economic measures. In a study released on July 28, the JSPC concluded that U.S. support of the British should be limited to diplomatic and economic support of Great Britain. The staff study was immediately rejected by Admiral Burke, General Taylor, and General Twining, all of whom held that Egyptian seizure of the canal was militarily unacceptable to the United States.[14] Moreover, Burke and Taylor were initially in favor of offering landing craft and other items for Britain's use, but they supported the chairman's position that the exigencies of the situation did not warrant immediate material support. Burke, however, notified northern Atlantic and Mediterranean commands to prepare for the evacuation of American nationals from the Middle East if the diplomatic situation deteriorated.

For the next two weeks, while British and French military leaders were laying the foundation for what ultimately was the Anglo-French invasion force, the Joint Chiefs of Staff prepared contingency plans in case diplomatic endeavors failed to relieve the escalating tension in London and Paris. In a memorandum on July 31, the Joint Chiefs informed the secretary of defense that they considered Nasser's seizure of the Suez Canal so detrimental to the interests of the United States that Eisenhower should consider the desirability of taking military action in support of Britain, France, and others as appropriate. Clearly taking a more bellicose stance than the president, the military chiefs proposed the allocation of one reinforced division from the Army; one fast carrier task force, one amphibious task force, and a regimental landing team from the Navy and the Marine Corps; and an air division headquarters, a fighter-bomber wing, and a tactical reconnaissance squadron and supporting airlift from the Air Force for use in the Middle East.[15]

14. Joint Chiefs of Staff action 2105/38. See 092 Egypt 7–28–56 Section 1, in Records of the Joint Chiefs of Staff, RG 218. See also galley proofs of Kenneth Condit, *The History of the Joint Chiefs of Staff: The Joint Chiefs of Staff and National Policy, 1955–56* (Washington D.C., 1992), 5, on file in Historical Office, Joint Chiefs of Staff, the Pentagon.
15. Galley proofs of Condit, *The Joint Chiefs of Staff and National Policy, 1955–1956*, pp. 6–8.

Robert Murphy arrived in London late Saturday, July 28, and quickly ascertained the warlike mood of the British statesmen. Following a meeting with Lloyd and Pineau, he confirmed that Great Britain and France had resolved to use military force to seize the Suez Canal if necessary. Taking his cue from Eisenhower's instructions on July 28, Murphy immediately informed his European counterparts that the United States' approach to the problem was a legalistic one and the question of eventual military intervention was inappropriate at the present and would depend on future developments. During a dinner with Chancellor of the Exchequer Harold Macmillan,[16] Murphy determined that the British government believed that only military action could resolve the crisis and that the French saw eye to eye with the British. As soon as the dinner was over, Murphy cabled Washington that Eden's position was that the entire Western position in the Middle East would be jeopardized if Nasser got away with his action. NATO, Western Europe, and other parts of the world would be at the mercy of a man who had shown himself irresponsible and faithless. Furthermore, Eden had taken the decision to arrange to have it within his power to use force. Turning his attention to the French, Murphy reported that France not only agreed with the British position, but also was prepared to give its full support for whatever was decided upon to bring Nasser down.[17]

When Secretary Dulles returned from Latin America on July 29, he immediately called a Department of State conference to study the potentially explosive Middle East situation. The following day, Dulles cabled new instructions to Murphy to guide his oral presentation with British and French leaders. By direction of the president, Dulles informed Murphy that Nasser should not be presented with an ultimatum requiring him to reverse his nationalization action under threat of force. Such an ultimatum would invariably make the Egyptian president stand firm, and war would accordingly become inevitable. Eisenhower had previously informed Eden that he had no authority to commit United States to military action without congressional authorization, and if there was no clear evidence that Nasser intended to impede vital traffic through the Suez Canal, the president doubted whether Congress would give him authority to commit military forces. At present, the United States preferred to act on a "more moderate though firm basis to achieve the desired results . . . therefore the United States believed that the best pro-

16. For account of this dinner party, see Alistair Horne, *Harold Macmillan,* Volume I: *1894–1956* (New York, 1989), 397. See also Murphy, *Diplomat Among Warriors,* 462–64.
17. Telegram, Murphy to Department of State, July 29, 1956, as quoted in Department of State, *Suez Crisis,* 37–39.

cedure would be to call a conference of the signatories of the 1888 convention," which had negotiated the original settlement by which the Suez Canal had operated.[18] Murphy submitted a proposed communiqué based on these instructions to Lloyd and Pineau on July 31 and promised to present the Anglo-French view to Dulles, who was scheduled to arrive in London the following day.[19]

Concerned with Murphy's reports outlining proposed Anglo-French military planning, Eisenhower summoned Dulles, Hoover, Secretary of the Treasury Humphrey, Burke, Allen Dulles, Legal Advisor to the Department of State Herman Phleger, and Assistant Secretary of Defense for International Security Affairs Gordon Gray, to the White House for consultation on July 31.[20] Secretary Dulles, Hoover, and Phleger had been with the president about fifteen minutes when the larger group entered the office. They and the president had read Murphy's last message that stated the British had made a firm, considered decision to "break Nasser" and to initiate hostilities at an early date (estimating six weeks to be required for commencing operations). Eisenhower typically took charge of the meeting and stated he considered military intervention to be a very unwise decision on Eden's part. Stating that to resort to arms would undoubtedly result in cutting off Middle Eastern oil supplies to Western Europe, Eisenhower thought the situation serious enough to send the secretary of state to London at once to state emphatically that only Congress, not the president, had authorization to commit military forces. In response to a question, Admiral Burke said the JCS were of the view that Nasser must be broken. The JCS thought this should be accomplished with economic and political means, but if this proved unsuccessful, the United States should declare itself in support of British armed intervention. Burke's views were in line with the Chiefs' previous rejection of the military staff study that urged diplomatic and economic support, vice military support, for Great Britain. Secretary Dulles then

18. See Telegram 574, July 30, 1956, top secret file 974.7301/7 3056, as quoted in Historical Division, Department of State, "The Suez Canal Problem, 1954–1958," Retired Office Files, 71D411, pp. 23–24, on file at the U.S. Department of State in Washington, D.C.

19. Throughout the crisis, Dulles conferred directly with Lloyd and Pineau, so the burden of conveying Eisenhower's views rested on the secretary of state, not the ambassadors of the respective countries. Dulles' personal diplomacy sometime annoyed American ambassadors, particularly Aldrich, who complained that the secretary often went over his head. See transcript of oral history by Winthrop Aldrich (OH 250) on file at Eisenhower Library and also at Columbia University Oral History Project.

20. See Memorandum of a Conference with the President, White House, July 31, 1956, prepared by Goodpaster, in folder marked "July 1956 (1) Misc.," Box 16, in DDE Diary Series, Ann Whitman File, EP, EL, for summary of this meeting.

informed Eisenhower that he had spoken to Senator Mansfield on July 30, and Mansfield hoped that the United States would not give in to Nasser, because the Egyptian president had all the attributes of an unstable dictator.[21] Dulles concurred and stated that Nasser must be made to disgorge his theft.

Weighing the alternatives and not prone to rash action, despite the bellicosity of some of his advisers, Eisenhower decided that the American response would be cautionary. Instructing Dulles to let the British know how gravely he viewed this matter, what an error the president thought their decision for military force was, and how this course of action would antagonize the American people, Eisenhower then stated that a divergence of views between himself and Eden might be extremely serious, but not as serious as letting a war start and not trying to stop it. If Nasser was to be made to disgorge what he had taken, it would be through international means—not by force. The president concluded by saying he wanted "not a whisper about this outside this room." Eisenhower's actions reflected a deep desire to prevent bloodshed and to solve the crisis at the negotiating table.

Later that evening, Eisenhower wrote a long personal letter to Eden in which he acknowledged the importance the prime minister attached to the Suez Canal. Additionally, he sought to dissuade Eden from using military force. Dooming any hope that Eden entertained about the United States supporting Great Britain in a combined military operation, Eisenhower stated:

> For my part, I cannot over-emphasize the strength of my conviction that some such method must be attempted before action such as you contemplate should be undertaken. . . . Public opinion here and, I am convinced, in most of the world, would be outraged should there be a failure to make such efforts [an international conference]. Moreover, initial military successes might be easy, but the eventual price might become far too heavy.
>
> I have given you my personal conviction, as well as that of my associates, as to the [un]wisdom even of contemplating the use of military force at this moment. . . . I realize that the messages from both you and Harold [Macmillan] stressed that the decision taken was already approved by the government and was firm and irrevocable. But I personally feel sure that the American reaction [to use of force without negotiations] would be severe and that the great areas of the world would share that reaction.
>
> I have given you only a few highlights in the chain of reasoning that compels us to conclude that the step you contemplate should not be undertaken until every peaceful means of protecting the rights and the livelihood of

21. Telephone Conversation Memoranda, July 30, 1956, in Box 5, Dulles Papers, Mudd Library, Princeton.

great portions of the world had been thoroughly explored and exhausted.[22]

To highlight his growing apprehension, the president directed Dulles to carry his letter to Eden and personally deliver it. Later that evening, Eisenhower sent a similar cable to Mollet.

Before Dulles departed Washington, British and French military leaders conducted preliminary discussions for armed intervention. It was evident because of the distances involved that Cyprus would have to be the staging base for any assault against Egypt, and the British government began preparations in that sector. On August 2, Whitehall issued a proclamation in which it summoned a large number of reservists to active duty. Additionally, Eden announced that the return of national servicemen from overseas might be delayed by extensive troop movements and precautionary measures in the Mediterranean area. The *Times* reported the departure of the aircraft carrier HMS *Theseus* from Portsmouth with the 16th Independent Parachute Brigade Group.[23] British newspapers also carried accounts of movements of French troops to Malta. The French had already alerted two divisions, the 10th Parachute Division and the 7th Mobile Mechanized Division, both of which were stationed in Algeria, for the upcoming invasion.

By August 11, the initial operational plans were complete, to include the formation of the command structure. General Sir Charles Keightley, commander in chief, British Land Forces Middle East, received the appointment as Supreme Allied Commander. His deputy was Vice Admiral Pierre d'Escadre, commander in chief, French Mediterranean Fleet. The operation envisioned a total of eighty thousand troops, the majority of whom were British. In spite of the militant rhetoric of the French and British diplomats, however, both nations were woefully unprepared to conduct immediate offensive operations. The British Chiefs of Staff had made this painfully clear to Eden during their initial meeting on July 26. Still, the military planning continued.

Serious tripartite negotiations at the foreign secretary level began immediately with Dulles' arrival in London on August 1. Dulles found the attitude of the British and French as Murphy had reported. For the next two days, Dulles laid the foundation for what eventually led to the first London Conference on August 16. In daily communication with the president, Dulles informed Eisenhower that Great Britain and France

22. Eisenhower to Anthony Eden, August 31, 1956, in Eden folder (1), Box 19, International Series, Ann Whitman File, EP, EL.

23. *Times* (London), August 3, 1956.

had already frozen Egyptian financial assets, and the diplomatic tone that prevailed in London was even more warlike than he had imagined. When Dulles met Macmillan on August 1, the chancellor of the exchequer vehemently argued that the final result of Nasser's action was to be the destruction of Great Britain as a first-class power and its reduction to a status similar to that of Holland. Comparing the seizure of the Canal to Munich, Macmillan stated that Great Britain would rather die fighting than slowly bleed to a state of impotence.[24]

When Dulles failed to share the anger that permeated Whitehall and the British community, the conservative British press vehemently attacked the United States and criticized American caution. To the *Times,* the main anxiety was that the American desire for conciliation might prevail over Anglo-French boldness and take the edge off effective action. An editorial claimed that if Nasser was allowed to get away with his coup, all the British and other Western interests in the Middle East would crumble. Taking offense at the president's legalistic stand, the editorial stated that "quibbling over whether or not he [Nasser] was legally entitled to make the grab will delight the finicky and comfort the faint-hearted, but entirely misses the point."[25]

In spite of this rhetoric and his known sympathy for Great Britain and France, Dulles urged calm. Unfortunately, he confused the issue by occasional references of the necessity to force Nasser to "disgorge" the Suez Canal region. Such remarks were typical of the secretary, who was prone to make inflammatory statements. Understandably, Eden and Lloyd were somewhat perplexed by this contradictory position, and they later cited this statement as proof that the United States had not eliminated the resolution of the dispute by military force. In all probability, Dulles had put a more bellicose face on United States policy than Eisenhower intended, but the president's personal messages to Eden left little room for doubt as to Eisenhower's position. Regardless of Eden's and Lloyd's later attempts at self-justification, Eisenhower had made it abundantly clear that the United States preferred a diplomatic, not a military, solution to the crisis.

In any event, the tripartite conferences terminated on August 3, and the members agreed to call an international conference to be held in London in mid-August to initiate steps toward establishing operating arrangements of the Suez Canal under an international system. The foreign min-

24. See Memorandum of a Conversation, 11 Downing Street, London, August 1, 1956, in Department of State, Central Files, 974.7301/8-156 Top Secret, as quoted in Department of State, *Suez Crisis,* 108–109.

25. *Times* (London), July 31, August 1, 1956.

isters agreed to invite twenty-four nations to participate, the eight surviving parties to the Convention of 1888 and sixteen other nations "largely
concerned in the use of the Canal either through ownership of tonnage
or pattern of trade."[26] The eight surviving parties to the 1888 agreement
were Egypt, France, Italy, the Netherlands, Spain, Turkey, the United
Kingdom, and the Soviet Union. The sixteen other nations that received
invitations were Australia, Ceylon, Denmark, Ethiopia, West Germany,
Greece, India, Indonesia, Iran, Japan, New Zealand, Norway, Pakistan,
Portugal, Sweden, and the United States.

Nasser's attitude toward the conference was soon clear. Having predicted the violent reaction to his nationalization of the waterway, Nasser
played for time, since he felt that if Great Britain and France failed to attack by the end of September, Egypt would be relatively safe and world
opinion would side with Egypt. When news of the tripartite conference reached him on August 3, he summoned American Ambassador
Henry A. Byroade and outlined Egypt's position. According to Nasser,
Egypt could not accept international control of the Suez Canal, nor could
Egypt accept participation in the proposed London conference. He therefore proposed the matter be settled without delay in the United Nations,
rather than at an international conference in London; and he was ready
to guarantee freedom of passage and uninterrupted use of Suez canal facilities, the sole exception being Israel, which had not been permitted
use of the Canal prior to the nationalization order.[27] Nine days later,
Nasser issued a lengthy statement in which he rejected the invitation to
the London conference on the grounds that the body was attempting to
interfere in Egypt's domestic affairs.

As Dulles returned to Washington, the president was confident that he
had made the correct decision in responding to Nasser's seizure of the
canal. In dealing only with a select group of advisers, Eisenhower ensured that he maintained the reins of foreign policy in the immediate aftermath of Nasser's nationalization order. Four times between July 27
and July 31, he chaired *ad hoc* meetings in the White House to solicit
recommendations and disseminate presidential directives. Prior to each
session, he had personally reviewed all appropriate diplomatic cables

26. See Tripartite Statement Issued at London, August 2, 1956, as quoted in Department of State, *Suez Crisis,* 126–27. See also Donald C. Watt, ed., *Documents on the
Suez Crisis* (London, 1957), 500. See also Selected Correspondence and Related Material, Suez Canal, 1956, Box 110, Dulles Papers, Mudd Library, Princeton.

27. Telegram from the Embassy in Egypt to the Department of State, August 4, 1956,
in Department of State, Central Files, 974.7301/8-456, Secret, as quoted in Department
of State, *Suez Crisis,* 133–35.

relating to the crisis. Eisenhower dictated the initial telegrams to Eden and outlined his official position directly to Eden in a lengthy letter on July 31 to remove any doubt concerning the president's aversion to using military force prior to attempting peaceful negotiations. Additionally, Dulles remained in daily contact with the president during the tripartite discussions of August 1–3, during which Eisenhower defined the American position that Dulles subsequently proposed in London.

In spite of Nasser's rejection of the London Conference, which Eisenhower fully anticipated, it was apparent that the president had succeeded in purchasing precious time in which he hoped to defuse the volatile situation. Aware of preliminary Anglo-French preparations for military action due to intelligence from U-2 surveillance flights, Eisenhower hoped that both his insistence on precautionary measures and emphasis on less militant solutions than those contemplated by his European allies would lead to a peaceful resolution of the crisis. What troubled Eisenhower most was a report from Allen Dulles, in which the Director of Central Intelligence informed him that the French Defense Minister, Maurice Bourges-Maunoury, had met Israeli Chief of Staff Moshe Dayan in midsummer. The result of that meeting was a French agreement to increase arms shipments to Israel to counter Nasser's alleged increased arms sales from the Soviet Union.[28]

Having assessed the crisis and selected a course of action aimed at resolving the dispute without resorting to violence, Eisenhower continued his personal involvement in the decision-making process. In the interest of avoiding war and obtaining a peaceful resolution to the crisis, he pondered what action he must undertake to enhance his bargaining leverage with his European allies to influence the outcome of the crisis. He believed that time was on his side, since the longer Eden waited to initiate military operations, the greater his possibility of finding a diplomatic solution. What Eisenhower needed now was time to prepare for the international conference, time to muster congressional support for the administration's stand, and time to monitor Anglo-French war preparations.

28. For the Israeli view of the crisis and the Franco-Israeli connection, see Moshe Dayan, *Moshe Dayan: Story of My Life* (New York, 1976), 213–327, and Rechavam Zeevy, "The Military Lessons of the Sinai Campaign: The Israeli Perspective," in Troen and Shemesh, eds., *Suez-Sinai Crisis, 1956,* 60–73.

4

DIPLOMATIC MARATHON:
THE LONDON CONFERENCES

While I am not going to comment on the action of any other government, for
ourselves, we are determined to exhaust every possible, every feasible method
of peaceful settlement, and we believe it can be done.
—Dwight D. Eisenhower, presidential address

A number of diplomatic attempts to reconcile Anglo-French interests
with the vigorous nationalistic policies of Nasser characterized the
first three months of the Suez crisis, August-October 1956. Eisenhower's
adroit supervision of his executive assistants had produced in his mind
a clear and unmistakable direction for American policymakers to fol-
low. In conversations with his cabinet and European allies, the president
sought to remove any doubt as to his opposition to the use of military
force to settle the Suez dispute. The American policy reflected the president's personal stamp on foreign policy. Following consultation with
his immediate advisers, Eisenhower, not Dulles or any executive agency,
dictated the course Murphy took to London for discussions with the European foreign ministers. As president, Eisenhower had directed
American policy from the onset of the Suez crisis. In the days ahead, he
maintained personal direction of the national security establishment as
well.

By August, Eisenhower had defined U.S. policy objectives that were
in sharp contrast to those of his European allies. As outlined in the president's correspondence with Nasser and the tripartite discussions with
Lloyd and Pineau, Eisenhower sought (1) to ensure the smooth and efficient operation of the Suez Canal, not the removal of Nasser as head
of state; (2) to establish an international agency to operate the Suez Canal,
presumably formed from the original signatories of the 1888 Convention and other states affected by the current crisis; (3) to repair the rift
with his European allies and to maintain the solidarity of NATO; and
(4) to exert diplomatic and economic pressure on Great Britain and
France to resolve the dispute by peaceful means, either by interna-

tional conference or within the United Nations. Eisenhower and Dulles had taken the lead in proposing and organizing meetings and conferences in which they strove to soothe Eden and Mollet by assuring them that Nasser would not be allowed to get away with his unilateral seizure of the canal, while on the other hand pressuring the allies to refrain from any immediate military expedition that might have longer-range political consequences.

The divergence between the Anglo-French approach and that of the United States was regrettable, because there were several points on which all agreed. All abhorred the manner in which Nasser had seized the waterway. All preferred an international board of supervisors to monitor and control the movement of shipping through the Suez Canal, and all feared the increasing influence of Nasser within the Arab world. Eisenhower, Eden, and Mollet differed in their interpretation of Nasser's motives and the methods by which the West should respond to the nationalization of the Suez Canal. Great Britain and France perceived Nasser pursuing policies inimical to their own vital interests. The prime minister saw nationalization as a direct threat to British economic, strategic, and political interests in the Middle East and concluded that Nasser's overall defiant posture justified military intervention to remove him from power.[1] Eden and Mollet felt the United States was not taking the Suez affair sufficiently in earnest. According to Eden, the Suez Canal "for them [United States] is not a matter of survival as it is to us and indeed to all Europe and many other lands."[2]

Contrary to Eden's perceptions, Eisenhower viewed the situation as irksome, but perhaps not as simple as Great Britain and France portrayed it. First, the president doubted the validity of the legal position the Europeans were using to justify their talk of resorting to force to settle the crisis. Herman Phleger, the Department of State's legal adviser, had originally voiced similar concerns in the White House meeting on July 31. Eisenhower also seriously questioned the Anglo-French denial of the inherent right of any sovereign nation to exercise the right of eminent domain within its own territory, provided that just compensation was paid to the owners of the expropriated property. Nasser's intention to continue the uninterrupted flow of commerce through the Suez Canal seemed to minimize any detrimental effects of his seizure of the Canal

1. For an elaboration on this theme see Peter L. Hahn, *The United States, Great Britian, and Egypt, 1945–1956: Strategy and Diplomacy in the Early Cold War* (Chapel Hill, 1991), 211.
2. M. Perlman, "Between the Devil and the Deep Red Sea," *Middle Eastern Affairs,* VII (December, 1956), 433. See also Lord Harlech, "Suez Snafu, Skybolt Saber," *Foreign Policy,* II (Spring, 1971), 39.

Company's assets. Eisenhower realized that under the terms of the 1888 treaty Nasser would have had complete title to the Suez Canal anyway, and it would not be necessary for him to make the kind of payments to the stockholders that he was offering to make at the present time.

Another reason Eisenhower was reluctant to support the Europeans centered on his revulsion to colonialism. Just as he had balked in 1954 during the Indo-China crisis when France had requested large-scale American intervention to bolster its position at Dien Bien Phu,[3] Eisenhower desired no part of any plan that had as its objective the reestablishment of European domination over Egypt. Writing to boyhood friend Swede Hazlett on August 3, the president said, "Nasser and the Suez Canal are foremost in my thoughts. . . . In the kind of world that we are trying to establish, we frequently find ourselves victims of the tyrannies of the weak." In the case of Suez, he noted that the Western nations had no choice but to swallow their pride, accept the insults, and attempt to work to bolster the underlying concepts of freedom, and he concluded that such a course was costly, but "there can be no doubt that in the long run such faithfulness will produce real rewards."[4] Moreover, the president firmly believed that any action should be taken within the framework of international law, preferably in the United Nations if direct negotiations failed. Eisenhower strongly opposed the unilateral use of force by Great Britain or France unless all other means were exhausted. To implement this policy, the president used adroit diplomacy, both on the international and domestic fronts, to obtain support for his convictions and defuse the explosive situation.

Although he had received only limited reports on the status of Anglo-French military preparations, Eisenhower remained extremely uncomfortable with the warlike statements emanating from London and Paris. His primary objective in dispatching Dulles to the tripartite meetings in London had been to divert the European allies from war by a series of

3. Although the French were intially against any united action with the United States against the Viet Minh, the rapidly deteriorating military situation around Dien Bien Phu prompted France to ask Washington to implement Operation Vulture, a plan that called for massive American air strikes consisting of conventional and small atomic bombs to save the beleaguered garrison. Eisenhower questioned the effectiveness of such air strikes in a jungle environment, and strong congressional opposition and British reluctance to become involved in the war convinced the president to abandon the project and limit American aid to munitions and technical assistance. See Parmet, *Eisenhower and the American Crusades,* 353–72; Eisenhower, *Mandate for Change,* 332–57; and Ambrose, *Eisenhower: The President,* 173–85.

4. Eisenhower to Hazlett, August 3, 1956, in Ann Whitman Name Series, Ann Whitman File, EP, EL, as quoted in Griffith, ed., *Ike's Letters,* 165. See also Ambrose, *Eisenhower: The President,* 333.

diplomatic initiatives aimed at settling the crisis without bloodshed. Since the chief result of the negotiations was the London Conference on August 16, the president had succeeded—at least temporarily—in achieving his policy objectives.

Suez also was a principal topic in the cabinet and National Security Council meetings in late July and August. Concerned with possible security leaks, Eisenhower informed the cabinet that the secretary of state was responsible for all press releases on the evolving crisis.[5] The National Security Council, on the other hand, discussed the Suez crisis on a routine basis. During the NSC meeting on August 9, Admiral Radford voiced the military chiefs' concerns of Nasser's increasing prestige. In this position of leadership, Nasser could exert an influence inimical to U.S. interests in all Third World countries. Likening the Egyptian president to another Hitler, Radford urged strong support for Great Britain and France. No commitment to a particular policy emerged from the NSC deliberations, but the president directed that, to provide the basis for decisions that might be required in the future, the Departments of State and Defense should jointly study all possible contingencies that might develop from the recent crisis in Egypt, what courses of action the United States might pursue under each of these contingencies, and the military, as well as the diplomatic, implications of each course of action. Additionally, Eisenhower directed that the newly instituted panel, named the Middle East Policy Planning Group (MEPPG), advise Arthur S. Flemming, the director of the Office of Defense Mobilization, as such studies progressed so that planning in reference to oil supplies could be coordinated with such state-defense studies.[6]

The MEPPG became the principal forum through which the Department of Defense coordinated its recommendations for the president's consideration. In August, the JCS proposed eight possible contingencies for the MEPPG's consideration. The most desirable course of action from the military perspective, should economic measures fail to place the Suez Canal under friendly control, was to "endorse publicly and support po-

5. See folder marked "Summary of August 3, 1956, Cabinet Meeting" in Box 7, Cabinet Series, Ann Whitman File, EP, EL. From the time Nasser nationalized the Suez Canal Company until the crisis was over in December, the cabinet met six times: July 27, August 3, September 28, November 16, November 21, and December 14. Only once, on November 16, did the subject of Suez dominate a significant portion of the meeting. With respect to the crisis, Eisenhower used the cabinet meetings to inform the members of the status of negotiations, not to solicit recommendations concerning policy.

6. See Summary of the 292nd Meeting of the NSC, August 9, 1956, in folder marked "NSC Summaries of Discussion," Box 8, National Security Council Series, Ann Whitman File, EP, EL. Lieutenant General Alonzo P. Fox, military adviser to the assistant secretary of defense (ISA), was named Defense Department representative.

litically, economically, and logistically, United Kingdom and French military action without direct participation by U.S. forces and guarantee publicly that the United States, in order to localize the conflict, will take appropriate action, including direct military action by U.S. forces as necessary, in the event of significant military intervention by third parties, when such intervention constitutes a threat of expanding the conflict either with respect to the area or the issue involved."[7]

This course of action reflected the JCS's assumption that the British and French could seize the Suez Canal without direct U.S. participation. Radford and the Joint Chiefs based their assumptions on combat assessments of the military capability of British, French, and Egyptian forces, as well as Israeli forces, which they assumed could reach the Suez Canal within days of the onset of hostilities. The possible involvement of Israeli forces in any hostile action in the region attracted more attention during the late summer, and the MEPPG and intelligence-gathering agencies focused their resources on monitoring radio traffic and high-altitude reconnaissance photography of potential mobilization centers.

Having organized the executive branch, Eisenhower next turned his attention to the legislative branch to muster domestic support for his stand against the use of force. Ever mindful of the importance of maintaining harmonious relations with the legislative branch and the American public during an election year, he held a press conference on August 1, during which he refused to give definite details of the American position until Dulles returned from London. Marshaling congressional support proved to be an easy task. Although Congress was in summer recess, Dulles called Vice-President Nixon, who was in charge of monitoring relations with the legislators, on August 8 and informed him that Eisenhower wanted bipartisan representation at the London Conference. The leading Democratic senators, including Johnson, Mansfield, George, and Fulbright, declined because it was an election year, and the issue had the potential to be highly volatile.[8] The next day, Eisenhower informed Dulles that he wanted Congress to share full responsibility in the crisis, "particularly if there should be any hostilities."[9] This

7. See galley proofs of Condit, *The Joint Chiefs of Staff and National Policy, 1955–1956*, p. 9, on file in Historical Office, Joint Chiefs of Staff, the Pentagon.

8. Telephone Conversation Memoranda, August 8, 1956, in Box 5, Dulles Papers, Mudd Library, Princeton. For specific reasons why Democrats refused the invitation to join Dulles in London, see letter from John Foster Dulles to Dwight D. Eisenhower, in White House Memoranda Series, Meetings with the President, 1956, Box 5, Dulles Papers, Mudd Library, Princeton. See also Eisenhower, *Waging Peace*, 45.

9. As reported in New York *Times*, August 11, 1956.

quest for joint responsibility with the legislative branch was again reminiscent of the Indo-China crisis in which the president made a concerted effort to obtain congressional authorization before he committed any American ground forces to the conflict.[10]

As part of his effort to keep Congress informed of the status of the Middle East crisis, Eisenhower hosted a full-scale bipartisan meeting with the legislators on August 12.[11] Twenty-two legislative leaders from both the Senate and House of Representatives joined the president, Nixon, Dulles, Arthur Flemming of the Office of Defense Mobilization, Gordon Gray, and Admiral Radford, who had just returned from a trip to East Asia. Prior to meeting with the congressional leaders, Eisenhower summoned his key aides to the White House to discuss the attendance of senatorial leaders at the forthcoming London Conference. For the next half hour, Eisenhower examined a wide range of alternatives concerning the potential success or failure of the proposed London Conference, the ramifications of the 1888 treaty governing the Suez Canal, and anticipated requests from the NATO allies for arms shipments. Most important, Dulles stated that he would point out to the congressional leaders that in the event of armed hostilities between Egypt and America's European allies, Great Britain and France would expect the United States to provide them with economic assistance and would hope that Eisenhower would neutralize Soviet Russia by indicating very clearly to the Soviet Union that if it should enter the conflict openly, the United States would enter it on the side of Britain and France.[12] The meeting soon adjourned as the attendees joined the congressional delegation that had arrived at the White House.

After expressing thanks to the congressional leaders for interrupting their activities to attend the meeting, the president began by stating that things were not going so well as to give "unbounded hope" for a peaceful solution. He noted the latest advice that Egypt probably would not attend the London Conference. Eisenhower then expressed his hope that one senator from each party would accompany Dulles to London, since the outcome might be in treaty form, and it would also be well to

10. *Public Papers of the President, 1954* (Washington D.C., 1960), 306. When asked if he would send American troops into Indo-China, Eisenhower responded that Congress would have to sanction any such move. See also Parmet, *Eisenhower and the American Crusades,* 363, and Eisenhower, *Mandate for Change,* 347.

11. For summation of the meeting, see Memorandum of a Conversation, August 12, 1956, noon–1:25 P.M., Notes on Presidential–Bipartisan Congressional Leadership Meeting, Box 2, Legislative Meetings Series, Ann Whitman File, and folder marked "August 1956 (1) Diary," Box 8, Ann Whitman Diary Series, Ann Whitman File, both in EP, EL.

12. Memorandum for Record, folder marked "August 1956 (1) Misc.," Box 17, DDE Diary Series, Ann Whitman File, EP, EL.

have the senators there so that the secretary might draw on them for advice. Much of the subsequent discussion centered on oil reserves and financial support to Great Britain and France. The president agreed that this was a serious problem, and Flemming noted that an emergency Middle East Oil Committee was being established to review the import statistics currently available. Throughout the conference, Eisenhower emphasized that the American position in London would be to contribute to a solution of the crisis with the objective of safeguarding the interests of those states dependent on the canal, as well as recognizing the legitimate interests of Egypt.

Most attendees immediately recognized the gravity of the situation and expressed appreciation to the president for soliciting their views on such an important subject. A lively debate then followed concerning the anticipated British and French use of force to settle the dispute. Dulles stated that he believed the British and French intended to reoccupy the former British base and station troops along the canal. Democratic Senators Johnson and George listened attentively while Eisenhower and Dulles briefed them on Western European reactions to Nasser's nationalization order, and left the briefing fully convinced that the United States' NATO allies contemplated military intervention. Republican Senator Styles Bridges concurred that Great Britain and France would not back down, and war would probably develop.[13] Before terminating the meeting, the president remarked on the confidential nature of the material presented, particularly in regard to statistics and the attitudes of the allies. A few minutes later he repeated this caution with particular regard to the military plan. Following the meeting, Eisenhower gave Dulles last-minute instructions, and the secretary flew to London to prepare for the upcoming conference.

Eisenhower's careful cultivation of congressional support was a vital component of his strategy management. Although he relied solely on a small group of intimate advisers in formulating national policy, the intricacies of election-year politics made congressional support all the more imperative since the president had no intention of presenting an image of an executive who was unable to control foreign policy. By bringing legislative leaders into the process, Eisenhower at least gave congressional leaders the impression that they were more involved than they actually were in the development of national policy during times of crisis. In submitting the Suez dispute to the legislative leaders in an atmosphere of crisis, the president was assured of almost universal support from both

13. For the reaction of the legislators, see CQ Weekly Report, No. 33 (August 17, 1956), 1044.

sides of the congressional aisle. Due to the logic of his policy, Eisenhower received the legislative support he desired.

In the interim between the end of the tripartite discussions on August 3 and the beginning of the London Conference, Eden tried to persuade Eisenhower and the British public that Nasser had to be destroyed. As recorded in Eden's personal memoirs, the official British position was that no arrangements for the future of the Suez Canal could be acceptable to Great Britain that would leave it in the unfettered control of a single power that could exploit it purely for purposes of national policy.[14] Addressing the British public in a radio broadcast on August 8, the prime minister again berated Nasser and compared him to Hitler. Referring to appeasement, Eden stated, "The pattern is familiar to many of us, my friends. We all know this is how fascist governments behave and we all remember, only too well, what the cost can be in giving into fascism."[15]

Unfortunately for Eden, public and parliamentary support for his Suez policy began to deteriorate by mid-August. The Labor party moved from enthusiastic support of Eden's conservatives, and a complete break occurred on August 14, when Labor spokesman Alfred Robins stated, "Neither the threat of force nor the use of force will solve the problem of the Suez Canal. This is not the time for banging drums or rattling sabers." Party leader Hugh Gaitskell joined the fray the following day and demanded assurances that the government's military measures "were precautionary . . . and not preparations for armed intervention outside and inconsistent with our obligations under the Charter of the United Nations."[16] Macmillan's diary entry for August 9 also gave a glimpse of the stresses building up in the cabinet as the British press became more critical. According to the chancellor of the exchequer, Eden was in a highly emotional state, making life very difficult all round him. Macmillan then wondered what Eden would do if Nasser was equivocal with respect to British demands. Would Eden negotiate with his invading armada at sea?[17] Macmillan could reach no conclusion, but it was obvious that the crisis was weighing heavily on the mind of the British prime minister.

Of the twenty-four nations invited to the Suez Canal Conference (also known as the 22-Power London Conference), all but Egypt and Greece

14. Eden, *Full Circle*, 483.

15. As quoted in Kennett Love, *Suez: The Twice-Fought War* (New York, 1969), 395.

16. As quoted in New York *Times*, August 13, 1956, and *Times* (London), August 14, 1956.

17. Horne, *Harold Macmillan*, I, 416–17.

accepted. Nasser had considered attending the conference, but changed his mind when he received reports of Eden's vitriolic attacks against him through the communications media. Nasser did, however, send Ali Sabri, the chief of Nasser's political cabinet, as an observer while relying on the Soviet Union and India to represent Egypt's interests. Greece declined the invitation because domestic public opinion was still inflamed against Great Britain over Cyprus.

The conference convened in London from August 16–23 in Lancaster House with British Foreign Secretary Lloyd as permanent chairman. Secretary of State Dulles headed the United States delegation, which included twenty-six members of the executive and legislative branches of government.[18] Throughout the conference, Dulles remained in constant contact with the president, often two or three times daily, keeping him fully abreast of both the formal and informal meetings with European leaders. On his arrival, the secretary happily reported to Eisenhower that the mood among the British and French was much more composed than two weeks earlier. He attributed this change to the growing realization of the magnitude of the task of military intervention and of the inadequacies of the British and French military establishments to conduct actual combat operations. Citing the domestic opposition that had been reported in the press, Dulles reasoned that the allies might still "take the plunge if things go badly here, but they were much less apt to do so."[19]

The attendees of the London Conference considered two principal proposals, one by the United States, the other by India. The American proposal stressed the establishment of a public international authority to operate the Suez Canal. Eisenhower had personally approved the plan that accorded equal recognition to the sovereign rights of Egypt and to the safety of the Suez Canal as an international waterway. Additionally, the proposal provided for negotiation of a new convention with Egypt to establish an international board for operating, maintaining, and developing the canal. The Indian proposal differed in that it gave primacy to the "recognition of the Suez Canal as an integral part of Egypt and as a waterway of international importance."[20] India then called for free navigation for all nations and due recognition of the Suez Canal users, but instead of prescribing a Suez Canal Board with real powers, India suggested a "consultative body of user interest," with advisory and liaison functions only.

18. The papers of the United States delegation are contained in Department of State, Conference Files, Lot 61 D 181, as cited in Department of State, *Suez Crisis,* 212.

19. Message from the Secretary of State to the President, August 16, 1956, Box 6, Dulles-Herter Series, Ann Whitman File, EP, EL. See also Department of State, *Suez Crisis,* 210.

20. Watt, ed., *Documents on the Suez Crisis,* 52–53.

On August 18, Dulles cabled Eisenhower, who reviewed both proposals. Considering the merits of each proposal, Eisenhower stated Nasser might find it impossible to swallow a Suez Canal Board with operating powers, instead of the Indian proposition of supervisory responsibility. On the other hand, the president realized that Dulles might have already written into the draft the minimum position that Great Britain and France felt they could take. Still, Eisenhower saw no objection to agreeing to a board with supervisory rather than operating authority, provided that the authority for supervision was clear. Uncharacteristically, the president gave Dulles *carte blanche* and assured the secretary his total support in whatever action the latter would take.[21] Eisenhower's delegation of authority in no way reflected his willingness to relinquish the reins of foreign policy to Dulles. Rather, Eisenhower looked to his secretary to sense how much the traffic would bear in attempting to find a basis for agreement and compromise. Consequently, Dulles rejected the Indian proposal, which was considerably more flexible and acceptable to Egypt, and began mustering support for his own proposal.

In permitting Dulles such broad latitude on a major foreign-policy decision, Eisenhower let a golden opportunity slip through his grasp. Whether Dulles could have convinced Great Britain and France to support the Indian proposal was unclear, but Egyptian acceptance was almost a certainty, since Nasser had approved the Indian plan in advance. The only suitable explanation for the president's lack of initiative was that he simply deferred to the man who was on the scene in the hope that the secretary would make the proper decision.

Despite Soviet opposition, eighteen of the twenty-two nations supported the American proposal as amended, with minor revisions. The amended text, known as the Five-Power Proposal, specifically acknowledged the sovereign rights of Egypt and called for just and fair compensation to be paid to the Universal Company of the Suez Maritime Canal, including a provision for arbitration in the event of disagreement, in accordance with a new convention to be negotiated with Egypt. The conference attendees agreed to call upon Nasser to present the eighteen-nation proposal. Eden and Macmillan then went to great lengths to have Dulles head a five-man delegation charged with presenting the London Conference proposal to Nasser, but Dulles prudently declined. Writing to Eisenhower on August 20, he stated, "I think it is preferable that we should become less conspicuous."[22] As a result of Dulles' refusal, Aus-

---

21. Message from the President to the Secretary of State, August 19, 1956, and August 20, 1956, in Department of State, Central Files, 974.7301/8-1956.

22. As quoted in Hoopes, *The Devil and John Foster Dulles,* 355.

tralian Prime Minister Robert Menzies journeyed to Cairo on September 3 to persuade Nasser to adopt a more conciliatory attitude toward a Suez solution.

Although the Menzies mission ultimately ended in failure, Eisenhower and Dulles were satisfied that they had halted any immediate use of military force by Great Britain and France. What disturbed Eisenhower were unofficial remarks made by Macmillan and Pineau to Dulles and Ambassador Dillon that the Europeans still considered the military option the most likely alternative to achieve their respective policy goals. What neither the president nor the secretary of state realized was that Admiral Andre Barjot, the French deputy commander for the proposed Anglo-French Expeditionary Force, had already contacted the Israeli military attaché in Paris on September 1 and had invited Israel to take part in the operation.[23] This invitation was the recommendation of the Egypt Committee, a special military-political commission established by Eden to prepare strategic plans for an invasion of Egypt. Eventually, the operation evolved to an amphibious landing at Port Said, supported by the Israeli armed forces.

Between the termination of the London Conference on August 23 and Menzies' arrival in Egypt in early September, Eisenhower's personal direction of national security policy reflected his growing trepidation that the British and French, despite their disclaimers that they were willing to await the outcome of the Menzies mission, were intent on military action. On August 29, the president met with Dulles and Radford to discuss the London Conference and review American military preparations in the event of armed hostilities in the Middle East. Dulles had already informed him that earlier in the morning Eden, Macmillan, and Lloyd had indicated that the British were determined to move militarily unless there was a clear acceptance of the Five-Power Proposal by Nasser by September 10. The secretary stated that Eden had indicated that their military planning would have to take a definite and irrevocable status by that date and could not be left appreciably longer in a state of indecision.[24] Radford then informed the president that he had alerted Chief of Naval Operations Burke to initiate planning for the possible evacuation of American nationals and the protection of American interests.[25] Additionally, the chairman discussed with Eisenhower the JCS meeting of August 29, in which the Joint Chiefs reviewed the current sta-

23. Dayan, *Moshe Dayan: Story of My Life,* 231.
24. See folder marked "Meetings with the President, 1956," White House Memoranda Series, Box 4, Dulles Papers, EL.
25. See Admiral Radford's Personal Files, entries dated August 17 and August 21, 1956, at Operational Archives Branch, Washington Navy Yard, Washington, D.C.

tus of their contingency plans pertaining to the Middle East. The MEPPG had previously accepted the courses of action prepared by the Joint Chiefs, and thereafter the JCS influence on policy decisions through the remainder of the crisis was negligible.

Convinced that Radford was preparing for all necessary alternatives, Eisenhower presided over the NSC meeting on August 30, during which the Suez issue was a principal topic of discussion.[26] The meeting lasted over three hours and included lengthy presentations by Dulles and Radford. Following introductory remarks by Special Assistant for National Security Affairs Dillon Anderson, Dulles initiated the discussion by summarizing the events surrounding the London Conference. Emphasizing that the British and French were feverishly continuing their own military preparations, the secretary concluded that the European allies seemed extremely serious in their intention to resort to military force if no other acceptable solution was found. Referring to European public opinion, Dulles stated that French public opinion was more wrought-up and more united over the canal issue than was British public opinion. Because the French were already fighting in Algeria, the secretary reasoned that they preferred to fight at the center of the trouble—namely Egypt—than fight on the difficulty. With the exception of the French Communist party, the French were united in favor of military action against Nasser. British public opinion, on the other hand, was less solid, because Labor party leader Gaitskell had already put the party on record as opposing the use of force outside the aegis of the United Nations. Summing up, Dulles continued his efforts to shape policy and stated that the situation was very grave, and he himself found it extremely difficult to take a strong stand against the British and French views since, after all, the British and French would be finished as first-rate powers if they did not somehow manage to check Nasser and nullify his schemes.

At the conclusion of Dulles' remarks, Radford briefed the council on the various courses of action outlined by the Joint Chiefs of Staff in early August and forwarded to the joint Department of State and Defense study group (MEPPG) by direction of the president. The general conclusion reached by the JCS was that the most desirable course of action for the United States was strong public, political, and logistic support for Great Britain and France, without direct military intervention by the United States unless a third party, obviously the Soviet Union, intervened in the hostilities. Such a course of action, Radford believed, would be most likely to prevent a war over Suez from spreading.

26. See discussion of the 295th Meeting of the National Security Council, folder marked "NSC Summaries of Discussion," Box 8, National Security Council Series, Ann Whitman File, EP, El.

When Radford concluded his presentation, Eisenhower added his own view that the Suez situation was so grave that it must be watched hourly. It seemed to the president that the limit of what the United States could do now was to take the necessary steps to prevent the enlargement of the war if it actually erupted. Several questions concerning the evacuation of American citizens from the Middle East followed, but Radford assured the NSC that the Joint Chiefs had developed emergency evacuation plans to cover just such a contingency. Arthur Flemming then concluded the discussion on Suez by assuring the council that the Office of Defense Mobilization was proceeding with plans for dealing with the oil situation in the event of trouble in the Suez Canal. Following Flemming's statement that he was talking with the British, who had provided him with a preliminary study of what the closure of the canal would do to their dollar position, Dulles turned to Acting Secretary of the Treasury W. Randolph Burgess and informed him that he better have his checkbook ready.

Congressional support for the administration's position against the use of force remained solid behind the president through late August. Moderate Democrats praised Dulles for his conciliatory efforts in London. Apparently convinced that Eisenhower and Dulles had restrained Britain and France, Senator Walter George, chairman of the Senate Foreign Relations Committee, declared, "while the danger of an actual collision of force is not entirely removed, it is more remote." Representative James Richards, George's counterpart in the House, told newsmen, "Our leadership at the London Conference was good." Senator Mansfield also applauded the secretary of state for "stopping the rush toward aggressive action on the part of France and England."[27] Although the Democratic leadership was definitely anti-Nasser, most members were content to support the administration if there was a chance to avoid violence; neither did they wish to oppose the Republicans on a popular stand in a presidential election year.

In September, Eisenhower reinforced this legislative support in a series of meetings with the Democratic party leadership, the most highly publicized being a ninety-minute briefing on September 6, in which Dulles presided. The secretary repeatedly stressed Eisenhower's insistence that military force be avoided in solving the crisis. The legislative leaders, knowing Menzies was currently in Cairo to negotiate with Nasser, generally lauded Dulles' efforts at seeking a peaceful resolution of the

27. Nashville *Banner,* August 29, 1956; Louisville *Courier Journal,* August 30, 1956; Great Falls *Tribune,* August 29, 1956, all quoted in Klingaman, "Congress and American Foreign Policy for the Middle East," 98.

problem. The meeting throughout was most cordial and no partisanship was injected, nor the secretary criticized, at any point. At one point the legislators asked Dulles about the Israeli role in the crisis, and he stated the Israelis were keeping quiet, undoubtedly on the calculation that whatever happened in the region would be helpful to them in one way or another. Asked if the United States was bound to assist the British and the French if the European states used force in the area, Dulles replied no, but that in a similar situation in both world wars, the United States had ultimately intervened in order to save France and Great Britain. As to whether that might happen again, Dulles said the congressmen were in a better position to judge than he, as it was Congress who declared war. The meeting adjourned in late afternoon, with all attendees satisfied with the administration's role in attempting to moderate the British and French positions.[28]

In spite of their initial efforts to end the crisis through negotiations, Eisenhower and Dulles met with total failure. The Menzies mission that arrived in Cairo on September 2 had little chance of success. Menzies, a strong Anglophile and an avowed anti-Nasserite, was probably not the best statesman to head the delegation. Because the unstated premise of the mission was that the Egyptians were unreliable and unable to operate the Suez Canal without international supervision, it was doomed to failure.[29] As Eisenhower suspected, Nasser was willing to make concessions on a wide range of issues, but he would never agree to international control of the Suez Canal. According to the Egyptian president, the proposals Menzies delivered envisaged the seizure of the canal by an international board, which could certainly be considered by the Egyptian people as "collective colonialism in regulated form." At one point, Menzies indicated that the refusal of an international adminis-

28. See Memorandum of a Conversation, Department of State, September 6, 1956, as quoted in Department of State, *Suez Crisis,* 396–98.

29. For a summary of the Menzies mssion, see Summary No. 2, Summary of Developments in Suez Situation, dated September 5, 1956, in Box 43, Special Suez Summaries, International Series, Ann Whitman File, EP, EL. On September 4, Under Secretary of State Hoover forwarded the first summary to Goodpaster under a cover memorandum that read: "I thought it would be helpful for you to have each day for use with the President a brief summary of the most important cables received and dispatched on the Suez situation." Between September 4 and November 1, forty-one of these reports, all entitled "Summary of Developments in Suez Situation," were forwarded to the White House for Goodpaster's daily brief to Eisenhower. The reports were discontinued on November 5, following the airborne invasion of Egypt by British and French troops. Hoover also sent copies of the summaries to the Departments of Defense and Treasury, the JCS, the Office of Defense Mobilization, and the Central Intelligence Agency.

tration would be the beginning of trouble. Nasser immediately closed the file on his desk and replied, "You are threatening me. Very well, I am finished. There will be no more discussions. It is all over."[30] Thus ended the first serious attempt to negotiate with Nasser.

In retrospect, the Menzies committee did not enjoy uniform support from the Western allies. Eden and Lloyd felt that Eisenhower's public statement of September 5, when the president disavowed the use of military force to settle the dispute, had destroyed any chance of success and had made the mission futile. With Eisenhower on record against military intervention, Eden never entertained any hope that Menzies would force concessions from Nasser. Indeed, British and French military leaders had scheduled the invasion for September 15, but logistical problems repeatedly forced the postponement of the operation. From the American perspective, Robert Murphy felt that Nasser had "burnt his bridges" and could not retreat from his intransigent position. The Egyptian president had staked his reputation on seizing the Suez Canal, and any weakening in the face of Western pressure would jeopardize his prestige within the Arab community.[31] What is surprising is that anyone in the administration believed that Nasser, whose primary claim to political legitimacy was Egyptian nationalism, would ever relinquish Egyptian territory to colonial European powers. Certainly Eisenhower and Dulles never entertained any such thought concerning Nasser's willingness to compromise with European leaders.

Unwilling to let the diplomatic initiative slip from his grasp and aware of the evacuation of British and French nationals from the Middle East, Eisenhower conferred with Dulles to determine the next step to resolve the crisis. Dulles mentioned the latest communication that Eisenhower had received from Eden, in which the prime minister again used the Hitler analogy concerning violation of territorial rights. Eisenhower then stated that the British had gotten themselves into a box in the Middle East and had chosen the wrong place in which to get tough. In summing up his personal views on the entire problem, the president stated that he did not want to alienate his friends and that he wanted to keep NATO strong, but he "could not agree with these people [British and French] in their extreme attitude."[32] Continuous communications between Eisenhower

30. Heikal, *Cairo Documents,* 102. Heikal, of course, is hardly an unbiased observer, but Department of State files also indicate that Nasser interpreted Menzies' statements as a veiled threat. Menzies claimed that Nasser had misinterpreted his meaning—that he certainly did not intend to make direct or implied threats, but merely to point out that the international tension would continue to exist until satisfactory arrangements for the future of the Suez Canal were concluded.

31. Murphy, *Diplomat Among Warriors,* 387.

32. Memorandum of a Telephone Conversation Between the President and the Sec-

and Eden, and Dulles and Lloyd, marked early September. The latest American plan to settle the dispute proposed a second London Conference to form a users' association, comprising the eighteen nations that had supported his earlier proposal, to negotiate rates and fees for the Suez Canal. The Suez Canal Users Association (SCUA) called for collective bargaining by the users, the employment of their own pilots to navigate the canal, and the payment of a fair share of fees to Nasser for use of the international waterway. In retrospect, the concept was ill-conceived and served only to buy additional time to defuse the crisis prior to the onset of armed hostilities. The Egyptian president immediately dismissed the idea as ludicrous, which it was, and countered with a proposal of his own, which called for the formation of an association of users of the port of London. Two could play Eden's game.

Great Britain and France received Dulles' latest plan with trepidation because it threatened another postponement of their military expedition, now scheduled for October 9. Lloyd had serious misgivings about the SCUA proposal, but Eden was willing to listen, particularly after he received a personal letter from Eisenhower on September 2. Succinctly outlining the administration's position, Eisenhower wrote:

I am afraid, Anthony, that from this point [safeguarding international rights of passage in the Suez Canal] onward our views on this situation diverge. As to the use of force or the threat of force at this juncture, I continue to feel as I expressed myself in the letter Foster carried to you some weeks ago. Even now military preparations and civilian evacuation exposed to public view seem to be solidifying support for Nasser which has been shaky in many important quarters. I regard it as indispensable that if we are to proceed solidly together to the solution of this problem, public opinion in our several countries must be overwhelming in its support. I must tell you frankly that American public opinion flatly rejects the thought of using force, particularly when it does not seem that every possible peaceful means of protecting our vital interests has been exhausted without result. Moreover, I gravely doubt we could secure Congressional authority even for the lesser support measures for which you might have to look to us.

I really do not see how a successful result could be achieved by forcible means. The use of force would, it seems to me, vastly increase the area of jeopardy. I do not see how the economy of Western Europe can long survive the burden of prolonged military operations, as well as the denial of Near East oil. Also the peoples of the Near East and of North Africa and, to some extent, of all of Asia and

retary of State, September 7, 1956, folder marked "Sept '56 Phone Calls," Box 18, in DDE Diary Series, September 7, 1956, Ann Whitman File, EP, EL. See also Memoranda of Telephone Conversations with the White House, Sept. 4 1956, to Dec. 31, 1956, Box 11, Telephone Calls Series, Dulles Papers, EL.

all of Africa, would be consolidated against the West to a degree which, I fear, could not be overcome in a generation. . . . Before such actions were undertaken, all our peoples should unitedly understand that there were no other means available to protect our vital rights and interests.[33]

Eisenhower's candid letter, much of which Dulles had drafted, revealed a sharp divergence with Eden's thinking on Suez. To the prime minister, Nasser's action symbolized the sharp decline in British international prestige. Still divesting itself of its former empire, Great Britain simply lacked the military and economic resources to bring Nasser to terms. Regarding the difference that separated Eisenhower's interpretation of the danger Nasser posed with his own interpretation, Eden viewed the dichotomy as a difference in assessment of Nasser's intentions and of the consequences in the Middle East of military action against him. Eden genuinely believed the Egyptian president was another Hitler intent on regional domination. For Eden, Suez became an issue of national survival, or at least the survival of what remained of the British Empire. Just as Britain had led Western Europe against the forces of fascism in 1939, the prime minister could not and would not accept the final dissolution of international prestige, which in his terms he equated to the ignoble end to Britain's long history.

Eisenhower's letter of September 2, and a subsequent missive on September 8, caused Eden anguish, but the French remained intractable. Mollet and Pineau viewed the SCUA proposal as an instrument intended to postpone the inevitable showdown with Nasser. Even the British were unaware of the true extent of French hatred of Nasser. Like the British, the French were in the midst of reluctantly relinquishing their colonial empire. A defeat in North Africa, coupled with the recent loss of Indo-China, most probably would result in the fall of Mollet's government. As early as September 1, the French had made overtures to the Israelis for the possibility of combined political and military action against Egypt, with or without British support. Barjot, the principal French representative at a secret meeting with a member of Israeli Chief of Staff Moshe Dayan's staff on September 7, discussed the feasibility of a joint attack on Egypt. Although Barjot stressed that the purpose of the talks was strictly exploratory, within a week, Shimon Peres, the director-general of the Israeli Ministry of Defense, flew to Paris to visit his French counterpart and discuss military cooperation against Egypt. When Eden advised Mollet that he was postponing Operation Musketeer, code name

33. Eisenhower to Eden, September 2, 1956, in folder marked "Egypt (1)," Box 8, International Series, Ann Whitman File, EL. For complete text, see Eisenhower, *Waging Peace*, 666–68.

for the planned invasion of Egypt, because he intended to accept Eisenhower's proposal to establish the Suez Canal Users Association, Mollet regarded this decision as Eden's abandonment of his former readiness to pursue the military option. France now turned to Israel, hinting at the desire to "do something" in defense of the interests of both countries against Egyptian aggression.[34]

On September 14, the Western pilots walked off their jobs at the Suez Canal. Egyptian pilots immediately brought through a convoy of thirteen ships, and by week's end traffic was proceeding through the canal at a normal pace. In the president's opinion, the very assumption on which the SCUA had been based had proven groundless. Nasser was operating the Suez Canal with his own pilots more efficiently than the British. Since the Egyptians were allowing the free flow of traffic through the waterway, Eisenhower remained convinced that not only was the use of military force unwise, it also was ridiculous.

The Second Suez Canal Conference met in London from September 19 to 21. All eighteen members invited by the United Kingdom to send delegations did so.[35] In daily reports to the president, Dulles confirmed Eisenhower's worst expectations. The British and the French had isolated themselves from even their closest allies. Ambassador Dillon also informed Dulles that he felt that the British still regarded military action as the only satisfactory solution to the Suez problem and that the British would take such action as soon as it was politically feasible. Dillon then notified the secretary that French President Mollet had expressed particular concern about the lack of support from his "American friends." Mollet felt that the British resolve was weakening and that the French government was nearing a constitutional crisis for failing to carry out the mandate of the Parliament to maintain its firm position.[36] With so much dissension within the Western camp, the Second London Conference naturally became a source of acrimony. Since Nasser was running the canal more efficiently than the British had, the Users Association merely kept alive the dispute concerning payment of fees and did

34. For a summary of French-Israeli negotiations, see Dayan, *Moshe Dayan: Story of My Life*, 231–36.

35. Dulles again headed the United States delegation. The records kept by the American delegation are in Department of State Conference Files, Lot 62 D 181. The Conference Files also contain copies of the verbatim record of the five plenary sessions and other documents prepared by the Conference's International Secretariat. See also Department of State, *Suez Crisis*, 516–57.

36. See Memorandum from C. Douglas Dillon to the Secretary of State, Subject: Deterioration of the Political Situation in France, September 21, 1956, as quoted in Department of State, *Suez Crisis*, 551–52.

nothing to resolve the dispute. Consequently, the conference limped to an unproductive conclusion on September 21, with the members agreeing that the Suez Canal Users Association would open on October 1 and would seek the cooperation of the Egyptian authorities toward a resolution of the crisis. Nasser, of course, rejected the Users Association and maintained national control of the Suez Canal.

In desperation, the British and French, without the concurrence of the United States and for what reason Eisenhower did not know, asked the United Nations to settle the dispute. The proposed resolution sought to have the Security Council reaffirm freedom of navigation in accordance with the Convention of 1888; urge Egypt to negotiate a settlement on the proposals of the First London Conference; and in the interim, recommend to Egypt that it cooperate with the Suez Canal Users Association. The Security Council initiated deliberations on the Anglo-French resolution on October 5. This action met with widespread acceptance in the British press. The Manchester *Guardian* exclaimed, "We are going to the United Nations at last!" The *Economist* shared the *Guardian's* view and praised Dulles for what it considered his ceaseless efforts to obtain a solution of the crisis in the United Nations. The *Times* had already concluded that the best thing to do was to refer the matter to the Security Council, but the newspaper accused the secretary of state of distorting the issue of the Suez question and vacillating in his support of Great Britain and France. The newspaper concluded that whatever difficulties might develop between the European and American partners of the Atlantic alliance would be the result of Dulles' inconsistent conduct.[37]

Why the British and French decided to submit the problem to the United Nations at this time mystified Eisenhower. Dulles had hoped to defer the discussion until a later date, because he felt that the problem might be resolved outside the United Nations and prevent an embarrassing situation for Great Britain. Moreover, debate in the Security Council might dissuade some states from joining the Users Association. Like Dulles, Eisenhower wondered if Britain and France had really intended the United Nations to reach a solution. If the Security Council failed to resolve the crisis, the European allies might claim that they had at least attempted to settle the dispute in the international forum before resorting to military force.

In an attempt to decipher European intentions, Dulles met with Lloyd and Pineau on the eve of the United Nations debate.[38] Convening the

37. Manchester *Guardian,* September 27, 1956; *Economist,* October 6, 1956; *Times* (London), September 24, October 2, and October 6, 1956.
38. Memorandum of a Conversation, Secretary Dulles' Suite, Waldorf Astoria, Oc-

meeting in the secretary's suite at the Waldorf Astoria, Dulles emphatically stated the need for clarification among the senior partners of the Atlantic alliance. Raising the question of Anglo-French intentions, the secretary inquired whether the Security Council debate was an attempt to find a peaceful settlement or an attempt to get the United Nations behind them to clear the way for a greater freedom of action and stronger measures. Dulles also confirmed Eisenhower's assessment that military action would start a war that would not only be extremely difficult to terminate, but also might lead to the irrevocable loss of sympathies of all the Middle Eastern, Asian, and African peoples. Lastly, Dulles assured Lloyd and Pineau that elections in the United States were not a factor in determining the American position against force, contrary to what was being said in some quarters in Britain and France.

Lloyd immediately denied any hidden agenda, adding that an Indian source had reported that the Russians were discussing the matter and intended to take it to the United Nations themselves. Stating that the British would favor economic pressure if it would show results within two weeks—not a likely prospect—Lloyd concluded that force was a lesser evil than tolerating regional anarchy caused by a "conspiracy" afoot in the Middle East. Pineau then joined in and attacked Eisenhower for not realizing the importance that France and the United Kingdom attached to Suez. It was not merely the canal, but all the Middle East that was involved. France, in Pineau's assessment, risked losing its influence in the Middle East if Nasser survived. Similar to Eisenhower's Southeast Asian "domino" analogy, Pineau foresaw the loss of British and French positions, followed by the loss of U.S. prestige.

The candid discussion between the Western foreign ministers failed to convince either party of the other's true intentions, but all agreed on the proceedings in the United Nations. Writing to Eisenhower, Dulles assessed that the next few days were the "make or break" point in the crisis.[39] Candidly outlining Lloyd's and Pineau's position that they did not believe any peaceful resolution possible and that only the use of force against Nasser would restore Western prestige in Africa and the Middle East, Dulles also informed the president that Egyptian Foreign Minister Fawzi had indicated his willingness to negotiate a settlement. Without a mandate to speak for Great Britain and France, Dulles agreed on a subsequent meeting at the legal advisor level to exchange views.

---

tober 5, 1956, in Department of State, Central Files, 974.7301/10-556. Top Secret. Copy also is included in Department of State, *Suez Crisis*, 639–45.

39. Message from the Secretary of State to the President, October 5, 1956, Box 6, Dulles-Herter Series, Ann Whitman File, EP, EL.

The Egyptian attempt to split the United States from Great Britain and France reflected Nasser's growing apprehension of the British and French military build-up on Cyprus. The Security Council welcomed Nasser's apparent willingness to consider an international advisory board in operating the Suez Canal. Fawzi suggested establishing a small negotiating body based on the principles of (1) guarantees of unimpeded transit, (2) cooperation between the Canal Authority and users, (3) a fair system of fixing tolls, and (4) allocating adequate revenues for development.[40] On October 12, following negotiations among Fawzi, Pineau, and Lloyd, the three foreign ministers agreed upon six principles to implement the administration of the Suez Canal.[41] The Six Principles called for free and open transit through the canal without discrimination, respect for the sovereignty of Egypt, and the use of arbitration to settle any disputes between Egypt and the Suez Canal Company. Although Eden, in telephonic communication with Lloyd, had the words *principles* changed to *requirements* in the introductory paragraph, the Egyptians proved to be surprisingly accommodating. The negotiations were seemingly acceptable to all parties, and the Security Council adopted them on October 13. The Security Council resolution, however, disrupted the planned military expedition against Egypt, and Great Britain and France attached a rider to the Six Principles that required Egypt to submit detailed implementing proposals in advance of any future negotiations. This ultimatum was totally unacceptable to Fawzi, and the Soviet Union vetoed the rider, leaving the resolution to stand alone.

Despite the failure of the United Nations to resolve the crisis, Eisenhower entered the last weeks of October confident that his efforts had succeeded in averting war. Heavily involved with the election campaign, the president relied on Dulles to keep him informed of British and French actions. During the month, the Suez problem definitely took a back seat to the election, but by mid-October, Eisenhower faced increasing attacks by Democratic nominee Adlai Stevenson, who attributed the spread of Soviet influence to the "dangerous drift in foreign affairs" resulting from the lack of a firm policy for Suez.[42] Democratic congressional candidates also criticized the president for his delaying tactics, which had not solved the impasse. Republican supporters were content to allow the president to defend his policy himself.

40. Bowie, "Eisenhower, Dulles and the Suez Crisis," in Louis and Owen, eds., *Suez 1956,* 206.
41. For complete text of the Six Principles, see Love, *Suez: The Twice-Fought War,* 445.
42. Washington *Post,* September 21, 1956.

Democratic criticism did not faze Eisenhower in his attempts to bring the crisis to a peaceful solution. Exercising the power of incumbency, the president was successful in presenting an image of a man of peace to the American public. As expected, Eisenhower's public statements made few concessions to the possibility of potential American military involvement in the Middle East. In numerous press conferences and speeches, he repeatedly urged a peaceful resolution to the dispute and disclaimed any intention of committing American troops should the situation deteriorate. In so doing, Eisenhower played to the domestic audience that was solidly against sending American forces to the troubled region. A Gallup poll conducted on September 28 asked Americans what they thought was the most serious problem facing the United States. Forty-six percent stated that the conflict over Suez constituted the most serious threat to the country, and 55 percent were against the dispatch of American armed forces to the Middle East if war erupted.[43]

As he embarked on the last leg of the campaign, Eisenhower firmly believed that the numerous diplomatic attempts to reconcile differences between the Europeans and the Egyptians that he and Dulles had implemented since the seizure of the Suez Canal had averted war in the Middle East. Although he was fully aware of the reluctance of Eden and Mollet to accept a peaceful resolution of the crisis, the president believed that the two London conferences, the Users Association, and the American stand in the United Nations had removed the immediate danger of hostilities. Speaking to a New York audience, Eisenhower noted, "It looks like . . . a very great crisis is left behind us."[44]

With respect to the security agencies of the government, Eisenhower kept tight reins on all major issues affecting his re-election campaign, Suez being foremost in his consideration. The president presided over all three NSC meetings in October, and Radford kept him informed daily on evacuation plans for American nationals in the Middle East. In the United Nations, Ambassador Lodge reported directly to the president and the secretary of state on ensuing negotiations.[45] Maintaining daily contact with Dulles, Eisenhower remained confident that a peaceful resolution of the crisis was at hand.

Unfortunately, two new crises erupted in mid-October. CIA Director

43. See Gallup polls released on September 28, October 27, and November 19, 1956, in Gallup, *The Gallup Poll: Public Opinion, 1935–1971*, II, 1447, 1451, and 1454 respectively.

44. As quoted in Chester Cooper, *The Lion's Last Roar: Suez, 1956* (New York, 1978), 144.

45. During international crises, Lodge worked directly with the president. See Henry Cabot Lodge, *The Storm Has Many Eyes* (New York, 1973), 130–37.

Dulles reported ominous rumblings in Hungary, and U-2 surveillance flights delivered the first hard intelligence of mobilization of Israeli ground forces on the Jordanian and Egyptian borders and of the presence of sixty French *Mystere* jets on Israeli airfields. To complicate matters, Dillon cabled Dulles about a conversation he had with Chaban Delmas, a minister of state in the French government, ranking above Pineau and a personal friend of the American ambassador.[46] According to Dillon, Delmas informed him that time was running out on the various alternatives that Dulles was pursuing to settle the dispute. What was needed was strong action by Eisenhower, or else military action would ensue within forty-eight hours of the American election. France simply could not allow the problem of Nasser to remain unresolved beyond Christmas at the latest. Although the date of the attack proved incorrect, Dillon's telegram was the first hard evidence that France had definitely decided to commence military operations. This news, coupled with the U-2 reports and National Security Agency monitoring of the traffic between Paris and Tel Aviv, heightened the president's anxiety over the increasing buildup of British and French forces on Cyprus.

Not yet sure of the extent of Anglo-French collusion with Israel, Eisenhower remained convinced that he had done all in his power to prevent armed hostilities in the Suez region. He had made it abundantly clear to his principal European allies that he regarded armed intervention against Egypt as unwarranted and self-defeating. Despite clear warning signs from Eden that the prime minister still considered the military option a viable alternative to diplomatic negotiations, Eisenhower chose to believe that Eden would never adopt a military campaign in Egypt without prior consultation with the United States. So convinced was he of Eden's loyalty to the Anglo-American partnership, that Eisenhower underestimated the prime minister's capacity and willingness to act in the crisis in contravention to the expressed desires of the president of the United States. It was a serious miscalculation on Eisenhower's part and led to an even greater crisis in the Atlantic alliance. His failure to anticipate Eden's next move created even more demands on Eisenhower's time and further taxed his ability as a crisis manager.

46. Interview with the author, June 29, 1982. See also Telegram from the Embassy in France to the Department of State, October 19, 1956, in Department of State, Central Files, 974.7301/10-1056, quoted in Department of State, *Suez Crisis*, 753–57.

5

THE OUTBREAK OF WAR

Bombs, by god. What does Anthony think he's doing? Why is he doing this to me?

—Dwight D. Eisenhower

The dual crises surrounding the events in Hungary and the Middle East could not have come at a more inopportune time for the president. With Stevenson attacking the administration's foreign policy record and the election less than three weeks away, Eisenhower was engaged in a full test of his ability as a crisis manager. The weeks that followed were the most demanding of his entire presidency and posed a serious threat to American prestige. Not only did he find himself interwoven in the Arab-Israeli conflict, but Eisenhower also risked alienating his principal Western allies. Despite the growing tide of anti-Americanism in Great Britain and France, Eisenhower remained adamant that he must not purchase favor by leading the Western European countries to feel that he would blindly support them in any course they might wish to pursue. Dulles had echoed similar sentiments earlier in the month in dispatches to American ambassadors in Great Britain and France. Aside from Hungary, an area in which the president felt powerless to influence events, Eisenhower demonstrated that he would not retreat from his position against the use of armed aggression to settle international disputes, even in the face of deteriorating relations with traditional partners. His performance at the height of the crisis marked him as a skillful chief executive who was tremendously effective in managing several crises simultaneously under the most difficult circumstances.

Nothing bothered the Eisenhower team more than the lack of intelligence surrounding the intentions of Great Britain, France, and Israel concerning possible military plans against Egypt. Although he had received routine cables from American embassies abroad and CIA reports concerning meetings between French and British military planners, Eisenhower received little information from his Atlantic partners. In fact, there was a virtual news blackout from the European side of the Atlantic. Eden had recalled Ambassador Roger Makins on October 11 to take up the top position at the treasury in London, and until November 8, Great Britain had no ambassador in Washington. His withdrawal marked the beginning of a deliberate attempt by Eden to mask his true intentions from the American president. Even some of the top officials within the British government were kept in suspense, although Makins and Macmillan, who knew of the collusion in broad outline, realized that the prime minister had made an important decision concerning the attack on Egypt.[1]

Unbeknownst to Eisenhower, Eden had met with General Maurice Challe, who had recently headed a French military mission to Israel, and Albert Gazier, the French Minister of Labor and close confidant of Mollet, on October 14. After being briefed on the clandestine Franco-Israeli negotiations for a joint strike against Egypt, the prime minister endorsed a plan that not only set the stage for the Israeli invasion of Egypt, followed by the intervention of an Anglo-French expeditionary force, but he also approved additional consultations among representatives of the three nations. According to Eden's private secretary, who attended the meeting,

The Prime Minister had . . . made up his mind to go along with the French plan . . . and we were to ally ourselves with the Israelis and the French in an attack on Egypt designed to topple Nasser and to seize the Suez Canal. Our traditional friendships with the Arab world were to be discarded; the policy of keeping a balance in arms deliveries as between Israel and the Arab States was to be abandoned; indeed . . . we were to take part in a cynical act of aggression, dressing ourselves for the part as fireman or policeman, while making sure that our firehoses spouted petrol and not water and that we belabored with our truncheons the assaulted and not the assaulter.[2]

As soon as Eden formally approved collusion with France and Israel, open communication across the Atlantic ceased.

As the Middle East situation deteriorated, Eisenhower summoned Dulles, Hoover, and Deputy Assistant Secretary of State Rountree to the White House on October 15 to discuss reports of a heavy Israeli concentration on the Jordanian border.[3] For weeks, Israeli patrols had violated Jordanian territory, allegedly in response to guerrilla raids against

1. For the details surrounding Makins' recall, see Horne, *Harold Macmillan*, I, 429–31. Horne is generous in his assessment that Macmillan knew little of the details of the invasion. Macmillan, who kept a meticulous diary throughout his public career, claimed he mislaid the volume that began around October 1, 1956. According to his biographer, Macmillan later admitted that he destroyed the volume outlining the British invasion of Egypt at the specific request of Eden.

2. Anthony Nutting, *No End of a Lesson* (New York, 1967), 94.

3. Memorandum for the Record by the President, October 15, 1956, folder marked "October 1956 (1) Diary," Box 8, Ann Whitman Diary Series, Ann Whitman File, EP, EL.

Israeli settlements. Eisenhower directed Dulles to warn Israeli Ambassador Abba Eban that the United States would condemn any military attack on Jordan. Moreover, Israeli aggression would lead to a United Nations resolution condemning Israel and would result in the diplomatic isolation of that country. Convinced that Israeli Prime Minister Ben Gurion's militant behavior was partially due to the belief that the American presidential campaign would prevent the United States from taking a firm stand against a preemptive strike in the region, the president directed Dulles to advise Eban that it was a grave error to believe that winning a domestic election was as important to him as preserving and protecting the interests of the United Nations and other nations of the free world in the Middle East.

Israeli troop concentrations were not the only bit of intelligence that Eisenhower found disturbing. The U-2 flights had also revealed the presence of sixty French *Mystere* pursuit planes, when France had reported the transfer of only twenty-four aircraft. The president had known since September 21 that France had possibly delivered additional aircraft to Israel, but the report could not be confirmed until aerial photography located the missing *Mysteres*. This was clearly a violation of the Tripartite Declaration of 1950, in which the United States, Great Britain, and France were committed to maintaining the *status quo* in arms and borders in the Middle East. Eisenhower knew that France was obviously lying to the United States and arming Israel in contravention to the 1950 agreement. Dulles expressed his concern to his brother, but the Director of Central Intelligence could not provide any additional information aside from the fact that French military officials had recently met with their British counterparts.[4] Allen Dulles also expressed his confidence that he had a handle on events in Egypt. Next, the secretary of state called Lodge at the United Nations, but all Lodge told Dulles was that British Ambassador Sir Pierson Dixon was reticent and more concerned with deteriorating Anglo-American relations. Clearly, something was amiss. To confront Great Britain and France directly, Eisenhower contemplated inviting Eden and Mollet to the United States, but decided to postpone the invitation until after the election lest the Stevenson camp view it as an election ploy. Left unsaid by the president was a more significant reason for delaying the invitation for a summit: a meeting between Eisenhower, Eden, and Mollet might convey U.S. complicity in any future military action against Egypt.

In retrospect, it seems inconceivable that the United States, with its

4. Telephone Conversations Memoranda, October 18, 1956, in Box 5, Dulles Papers, Princeton.

highly sophisticated intelligence system and its global contacts in the diplomatic and military arena, could remain in the dark about British intentions. On the surface it would appear that Eisenhower was either incredibly naive or he suffered a massive failure of intelligence. The answer was not so simple. Sometimes one could have too much information, and the question was not so much lack of intelligence as it was a question of interpretation. Such was the case during Suez. The CIA employed a full network of operatives in most foreign capitals and U-2 surveillance flights flew constantly over the Atlantic and Mediterranean Sea, sending back aerial photographs that clearly outlined the scale of mobilization on Malta and Cyprus, and in Israel. Ambassadors Dillon and Aldrich also dispatched routine cables to the Department of State, in which they outlined British and French domestic support for armed intervention, as well as unofficial conversations with diplomatic friends who freely admitted something was in the air. Moreover, American newspapermen supervised an extensive information network in Paris, London, and Tel Aviv. Surely the president and Dulles must have suspected their European allies were concealing their true intentions.

Why then was the president surprised? First, Eden and Mollet deliberately lied to Eisenhower to conceal the extent of their collusion with Israel. By withdrawing Makins to Britain, Eden purposely left the United States without a British ambassador, thus severing a valuable source of information and communication with Washington. Additionally, Mollet, who conspired with Israel to attack Egypt from the start, kept Eden in the dark about the detailed military planning until mid-October. Thus, there existed as much confusion in the European camp as there was between the United States and its European allies. The prime minister, in turn, confided only in a select group of advisers—excluding a number of key Cabinet members whom he felt would oppose his conspiracy—thereby eliminating another source of information to the Eisenhower team. For his part, Allen Dulles failed to interpret correctly what intelligence the agency had gathered. He advised Eisenhower that the Israelis were mobilizing against Jordan, not Egypt. By their nature, intelligence experts are loathe to admit failures; Dulles and the CIA were no exceptions. Last, Eisenhower must share a portion of the blame. Presented with hard evidence of French deceit concerning arms shipments and convinced that Eden would not double-cross him, the president failed to act as vigorously as he should have to remove the cloak of secrecy. As a result, he was taken by surprise.[5]

5. See Ambrose, *Eisenhower: The President*, 353. Ambrose faults Eisenhower for not remaining in touch with his close personal friends, such as Macmillan and Mountbatten, both of whom opposed Eden's adventurism.

What Eisenhower failed to understand was the exact extent of the conspiracy against Egypt. From the moment Eden approved the French-Israeli plan, Eden took the most elaborate precautions to preserve absolute secrecy, even to the point of misleading the United States government. After his conference with Challe and Gazier, Eden treated Eisenhower as an unreliable ally. The more the president warned the prime minister that the American public would not tolerate wanton aggression, the more determined Eden became in concealing his intentions from the Americans. Following his meeting with French leaders, Eden said nothing at all. It was a deliberate attempt to dupe the American president, and Eden took the additional precaution of not informing the British chargé d'affaires in Washington of the operational plans to preclude his inadvertently disclosing the details of the collusion.[6] So appalled by the immorality of Eden's role in the conspiracy was Anthony Nutting, Eden's protégé and personal secretary, that he submitted his resignation.

Unswayed by the departure of his trusted adviser, Eden met Mollet and Ben Gurion at Sevres, midway between Paris and Versailles, from October 23–24. It was the first time the chief conspirators met face to face. Rapidly reaching an accord, the heads of state agreed that Israel would initiate hostilities at dusk on October 29 with an airborne assault on the Mitla Pass to create the appearance of an immediate threat to the Suez Canal. When Great Britain and France "learned" of the threat to the waterway, Eden and Mollet would issue an ultimatum demanding a "temporary occupation" of the Suez Canal zone and a buffer zone of ten miles on each side of the canal. Egypt and Israel would have twelve hours to respond to the ultimatum. If either nation rejected the demand, British and French troops would land at Port Said at the mouth of the Suez Canal and move down its length to block the Egyptian army's withdrawal from the Sinai. The document also provided for the Israeli occupation of the western shore of the Gulf of Aqaba, and the islands of Tiran and Sanafir, and contained a promise from Israel not to attack Jordan during the period of operations against Egypt. Eden also consented to assist Israel in gaining an advantageous peace settlement.[7] Before returning to their re-

6. For a British view of Eden's deceit, see Nutting, *No End of a Lesson*, 110–13.

7. The Israeli Delegation, headed by Ben Gurion and including Dayan and Peres, arrived in France and began discussions with Mollet, Pineau, and Defense Minister Bourges-Maunoury on October 22. That evening Lloyd met briefly with the others, and Lloyd and Pineau flew to London to discuss the matter directly with Eden. The next day, the document was signed by Ben Gurion, Pineau, and Deputy Under Secretary of the British Foreign Office Patrick Dean, who attended the final discussions in Lloyd's place. For a summary of the Sevres conference, see Hoopes, *The Devil and John Foster Dulles*, 371–72; Robertson, *Crisis: The Inside Story of the Suez Conspiracy*, 157–63; and Neff, *Warriors at Suez*, 342–45. See also Department of State, *Suez Crisis*, 776–77.

spective capitals, the conspirators drafted the ultimatum that they intended to present to the warring parties. Although there is frequently an element of political intrigue in the conduct of international relations, Europe had not witnessed such naked collusion since the Nazi-Soviet Non-Aggression Pact of 1939.

The final weeks of October were extraordinarily busy for Eisenhower and his secretary of state. Political speeches and campaign appearances filled the president's agenda, but he still found time to manage the twin crises of Hungary and Suez. On October 20, he presided over the 301st meeting of the National Security Council, at which Hungary was the principal topic of discussion. Until October 29, Eastern Europe, rather than the Middle East, dominated the Eisenhower agenda. Still, the president sought to penetrate the Anglo-French screen, but he and his advisers misinterpreted the available intelligence. Eden and Mollet had woven their web of conspiracy too well. The situation further deteriorated on October 25, when Jordan, Egypt, and Syria announced the signing of the Pact of Amman to increase their mutual military cooperation. Ben Gurion immediately announced that Israel was in direct danger, and he issued a call for Israeli mobilization. Colonel Leo J. Query, the Army attaché in Tel Aviv, relayed this information to Washington, along with additional intelligence concerning Israeli troop concentrations in the border regions.[8] Query described the mobilization as "very large scale," exceeding the extent of every Israeli mobilization since the 1948 Israeli War of Independence. Query also reported that the French might be working with the Israelis, and he speculated that an Israeli move against the Straits of Tiran was a good possibility.

By now it was evident to both Eisenhower and Dulles that chances for a peaceful resolution of the Middle East crisis were evaporating quickly. Dulles cabled Aldrich in London to express the administration's concern that Eden was deliberately keeping the president in the dark as to his intentions in the Middle East generally and in Egypt in particular. With no high-level contacts on these matters with the British Embassy in over a week, Dulles raised the question of possible French conspiracy with Israel, and possible United Kingdom complicity with France and Israel. Aldrich replied that the absence of information was due essentially to Eden and Lloyd handling Suez-related issues personally, along with a detectable reticence among government officials to express opinions as to prospects of a resolution of the crisis. Completely misread-

8. See Chronology of Significant Events Relating to the Current World Crisis, October 23–31, 1956, in the Operational Archives Branch, Naval Historical Center, Washington Navy Yard, Washington, D.C.

ing Eden's intentions, Aldrich stated that he was sufficiently optimistic that negotiations with the Egyptians were on track.[9]

Back in Washington after a campaign trip, Eisenhower summoned Dulles, Hoover, Rountree, and Goodpaster for a meeting in the Oval Office to discuss Hungary and Suez. Turning to the Middle East, Eisenhower inquired about the Israeli mobilization and what direction the secretary thought it would take. Rountree suggested that Jordan was the most likely target, and Dulles recommended that the president immediately send a message, expressing his grave concern over recent developments, to Ben Gurion.[10] Eisenhower's subsequent missive renewed his plea that there be no forcible initiative on the part of the Israeli government that would endanger the peace and the growing friendship between the United States and Israel.

The following day, October 28, brought ominous warnings of impending military action. After examining the latest evidence, the CIA's Intelligence Advisory Committee concluded that the heavy Israeli mobilization would allow Israel to occupy Jordan west of the Jordan River; penetrate Syria as far as Damascus; invade Egypt to the Suez Canal and hold parts of Sinai for a considerable time; gain air superiority over the Egyptian air force alone, or in combination with air forces of the other Arab States; and probably execute all of the above, even in the face of combined resistance of contiguous Arab states. More important, the CIA speculated that Israel would launch its attack against Egypt in the very near future, under the pretext of retaliation, exceeding past raids in strength.[11] Eisenhower had clearly guessed wrong with respect to Ben Gurion's objective. Again he cabled the Israeli prime minister, emphasized the dangers inherent in the present situation, and urged Israel to do nothing that would endanger the peace.

To amplify his concern, the president issued a public statement, which Dulles personally handed to French Ambassador Herve Alphand and to Sir John E. Coulson, minister of the British Embassy in the United States. The statement outlined the confirmed reports of Israeli mobilization and Eisenhower's recent correspondence with Ben Gurion. When questioned

9. See Telegram from the Department of State to the Embassy in the United Kingdom, October 26, 1956, and Aldrich's reply, in Department of State, *Suez Crisis,* 790–92.

10. Memorandum of a Conference with the President, White House, Washington, October 27, 1956, in folder marked "October 1956 Staff Memoranda," Box 19, DDE Diary Series, Ann Whitman File, EP, EL. A copy of the president's telegram is in Department of State, Central Files, 684A.86/10-2756, as quoted in Department of State, *Suez Crisis,* 795.

11. CIA Files, Top Secret, as quoted in Department of State, *Suez Crisis,* 798–99, and Condit, *Joint Chiefs of Staff and National Policy, 1955–1956,* pp. 16–17.

by Dulles about the movement of French ships to the Eastern Mediterranean, Alphand denied any knowledge of ship movements toward the Middle East. Coulson, who had just assumed his ministerial duties on October 27, reiterated that he had no information from his government regarding Israeli mobilization measures of a kind similar to that in Eisenhower's possession. The meeting ended with a brief exchange of information on Hungary.

Following a brief discussion with Hoover, Murphy, Phleger, and Rountree, the secretary then called Eisenhower and recommended he authorize the evacuation of American citizens from Egypt, Jordan, and Israel.[12] Eisenhower asked Dulles if the secretary thought that, by initiating the evacuation, the United States would exacerbate the situation, but Dulles said no, as the British and French had already withdrawn their nationals from the troubled region. Assured by the secretary of state, the president ordered the evacuation, whereupon Dulles prepared a communiqué to announce that "as a matter of prudence, persons not performing essential functions will be asked to depart until conditions improve."[13]

After the discussion on evacuation, Eisenhower and Dulles examined the increase of troop transports around Cyprus—30 to 63 in the last 48 hours from Great Britain and an increase of 3 to 21 French transports. The president said he could not believe that Britain would be dragged into this, but Dulles replied that Coulson's and Alphand's professed ignorance of the Israeli mobilization and ship movements around Cyprus was a sign of a guilty conscience. Eisenhower concurred and stated that he expected an Israeli attack the next day. Dulles remained more optimistic, but promised to keep Eisenhower, whose schedule included a southern campaign swing the following day, informed of any new developments.

At precisely 1630 hours, October 29, the date agreed upon at Sevres to commence hostilities, the Israeli assault on the Egyptian forces in the Sinai began. When the attack began, Eisenhower was in the middle of a campaign tour of the South. Forty minutes after the initial assault, Dulles phoned Lodge at the United Nations and informed him of the outbreak of hostilities. Unsure of Israeli intentions, Dulles instructed Lodge to "smoke out" the British and French to see where they stood; meanwhile, he would confront the European ministers in Washington.

12. Telephone Conversations Series, Box 11, in Dulles Papers, EL. See also folder marked "October, 1956 Phone Calls," Box 19, DDE Diary Series, Ann Whitman File, EP, EL.

13. Eisenhower, *Waging Peace*, 70. For text, see Department of State *Bulletin*, November 5, 1956, 700.

Shortly thereafter, Senator Knowland called, and the secretary told him that the French, and possibly the British, had conspired with Israel. Soon Richard Rountree was on the line to inform Dulles that the 6th Fleet was proceeding with contingency plans outlined by Radford and Burke for the evacuation of American nationals.[14] Eisenhower did not receive word of the Israeli aggression until he landed in Richmond, the last stop on his tricity tour. With customary calmness, he delivered his speech and returned to Washington.

Awaiting the president on his return to the White House were the Dulles brothers, Hoover, Charles Wilson, Radford, Goodpaster, Sherman Adams, and General Persons, the deputy assistant to the president for congressional affairs. Entering the Oval Office, Eisenhower was absolutely livid over Ben Gurion's deceit, and he instructed Dulles to send a scathing cable condemning the unwarranted aggression. Speaking in an irate tone, the president allegedly added, "Foster, you tell them, goddamn it, we're going to the United Nations. We're going to do everything that there is so we can stop this thing."[15] Following this emotional outburst, Eisenhower presided over the meeting, which considered the American response to the outbreak of war.

Secretary Dulles initiated the conference with an account of French military assistance to Israel prior to October 29, referring to the sizable number of *Mysteres* given to the Israelis in excess of agreed figures and without the notifications called for in the Tripartite Declaration. Next, Allen Dulles reviewed the intelligence reports regarding Egyptian military forces, which caused the president to inquire as to what was the best method to support the victim of aggression in accordance with the U.S.–U.K.–French pact of 1950. Radford expressed his conviction that Israel would be on the Suez Canal in three days, and there was little the United States could do before that time except in the diplomatic arena. He also informed Eisenhower that the 6th Fleet was proceeding with the evacuation plans and that Burke had moved the fleet to the vicinity of Cyprus, if the president desired to use the fleet for any other purposes.

After hearing the recommendations of his civilian and military advisers, Eisenhower made the decision to bring the matter to the United Nations before the Soviets did so the following morning.[16] Staking his

14. Transcripts of telephone messages between Dulles and Lodge, Knowland, and Rountree are in Telephone Conversations Memoranda, October 29, 1956, Box 5, Dulles Papers, Mudd Library, Princeton.

15. As quoted in Neff, *Warriors at Suez,* 365.

16. The Dulles Papers at the Eisenhower Library contain memoranda of several telephone conversations that preceded this meeting. On his own initiative, Dulles had

reputation, as well as that of his country, on a principled approach to the crisis, he stated that under the circumstances, the United States could not be bound by its traditional alliances, but must instead face the question how to make good on its pledge [Tripartite Declaration]. The president then instructed Dulles to explain to the British, whom he suspected were more knowledgeable of the Israeli intentions than they professed, that the United States recognized that there was much on their side in the dispute with Egypt, but nothing justified double-crossing him. Considering convening Congress on the eve of the election, Eisenhower deferred until he could learn more about the military situation.

Immediately following the meeting, Eisenhower summoned British Chargé d'Affaires Coulson to the White House to receive the American position relating to the crisis. Joining the president were Secretary Dulles and the ever-present Goodpaster. In no uncertain terms, Eisenhower stressed that the United States and the United Kingdom must stand by the Tripartite Declaration. Lacking concrete proof of Britain's role in the collusion, of which Coulson was totally unaware, Eisenhower invited Great Britain to join the United States before the Security Council. Asking Coulson to communicate these ideas urgently to London, the president again reiterated his belief that he would not betray the good word of the United States by condoning aggression in the Middle East.[17] Moreover, he informed Coulson that he insisted that the British government provide the United States with a statement as to what the British government thought it was doing. That evening Dulles directed Lodge to give notice to the president of the Security Council that Eisenhower desired to introduce an item on the Israeli attack into the next morning's agenda. Eisenhower had beaten the Soviet Union to the United Nations.

Eisenhower's actions on October 29 highlighted one of the supreme moments of his presidency. Abandoned by his allies and faced with naked aggression against a state whose leader he personally distrusted and whom he believed was at the root of most of the problems in the Middle East, Eisenhower placed America's prestige on the side of justice and

---

asked Radford and Allen Dulles to attend the meeting. The president approved and informed Dulles to schedule the meeting for the early evening. See Department of State, *Suez Crisis,* 833–34, for Dulles' telephone conversations and Memorandum of Conference with the President, October 29, 1956, folder marked "October 1956 (1) Staff Memoranda," Box 19, DDE Diary Series, Ann Whitman File, EP, EL, for a summary of the actual meeting.

17. Memorandum of a Conference with the President, October 29, 1956, folder marked "October 1956 (1) Staff Memoranda," Box 19, DDE Diary Series, Ann Whitman File, EP, EL.

against unwarranted aggression. Eisenhower's position was a principled approach that happened to coincide with his interest in retaining friendly terms with the Arab community to forestall Soviet intervention in the region. The events of October 29 also revealed something about Eisenhower's role as a crisis manager. Although he expected most operations to be carried out at departmental level within the guidelines of policy developed by the NSC staff and coordinated at the interagency level by the Operations Coordination Board during crisis operations that required Eisenhower's direct participation, the decision-making forum was a small group of intimate advisers, who furnished the president with a wide range of recommendations on the specific aspects of a rapidly evolving situation. Carefully weighing the merits of each recommendation, he then opted for a strategy that would achieve his long-term policy objective, namely, a return to the *status quo ante bellum* to promote regional stability and the denial of the region to Soviet incursions. Only by taking a firm stand in the United Nations against the aggressor nations could Eisenhower attain his political goals. Personal political considerations, such as the presidential election, simply did not enter the equation. As he stated to his advisers during the White House conference, he did not really think the American people would throw him out in the midst of a crisis, but if they did, so be it. The United States would stand on principle and keep its word, regardless of the consequences. It was one of Eisenhower's finest hours and a testament to his moral courage in time of crisis.

When he arrived at the White House the following morning, the president immediately called Dulles, who related what the secretary termed a rather "bizarre" conversation that Cabot Lodge had had the previous evening with his British counterpart at the United Nations. Lodge reported that although Sir Pierson Dixon was normally an amiable fellow, "last night it was as though a mask had fallen off; he was ugly and not smiling." When Lodge spoke of living up to the Tripartite Declaration, Dixon replied, "Don't be silly and moralistic. We have got to be practical." Adding that Great Britain would never go along with any move against Israel in the Security Council, Dixon stated that London regarded the Tripartite Declaration as ancient history and without current validity.[18]

Criticizing Dixon's response, Eisenhower asked Under Secretary of

18. Memorandum of Telephone Conversation, October 29 1956, in General Telephone Conversations, Box 11, Dulles Papers, EL. See also Lodge, *The Storm Has Many Eyes,* 131; and Neff, *Warriors at Suez,* 371.

State Hoover and legal adviser Phleger to join Dulles and himself to discuss courses of action available to the United States and to examine a letter he had drafted to Eden. Dulles opened the meeting with a report that Lodge had given notice to the president of the Security Council regarding Eisenhower's desire to include an item on the Security Council's agenda regarding the Israeli attack. The president at this point read aloud a message he had been drafting to Eden and asked Dulles to edit it prior to immediate dispatch. At the close of this missive, Eisenhower read an International News Service report of imminent French and British landings in the canal region. Debating the merits of any Anglo-French invasion, the president concluded that he did not see much value in an unworthy and unreliable ally [Great Britain and France] and that the necessity to support them might not be as great as Great Britain and France believed. Interrupted briefly with the news that a message from Eden had been received by the British Embassy, Eisenhower adjourned the meeting until its arrival.[19]

Eden's message revealed the true extent of British deceit. Claiming that he had urged restraint when he received the initial news of Israeli mobilization, the prime minister fixed the blame for hostilities on Nasser, who had to a large extent brought the attack on himself by insisting that a state of war persisted between Egypt and Israel, by defying the Security Council and declaring his intention to marshal the Arab states for the destruction of Israel, and by announcing the joint command between Egypt, Jordan, and Syria. To preclude closing the canal, Eden claimed he was forced to take decisive action to halt hostilities.[20] It was now increasingly obvious to Eisenhower that Eden was being neither totally candid nor sharing his actual views with Washington.

When the White House meeting resumed, Eisenhower read Eden's message, commenting that the prime minister stated that the attitude of Egypt over the past years had relieved the signatories of the three-power declaration from any obligation. Dulles and the State Department group then left to work on the United Nations resolution, but Dulles called soon with the news that Eden was announcing in the House of Commons the landing of British and French forces in the Suez Canal area. Dulles' report was erroneous—what Eden was announcing was the ultimatum upon which the conspirators agreed at Sevres, and Eden's cabinet had already approved the text. Dulles' call deeply disturbed the pres-

19. Memorandum of a Conference with the President, October 30, 1956, folder marked "October 1956 (1) Staff Memoranda," Box 19, DDE Diary Series, Ann Whitman File, EP, EL.

20. Eden to Eisenhower, October 30, 1956, in Box 19, International Series, Ann Whitman File, EP, EL.

ident, who now understood Eden's complicity in the collusion. Eisenhower decided the most prudent course at that time was to take a "hands off" attitude by the United States and to issue a public statement disassociating the United States from the French and the British in their activities.

In writing to Eden, Eisenhower made a final attempt for Anglo-American cooperation. Greatly troubled by what he perceived as a major split with his most trustworthy ally, Eisenhower wrote:

> I address you in this note not only as head of Her Majesty's Government but as my long time friend who has, with me, believed in and worked for real Anglo-American understanding.
>
> Without bothering here to discuss the military movements themselves and their possible grave consequences, I should like to ask your help in clearing up my understanding as to exactly what is happening between us and our European allies—especially between us, the French and yourselves. . . . When on Monday [October 29] actual military moves began, we quickly decided that the matter had to go immediately to the United Nations, in view of our Agreement of May, 1950, subscribed by our three governments.

After summarizing Lodge's conversation with Dixon at the United Nations, Eisenhower continued:

> Without arguing the point as to whether or not the tripartite statement is or should be outmoded, I feel very seriously that whenever any agreement or pact of this kind is in spirit renounced by one of its signatories, it is only fair that the other signatories should be notified . . . it seems to me of first importance that the UK and the US quickly and clearly lay out their present views and intentions before each other, and that, come what may, we find some way of concerting our ideas and plans so that we may not, in any real crisis be powerless to act in concert because of misunderstanding of each other. I think it important that our two peoples, as well as the French, have this clear understanding of our common or several viewpoints.[21]

When Eisenhower read the text of the Sevres ultimatum on October 30, his first reaction was that the ultimatum was unduly harsh and unacceptable to Egypt. Dulles termed it about as crude and brutal as anything he had ever seen. Confronted with the first real evidence of collusion, the president cabled stern warnings to Eden and Mollet about the inadvisability of taking such action independently of the United Nations.[22] He also expressed his deep concern at the prospect of this dras-

---

21. Text is in Eisenhower, *Waging Peace*, 678–79. See also Department of State, *Suez Canal Crisis*, 848–50.

22. Miscellaneous Papers—UK (Suez Crisis), in Dulles Papers, EL, as quoted in Department of State, *Suez Crisis*, 866.

tic action at the very time when the Suez issue was under consideration by the Security Council. Knowing his cable would fall on deaf ears, Eisenhower again expressed his belief that peaceful processes could and should prevail.

Throughout the remainder of the day, Eisenhower remained in telephonic contact with Dulles and cable communication with Eden. Eden sent a second message to Eisenhower in which the prime minister outlined a conference between the British and French heads of state on October 30. Still attempting to deceive the United States, Eden stated that he did not wish to support or even condone the action of Israel. Eden then discussed the Anglo-French declaration, which he intended to present to Parliament that afternoon. Correctly anticipating Eisenhower's reaction to the ultimatum when the Security Council had already scheduled a debate on the Suez issue, the prime minister incredibly sought to portray his government's action as an opportunity for a fresh start between the United States and Great Britain to strengthen the weakest point in the line against communism in the Middle East.[23] That Eden actually believed his own message seemed unbelievable.

As a chief of state, Eisenhower was incredulous at Eden's apparent dismissal of the economic repercussions if the Arabs united against Britain. Would the Arab states cut off all petroleum shipments to Great Britain and France? The question of oil shipments to Western Europe had been a critical concern to Eisenhower for months. As early as July, he had raised this issue in the NSC, and the Office of Defense Mobilization had prepared several memoranda outlining anticipated oil needs, alternate sources of petroleum, and possible solutions if Western Europe found itself in dire economic straits. Flemming, director of the Office of Defense Mobilization, now joined Eisenhower and Goodpaster in the White House to consider an appropriate American response to the Anglo-French ultimatum. According to Goodpaster, "The President said he was inclined to think that those [Great Britain, France, and Israel] who began this operation should be left to work out their own oil problems—to boil in their own oil, so to speak." Despite his obvious disagreement with his European allies, Eisenhower realized he could not abandon them in an hour of economic need. Anticipating that the United States would probably be receiving requests for assistance, he suggested

23. Message from Eden to Eisenhower, October 30, 1956, in Box 19, International Series, Ann Whitman File, EP, EL. According to Eden, the purpose of the declaration was to make similar requests upon each party. First, all hostilities by land and air should cease. Second, the Canal Zone should be left free so that no fighting or incidents could take place there. To ensure the effectiveness of a ceasefire, British and French troops would temporarily occupy Port Said, Ismailia, and Suez.

that Flemming look into the possibility of fleet oilers (which did not in-
cur dollar costs) to help meet the British shipping problem, if he
should decide to assist his European ally. Still, Eisenhower seemed
content to let Eden and Mollet sweat a bit for their obvious perfidy.[24]

The Eisenhower administration was not the only political body
confused by British and French intentions. In spite of the warlike rhetoric
from Paris and London since July, Nasser and his cabinet were reluctant
to believe that either the British or the French would actively support Israeli aggression. Assistant Secretary of State Rountree called the Egyptian ambassador to express Eisenhower's surprise at the British and
French ultimatum to Israel and Egypt. Rountree added that the president had learned of the ultimatum only from press reports and that he
had no direct confirmation of the text. Rountree continued that Eisenhower, on learning of the ultimatum, had addressed personal messages
to Eden and Mollet in which he requested both countries not to take the
action contemplated. Hussein then inquired as to what steps the United
States intended to take. Rountree said two developments were pending:
the United States' appeal to the Security Council and the presidential appeals to the British and the French, to which there had not been a response. Hussein was visibly impressed with Rountree's statement and
added that he suspected that the Israelis, the British, and the French had
hatched a devious plot against Egypt. Why else would the Anglo-French
ultimatum call for a withdrawal of forces to a point ten miles from the
canal? The Israelis were not yet within ten miles of the Suez Canal.[25]

If Eden correctly judged Eisenhower's reaction to the ultimatum, he
failed to anticipate the sharp criticism he encountered from the Labor
party in the House of Commons. When the prime minister submitted his
proposal outlining the temporary occupation of the Suez Canal by
Anglo-French forces, the Laborites, led by Gaitskell, launched a vicious
attack on the government's policies. Had Eden consulted with the United
States? Was Eden planning to submit the matter to the United Nations? If Egypt rejected the ultimatum, would the British and French
forces actually intervene or was it only a threat? Gaitskell demanded details of the military plan of operations. In defense of their policies, Eden
and Lloyd presented conflicting testimony before the House of Com-

24. Memorandum of a Conference with the President, October 30, 1956, folder marked
"October 1956 (1) Staff Memoranda," Box 19, DDE Diary Series, Ann Whitman File, EP,
EL.

25. Memorandum of a Conversation Between the Egyptian Ambassador (Hussein)
and the Assistant Secretary of State for Near Eastern, South Asian, and African Affairs
(Rountree), Department of State, Washington, October 30, 1956, as quoted in Department of State, *Suez Crisis*, 877–79. See also Heikal, *The Cairo Documents*, 108–109.

mons, prompting Gaitskell to state, "We are still left to some extent in the dark as to what her Majesty's Government has done. I must ask the Prime Minister . . . to tell us 'yes or no' whether on the expiry [sic] of the ultimatum, instructions were given to the British and French forces to occupy the canal zone." Eden refused to divulge any details, leaving Gaitskell to conclude, "All I can say is that taking this decision, it is the view of the Opposition that the Government have committed an act of disastrous folly whose tragic consequences we shall regret for years because it will have done irreparable harm to the prestige and reputation of our country."[26] The House then took a vote of confidence, which Eden won along straight party lines, 270–218.[27] In France, the National Assembly gave Mollet a greater majority, 368–182, the chief dissenters being members of the French Communist party.

Eden's problems did not confine themselves to Parliament. Popular support in Britain for his policy of armed intervention also was lacking. The Manchester *Guardian* considered the Anglo-French action "an act of folly without justification." The *Times,* normally a Conservative newspaper, expressed a feeling of "deep disgust" and was astonished that the prime minister had committed himself without the support of the Commonwealth and the United States. No possible reasons of speed or expediency could necessitate a situation in which the president of the United States had to hear about actions of his British ally from press reports. The *Economist* questioned Eden's motives and criticized the strange union of cynicism and hysteria that gripped the prime minister and his followers.[28] It was now evident to Eden that the public support he had enjoyed when the crisis began in July was rapidly vanishing.

That Eden would risk committing British forces without unqualified support from Parliament and the British public also was inconceivable to Eisenhower, who felt that the prime minister was making a major political error. Though he understood Eden's desire to maintain Great Britain's international prestige, Eisenhower knew that the prime minister must face political reality, as lack of public support would doom any international enterprise. Writing to General Alfred M. Gruenther, a close personal friend and the Supreme Allied Commander, NATO, the president expressed his bewilderment at the fragility of domestic sup-

26. *Hansard's Parliamentary Debates,* Vol. 558, pp. 1273–98. The *Times* (London) also carried the full text of the parliamentary debate, November 1, 1956.

27. On hearing of Eden's small majority, Eisenhower stated, "I could not dream of committing this nation on such a vote." As quoted in Ambrose, ed., *The Wisdom of Dwight D. Eisenhower,* 33.

28. Manchester *Guardian,* November 1, 1956; *Times* (London), October 31 and November 1; and *Economist,* November 3, 1956.

port for Eden, "If one has to have a fight, then that is that. But I don't see the point in getting into a fight to which there can be no satisfactory end, and in which the whole world believes you are playing the part of the bully and you do not even have the firm backing of your entire people."[29]

On October 30, the United Nations Security Council convened to consider the American draft resolution calling upon Israel to withdraw its armed forces behind established armistice lines and requesting that all members of the United Nations refrain from using military force, or the threat of force, in any manner inconsistent with the purposes of the United Nations in the Middle East.[30] Reports that Washington was contemplating restricting economic aid to Israel reinforced the impact of the American resolution. During the second session of the Security Council, Egypt was successful in requesting the council to consider the Anglo-French act of aggression in sending Egypt an ultimatum. As expected, Great Britain and France vetoed both the American resolution and a similar resolution sponsored by the Soviet Union to substitute a United Nations force for the Anglo-French expeditionary force. This was the first time that Great Britain and France had exercised their option of veto since the establishment of the United Nations. The end of the debate found the United States curiously aligned with the Soviet Union against America's traditional allies. Eisenhower was uncomfortable with this arrangement, but totally convinced of the righteousness of his cause.

With the election less than a week away, the president sought to have his administration present a calm and united front to the American public. Eisenhower, unlike Eden, realized the importance of maintaining strong public support for his position. Eisenhower's initial step was to ensure that no one, other than himself, spoke for the administration. The first item on the president's agenda was to rein in Vice-President Nixon, who called Dulles early on October 31. Nixon wanted to "hit" the Suez issue during the final week of the campaign, but the secretary of state urged a more moderate approach. Nixon also urged strongly against convening Congress, which Dulles said was not the president's intention. Turning his attention to the election, Nixon said that the admin-

29. Eisenhower to Alfred Gruenther, November 2, 1956, in folder marked "Eisenhower, DD—1956 (1)," Box 1, Eisenhower Correspondence Series, Alfred M. Gruenther Papers, 1941–83, EL.
30. For text of the United States draft resolution, see Department of State, *Suez Crisis*, 881.

istration's stand against Israeli aggression would probably cost Eisenhower some votes, but in times of crisis, the country did not want a "pipsqueak" for president.[31] Dulles agreed and lauded the president for not sacrificing foreign policy for political expediency.[32]

By this time, Eisenhower decided to cancel the remainder of his campaign appearances to prevent events from getting out of hand. Adlai Stevenson soon began attacking the administration's policy, labeling the president's assurances that there would be no war as "tragically less than the truth."[33] Continuing his attack, Stevenson stated, "Our Middle East policy is at absolutely dead end. The hostilities going on . . . reflect the bankruptcy of our policy."[34] On November 2, he criticized the "lack of principle" in the administration's foreign policy and claimed that Eisenhower and Dulles were responsible for the Middle East fighting and the decline of the Atlantic alliance. Appealing for support from a Detroit audience, Stevenson even went so far as to question whether Eisenhower was actually in charge of foreign policy. He ended his verbal tirade by accusing the president of "getting in bed with Communist Russia and the dictator of Egypt."[35]

In addition to the party's presidential nominee, Democratic senators, including Kefauver of Tennessee, ridiculed the absurd situation in the United Nations where the United States was allied with the Soviet Union against Great Britain and France, blaming Eisenhower's "confusion and inconsistency." Although the Senate Foreign Relations Committee did not meet in formal session from July 26 to November 12, six Democratic senators, namely Mansfield, Green, Fulbright, Humphrey, Sparkman, and Morse, joined the attack by accusing Eisenhower's Middle East policy for producing the worst diplomatic disaster in memory.[36]

The president was certainly aware of how the volatile events in the Middle East might influence the election, but he refused to alter his position that naked aggression was immoral. Writing to Gruenther, Eisen-

---

31. In his memoirs, Nixon wrote: "In retrospect I believe that our actions were a serious mistake. Nasser became even more rash and aggressive . . . Britain and France were so humiliated . . . they lost the will to play a major role. . . . I have often felt that if the Suez crisis had not arisen during the heat of a presidential election campaign a different decision would have been made." Quoted in Stephen Ambrose, *Nixon: The Education of a Politician, 1913–1962* (New York, 1987), 420.

32. Telephone Conversation Memoranda, October 31, 1956, in General Telephone Conversations, Box 5, Dulles Papers, Mudd Library, Princeton.

33. New York *Times,* October 30, 1956.

34. *CQ Weekly Report,* No. 45 (November 9, 1956).

35. *Ibid.*

36. Great Falls *Tribune,* November 3, 1956, as quoted in Klingaman, "Congress and American Foreign Policy for the Middle East," 99–101.

hower said, "Respecting the election, I have one comment only for my good friends. If the American people decide that in the record, they don't want me—that they think I have made too many mistakes to be trusted again—then you can be sorry for anyone you want in this world *except me!!*"[37] In a separate conversation with Dulles, Eisenhower voiced his growing dissatisfaction with Democratic attacks on his policy, saying "We'll do what we think is right regardless of how it affects the election. If they [the people] don't want me, let them get someone else."[38]

The week preceding the election demonstrated the powers of the incumbent. Remaining in Washington to maintain control over a rapidly deteriorating situation, Eisenhower delivered a nationally televised address to the American people during prime time viewing hours on October 31. Dulles' promised draft failed to reach the president until late afternoon, and when it finally did arrive, Eisenhower junked it and issued specific instructions for revision to speech-writer Emmet Hughes. The address, which Eisenhower delivered with calm and strong assurances, reiterated his basic rejection of force. Summarizing the events of the previous three days, he emphasized that America's allies had not consulted the United States before attacking Egypt. Aware that the British and the French had begun bombarding Egyptian airfields, Eisenhower demanded an immediate cessation of hostilities. Under the present circumstances, the president stated:

There will be no United States involvement in these . . . hostilities. I therefore have no plan to call the Congress in special session. Of course, we shall continue to keep in contact with Congressional leaders of both parties. . . . At the same time, it is—and it will remain—the dedicated purpose of your government to do all in its power to localize the fighting and to end the conflict. . . . The processes of the United Nations, however, are not exhausted. It is our hope and intent that this matter will be brought before the United Nations General Assembly. There, with no veto operating, the opinion of the world can be brought to bear in our quest for a just end to this tormenting problem. In the past, the United Nations has proved able to find a way to end bloodshed. We believe it can and that it will do so again.[39]

The speech was a tremendous public relations success for the president. By appealing directly to the American public and presenting the image

37. Eisenhower to Gruenther, November 2, 1956, in Eisenhower Correspondence Series, Box 1, Gruenther Papers, EL.

38. As quoted in Parmet, *Eisenhower and the American Crusades*, 485.

39. For text, see *Public Papers of the President, 1956*, (Washington, D.C., 1958, 1060–66. See also New York *Times*, November 1, 1956, and Magnus, ed., *Documents on the Middle East*, 169–71. Emmet Hughes discusses his preparation of the speech in *The Ordeal of Power: A Political Memoir of the Eisenhower Years*, 218–22.

of serenity in the midst of chaos, Eisenhower in effect disarmed his political critics and maintained his personal popularity. A New York *Times* poll conducted after the address concluded that Eisenhower was still the right man in time of crisis.[40]

The Anglo-French ultimatum expired on Wednesday, October 31, at 0600 hours, Cairo time. British and French bombs began falling on Egyptian airfields by early evening and continued for several days. Israel's co-conspirators had fulfilled their part of the Sevres accords. The Egyptians immediately blocked the Suez Canal by sinking the Egyptian ship *Akka* in the canal near Lake Timsah. Nasser also severed diplomatic relations with the British and French governments. Both the president and secretary of state were aghast when they received notification of the unprovoked attack. Had Nasser closed the Suez Canal prior to the initiation of hostilities, that would have been a different matter. The news totally unnerved Dulles, who had been ill for a week. According to Hughes, Dulles appeared "almost completely exhausted, ashen gray, and heavy lidded."[41]

Eisenhower was equally opposed and deeply saddened at Eden's rashness. The president himself was an emotional man, but Eden's unbridled emotion was a poor substitute for adroit British diplomacy. Privately, Eisenhower expressed his amazement that Britain had made "such a complete mess and botch of things." Confiding to Hughes, he lamented, "I just don't know what got into those people. It's the damnedest business I ever saw supposedly intelligent governments get themselves into."[42]

Did Eisenhower's failure to prevent Anglo-French aggression signal a failure of his techniques of crisis management? Not at all. From the inception of the crisis, Eisenhower had personally directed the American response and had done virtually everything in his power to dissuade Eden and Mollet from taking such drastic action. In message after message, Eisenhower had reiterated his opposition to using military force to settle the dispute. Moreover, the president ensured that he maintained control of foreign policy to prevent any misinterpretation of presidential intentions. In return, his European allies had deliberately deceived him as to their plans to topple Nasser by armed intervention. Although Eisenhower could control his own administration, he could not enforce his will on allies, who pursued policy objectives inimical to U.S. interests.

40. New York *Times*, November 2, 1956.
41. Hughes, *The Ordeal of Power*, 220.
42. *Ibid.*, 219.

Not yet anyway; but now that Eden and Mollet had shown their hand, it was a different matter. From now on, Eden and Mollet would have to contend with Eisenhower, not as a supportive partner, but as a crisis manager intent on utilizing the natural pressures that existed—the need for oil and the need for financial support—which were inherent in the situation the French, British, and the Israelis had created by making it unmistakably clear that these economic requirements could not and would not be met unless there was an immediate cessation of hostilities. The preliminaries were over; henceforth, the president intended to play hardball. How to terminate hostilities, while soothing frayed relations with traditional allies over a policy that Eisenhower diametrically opposed, presented new challenges for the president as he entered the final week of the presidential campaign.

6

THE ALLIANCE IN PERIL

It has always been true that the British and French can not get along whenever they try to combine forces.

—Dwight D. Eisenhower

During the weeks following the Anglo-French invasion, the president doubled his efforts to end the crisis and thus prevent the Soviet Union from exploiting an opportunity to introduce its own forces into the Middle East. To accomplish his goals, Eisenhower utilized the diplomatic and economic pressure that already existed to bring hostilities to an end. At the same time, he used American military forces to underscore verbal and diplomatic expressions of American foreign policy.[1] This interaction among the political, economic, and military dimensions of foreign policy marked Eisenhower as a skilled practitioner of crisis management. By his bold actions in the face of opposition by his allies and domestic Democrats, the president succeeded in securing a cease-fire in the Middle East, keeping the Atlantic alliance intact (albeit somewhat tattered), preventing the Soviets from gaining ground in the Middle East, and enhancing the prestige of both the United States and the United Nations within the Arab world and among the nations of the developing Third World.

When Great Britain and France intervened militarily on October 31, Eisenhower's critics charged that the administration's Middle East policy had collapsed completely. It was one thing for Israel to attack Egypt, but the entry of America's most trusted allies into the conflict seemed to make a mockery of the president's efforts to achieve a peaceful resolution of the crisis. The British and the French had conspired with Israel, deliberately misinformed the United States, and initiated hostilities at a time when they felt Eisenhower would be powerless to act due to the presidential election. Both Eden and Mollet anticipated Eisenhower

1. For an elaboration of this theme, see Barry Blechman and Stephen Kaplan, *Force Without War* (Washington, D.C., 1978), and the Ph.D. dissertation of Diane Kunz, "The Economic Diplomacy of the Suez Crisis" (Yale University, 1989).

would oppose their attack on Egypt. The later charges that Eisenhower and Dulles had misled the Europeans as to the United States' position in the crisis were groundless. The president had made it quite clear in all his statements since July that he did not believe the situation warranted the use of military force. In this regard, the European leaders correctly gauged the American response. Unfortunately, they did not calculate the intensity of Eisenhower's reaction. Eden hoped the United States would remain neutral; at best, he and Mollet expected passive resistance.[2] What Eden and Mollet failed to comprehend was that Eisenhower did not consider his policy a shambles and, election or not, he intended to stand on moral principle against military aggression to settle an issue that less violent means might resolve.

The immediate problem confronting Eisenhower on November 1 was the official response to the introduction of British and French military forces in Egypt. Because the General Assembly was scheduled to meet at five o'clock that afternoon to discuss the situation, the president met with the National Security Council in the morning to obtain recommendations on the formulation of a clear policy outlining the American position.[3] Present were not only the regular members of the NSC, but also the service secretaries and the Joint Chiefs of Staff. On entering the cabinet room from his office, the president informed the members of the council that he did not wish the council to take up the situation in the Soviet satellites, but rather he wished to concentrate on the Middle East. Allen Dulles opened the session with an intelligence summary of the events from the preceding weeks and stated that Eden had not received wide support from the British Commonwealth for his intervention. Indeed, grave disagreements during the House of Commons debate on Suez had recently led to a suspension of discussion.[4] Additionally, London witnessed numerous demonstrations calling on the prime minister to cease the aggression. Deferring discussion on the American military posture in the Middle East to Radford, Dulles concluded his briefing by stating that from reports received to date, the Israelis appeared to have gained a substantial victory over the Egyptians. Eisenhower then interrupted to

2. Herbert Feis, "Suez Scenario: A Lamentable Tale," *Foreign Affairs,* XXX (July, 1960), 606, and Lord Harlech, "Suez Snafu, Skybolt Saber," *Foreign Policy,* II (Spring, 1971), 44.

3. See Discussion of the 302nd Meeting of the National Security Council, in folder marked "NSC Summaries of Discussion," Box 8, National Security Council Series, Ann Whitman File, EP, EL, for all references to the NSC meeting on November 1.

4. For this unusual occurrence, see *Hansard's Parliamentary Debates,* Vol. 558, p. 1625.

say he did not wish to discuss the military situation at that time, but desired to concentrate on the policy problem.

Eisenhower announced that he would start the discussion of policy issues by asking the secretary of state to bring the council up to date on diplomatic developments as Dulles saw them. Dulles hastily outlined the diplomatic background of the crisis, describing the collusion of the aggressors. He stated that the French actually conducted the operational planning with the Israelis, and the British generally acquiesced. Moreover, the French had for some time been supplying the Israelis with far more military equipment than the United States had been aware, in clear violation of the Tripartite Declaration, in which each of the Western powers had promised to inform the others of the extent of military assistance each was providing Israel. Following this indictment, Dulles stated that the matter was now before the General Assembly because both Great Britain and France had vetoed the American-sponsored cease-fire resolution in the Security Council. Summarizing this portion of his presentation, the secretary said that the American position against the use of force had evoked greater international support for the United States than any time in history, and the entire world was looking toward the United States for firm leadership in this critical situation.

Dulles based his assessment of international support on a telephone call that Eisenhower received from Lodge at the United Nations, in which Lodge had given the president a first-hand report of the "flavor of reaction" at the international forum. Lodge confirmed that Ambassador Urrutia of Colombia reported that twenty-one Latin American republics were behind the president. The secretary general had handed Lodge a note, in which he stated, "This is one of the darkest days in post-war times. Thank God you have played the way you have." Additionally, an Afro-Asian delegation had met and had endorsed the moral courage of the United States. Even the busboys, typists, and the elevator operators, said Lodge, had been offering their congratulations.[5]

Summing up, Dulles stated that the United States had reached a point of deciding whether "we think the future lies with a policy of reasserting by force colonial control over the less developed nations, or whether we will oppose such a course of action by every appropriate means." Concluding on a gloomy note, the secretary said that it was nothing less than tragic that at this very time, when "we are on the point of winning an immense and long-hoped-for victory over Soviet colonialism in Eastern Europe, we should be forced to choose between following

5. See folder marked "October, '56 Phone Calls," Box 19, DDE Diary Series, Ann Whitman File, EP, EL.

in the footsteps of Anglo-French colonialism in Asia and Africa, or splitting our course away from their course."

Eisenhower broke the tension that followed Dulles' statement by stating that if anybody wanted to know how "political" the issue had become, they could read the telegram the president had received from Stevenson, in which the Democratic candidate cautioned Eisenhower about introducing American military forces into the troubled region. Although the president never considered dispatching American ground forces into the Middle East to halt the fighting, Stevenson based his appeal on a recent Gallup poll in which 55 percent of the people polled were against sending American troops into Egypt.[6] Returning to the primary purpose of the meeting, the president inquired if it were necessary for the United States to introduce the resolution demanding a cease-fire to the General Assembly or if the secretary general could introduce it. Dulles declared that by law any nation could introduce a resolution, and that the Soviet Union would do so if the United States demurred.

For the next hour, various members of the council debated the contents of the proposed resolution, differing widely on the intensity of the condemnation of the aggressors. Secretary Humphrey opined that the United Kingdom was the real aggressor, and Israel only a pawn. Governor Stassen, special assistant to the president and representative on the United Nations Disarmament Commission, expressed the opinion that Britain had legitimate interests in the region and that there was some justification for their action. With this, the president could not agree, pointing out that transit through the canal had increased rather than decreased since the Egyptians took over and that Nasser had agreed in principle that the canal must be insulated from the politics of any nation. Undeterred by Eisenhower's rebuff, Stassen emphasized that he could not see how it would serve the interests of the United States to strike now at Britain and Israel. In the NSC notes prepared by S. Everett Gleason, deputy executive secretary of the council, Dulles interrupted and "with great warmth," reminded Stassen that it was the British and French who had just vetoed the proposal for a cease-fire. As Dulles and Stassen continued to debate the merits of a new resolution, Eisenhower had had enough and asked what the argument was really all about. Dulles was asking for a mild resolution in the United Nations, and the president couldn't agree more. The United States would offer a resolution calling for an immediate cease-fire and the withdrawal of foreign troops from Egypt. In addition, the United States would halt the shipment of

6. Gallup, *The Gallup Poll: Public Opinion, 1935–1971*, II, 1454. Gallup conducted this survey September 20–25, 1956.

military supplies and assistance to Israel. When asked if he intended to
include Britain in the embargo, Eisenhower replied that he would continue to assist Britain in order that it might meet its NATO requirements.
If the British actually diverted these supplies to other purposes, he would
consider such an action to represent another case of "perfidious Albion."
Having received presidential guidelines for preparing the resolution,
Dulles asked and received permission to depart the cabinet room to draft
the resolution.

Eisenhower terminated this phase of the discussion by requesting that
Radford present his report on the military situation and the status of the
evacuation of American citizens from the region. Radford read his report, which gave a detailed appreciation of the military situation. When
he finished, Radford stated that the U.S. forces in the area had largely
completed their first responsibility of evacuating American citizens from
the area of hostilities. He also pointed out that the Joint Chiefs of Staff
were currently very concerned over the possibility of uprisings against
Europeans in the neighboring Arab states, and therefore he intended
to keep the 6th Fleet on station in the Eastern Mediterranean. Satisfied
with the chairman's analysis of the American military state of readiness,
Eisenhower brought the meeting to a conclusion by declaring that the
United States would do what was decent and right, but it would not condemn Great Britain and France more bitterly than was necessary. The
council then directed that the secretary of state draft appropriate action
papers in light of the discussion for subsequent consideration by the president.

This particular NSC meeting revealed a great deal of how Eisenhower
employed the National Security Council in times of crisis. Preferring to
work with an informal group of close advisers for daily operations,
Eisenhower convened few formal meetings during the height of the Suez
crisis. Having already decided on the broad outlines of the American
response to Israeli aggression and Anglo-French intervention in informal meetings with Dulles and others, the president used the council as
a sounding board for his position and for the free exchange of ideas on
all aspects of the Suez dispute. Although he focused the discussion on
specific areas, Eisenhower fostered lively debate among the council
members, even to the point of listening patiently—yet this had its limits—to conflicting recommendations from council members. Having
heard the recommendations of the council, he adjourned the session,
concluding with the very position he had before the council convened—
that the United States would do what was decent and right, but not condemn traditional allies any more than it had to. Following the meeting,

he sent Dulles a memorandum, in which he outlined the position he wished Dulles to take in the United Nations. It was vintage Eisenhower.

The military evacuation of American citizens, to which Radford had referred, was an unqualified success and reflected immense credit on the planning of the Joint Chiefs of Staff and the 6th Fleet. It also reflected the president's keen insight into the contingencies that might arise as a result of increased tension in the Middle East. Indeed, Eisenhower had discussed noncombatant evacuation with the Joint Chiefs as early as late August, long before he was aware of Anglo-French plans for military operations. In the interim between his initial consultations with Radford and the execution of the evacuation, Eisenhower remained abreast of the situation through periodic reports from Radford and the written Suez summaries issued by the Department of State. This process permitted the president to keep a military option of his own in the event that he had to support diplomatic initiatives with military action. Maintaining a wide array of options was a critical component of Eisenhower's management of international crises.

Having issued guidance to Radford on planning for the evacuation of American nationals from the troubled region, Eisenhower left detailed planning to his subordinates. Radford responded splendidly. Ever since the Department of State had notified him that hostilities were imminent (October 28), Radford had conferred daily with the other Chiefs. The chairman not only finalized plans for the evacuation, but directed the Chief of Naval Operations to ready the 6th Fleet for possible engagement. On October 29, the Joint Chiefs agreed to take the following steps to increase American readiness in the area: (1) alert two Army regimental combat teams and one Marine battalion landing team in the United States for emergency deployment; (2) alert one C-124 Air Force wing for movement to the Middle East from the United States; (3) issue instructions for loading one Marine battalion landing team from the Far East; (4) order one Navy hunter-killer group, consisting of one antisubmarine carrier, six destroyers, two submarines, and an oiler to report to the 6th Fleet; (5) cancel the 6th Fleet's participation in NATO exercise "Beehive"; and (6) direct Admiral Boone, the Commander of Naval Forces, Eastern Atlantic and Mediterranean, to establish his command headquarters on the USS *Pocono* by November 2. Boone's normal headquarters was in London, but Burke felt he should be on station in the Eastern Mediterranean.[7]

7. For actions by the Joint Chiefs of Staff, see JCS 091 Palestine, Records of the Joint Chiefs of Staff, RG 218. For actions relating strictly to the navy, see Chronology of Naval Activities—Suez Incident, Operational Archives Branch, Washington Navy Yard, Washington, D.C.

The evacuation commenced on October 31, with USN and USAF aircraft evacuating citizens from Tel Aviv, while two naval task forces extracted American nationals from Alexandria and Haifa. A total of eight ships participated in the actual exercises: The *Chilton* (APA), *Thuban* (AKA), *Fort Snelling* (LSD), *Summer* (DD), and *Sperry* (DD) went to Alexandria; the *Burdo* (APD), *Dickson* (DD), and *Purvis* (DD) went to Haifa. The aircraft carriers of the 6th Fleet remained in position to cover the two evacuation groups. As of November 2, the military had evacuated 2,857 American citizens from the Middle East and the United Nations observer team at Gaza, but the multinational team returned to Gaza on November 4. On November 3, Vice Admiral Brown, commander of the 6th Fleet, cabled Burke that the evacuation was complete.[8]

Meanwhile, Burke gradually increased the strength of the 6th Fleet. Unable to project what might occur amid the confusion and concerned that the Soviet Union might attempt to disrupt the Anglo-French amphibious forces steaming toward Egypt, he prepared for all contingencies. On October 30, he cabled Brown: "Situation tense, prepare for imminent hostilities." The 6th Fleet commander, who was as confused as his superior in Washington, answered: "Am prepared for imminent hostilities, but which side are we on?" Unsure of who the enemy actually was, Burke responded: "If U.S citizens are in danger, protect them—take no guff from anyone."[9] Burke was taking no chances that the Navy would be unprepared for any contingency.

Throughout the crisis, Burke was the most vocal of the Joint Chiefs in presenting his view that the United States should provide landing craft and other support to the Anglo-French expeditionary force. Well aware of the logistical problems from which the European force was suffering, Burke remained a vigorous proponent of military cooperation with Great Britain and France. Though he was careful not to voice his private support to his British colleagues, Burke sympathized with the Anglo-French efforts to depose Nasser. He failed, however, to convince Eisenhower, who continued to oppose the use of force to settle the dispute. In opposing the advice of Burke, and to a lesser degree Army Chief of Staff

8. For details of the Sixth Fleet's role in the evacuation exercise, see William B. Garrett, "The U.S. Navy's Role in the 1956 Suez Crisis," *Naval War College Review,* XXII (March, 1970), 66–78. See also JCS 091 Palestine, Records of the Joint Chiefs of Staff, RG 218. For the role of the United States Marine Corps, see J. Robert Moskin, *The U.S. Marine Corps Story* (New York, 1977), 819, and Allan R. Millett, *Semper Fidelis* (New York, 1980), 539.

9. Burke interview by the author, June 18, 1981. See also David Rosenburg's biographical sketch of Burke in Robert W. Love, Jr., ed., *The Chiefs of Naval Operations* (Annapolis, 1980), 283.

Taylor, the president found himself in a position similar to the Quemoy-Matsu crisis in 1954–1955,[10] in which he rejected the advice of his military advisers concerning the defensibility of the off-shore islands and used the threat of nuclear retaliation to deter the Chinese communists. Just as he had done in the case of Quemoy-Matsu, Eisenhower carefully evaluated the political and military options available to the United States in the current crisis in the Middle East and rejected the use of American military resources to resolve the crisis.

Following the National Security Council meeting, Eisenhower sent Dulles a memorandum outlining the course he wanted the secretary to take at the United Nations. The president stated that the first objective of the United Nations should be to achieve a cease-fire, because a cessation of hostilities would keep the war from spreading, give time to find out what each side was trying to gain, and allow the General Assembly to develop a final resolution that would represent the considered judgment of the United Nations respecting past blame and future action. The United States must lead, Eisenhower informed Dulles, to "prevent the immediate issuance by the United Nations of a harshly worded resolution that would put us in an acutely embarrassing position, either with France and Britain or with all the rest of the world." At all costs, Eisenhower remained determined to prevent the Soviets from "seizing the mantle of world leadership through a false but convincing exhibition of concern for smaller nations. Since Africa and Asia almost unanimously hate one of the three nations Britain, France and Israel, the Soviets need only to propose severe and immediate punishment of these three to have the whole of two continents on their side." Last, he instructed Dulles to ensure that the United States "not single out and condemn any one nation, but to emphasize to the world our hope for a quick cease-fire to be followed by sane and deliberate action on the part of the United Nations."[11]

The president's memorandum to Dulles on the eve of the General Assembly debate refutes Sherman Adams' claim that Eisenhower delegated to Dulles the responsibility of developing the specific policy, including the decision where the administration would stand and what course of action would be followed in each international crisis. The memorandum, to which Eisenhower attached a note, "Just some simple thoughts

10. For an analysis of Eisenhower's disagreement with his military advisers during the Quemoy-Matsu crisis, see Bennett C. Rushkoff, "Eisenhower, Dulles and the Quemoy-Matsu Crisis, 1954–1955," *Political Science Quarterly*, XCVI (Fall, 1981), 470–71. See also Ambrose, *Eisenhower: The President*, 231–45.

11. Memorandum by the President, November 1, 1956, in Box 5, White House Memoranda Series, Dulles Papers, EL.

that I have jotted down since our meeting this morning," removed any doubt in the secretary's mind as to what course of action to take. Eisenhower could not have been more succinct with respect to policy objectives, the rationale behind the American position, what he wanted Dulles to do and not do, and the alternatives the secretary should consider for future action. "We should be expected," Eisenhower continued, "to suspend governmental shipments, now, to countries in battle areas and be prepared to agree, in concert with others, to later additional action."[12] How could one be more clear? The specific guidance the president gave Dulles during the most demanding week of his presidency revealed a president who remained clearly at the helm of the ship of state and did not delegate major foreign policy decisions to the secretary of state.

Dulles followed his orders to the letter. The first emergency session of the United Nations General Assembly convened at 5 P.M. on November 1. Speaking before the international forum, Dulles appeared ill and feeble. Addressing the General Assembly in tones that frequently revealed his anger at allies whom he felt had betrayed him, he declared:

I doubt that any delegate ever spoke from this forum with as heavy a heart as I have brought here tonight. We speak on a matter of vital importance, where the United States finds itself unable to agree with three nations with whom it has ties, deep friendship, admiration and respect, and two of whom constitute our oldest, most trusted and reliable allies.

The fact that we differ with such friends has led us to reconsider and reevaluate our position with the utmost care, and that has been done at the highest levels of our government. Even after that reevaluation, we still find ourselves in disagreement. Because it seems to us that that disagreement involves principles which far transcend the immediate issue, we feel impelled to make our point of view known to you and through you to the world.[13]

The proposed resolution, which Eisenhower had previously approved, urged an immediate cease-fire, the withdrawal of all forces behind the armistice lines, a ban on all military aid to the belligerents, and action to reopen the Suez Canal, which the Egyptians had blocked at the beginning of the war. Egypt immediately accepted the cease-fire and, following an exhausting debate, the General Assembly adopted the U.S. proposal by a vote of 64–5—Great Britain, France, Israel, Australia, and

12. *Ibid.*

13. The secretary was suffering from cancer at the time. For complete text of Dulles' address, see Department of State Press Release, unnumbered, November 1, 1956, in Selected Correspondence and Related Material, 1956, Suez Canal, 1956, Box 10, Dulles Papers, Mudd Library, Princeton.

New Zealand dissenting. Canada, South Africa, Belgium, Laos, the Netherlands, and Portugal abstained. Eden had lost the support of a large portion of the Commonwealth.

Satisfied with the vote, but still disgusted with British and French treachery, Eisenhower delivered his last major campaign address in Philadelphia. Attempting to prevent the further deterioration of the Atlantic alliance, he soothed Anglo-French feelings, but maintained his unequivocal stance against aggression. Pleading for cooperation with his European allies, the president stated, "We cannot—in the world, any more than in our own nation—subscribe to one law for the weak, another law for the strong. There can be only one law, or there will be no peace. We value—deeply and lastingly—the bonds with those great nations, those great friends, with whom we now so plainly disagree. And I, for one, am confident that those bonds will do more than survive. They can, my friends, they must, grow to new and greater strength. But this we know above all: There are some firm principles that cannot bend—they can only break. And we shall not break ours."[14]

The president then took leave from more important business and wrote letters to two close associates, Gruenther at NATO and "Swede" Hazlett, a boyhood friend from Abilene. To Gruenther, he expressed his dismay at Eden's persistence in employing military force. "I believe that Eden and his associates have become convinced that this is the last straw and Britain simply <u>had</u> [underlined by Eisenhower] to react in the manner of the Victorian period." Writing to Hazlett, the president expressed similar fears concerning the inadvisability of military intervention:

> I think that France and Britain have made a terrible mistake. Because they had such a poor case, they have isolated themselves from the good opinion of the world and it will take them many years to recover. France was perfectly cold-blooded about the matter. She has a war on her hands in Algeria, and she was anxious to get someone else fighting the Arabs on her Eastern flank so she was ready to do anything to get England and Israel in that affair. But I think the other two countries have hurt themselves immeasurably and this is something of a sad blow because, quite naturally, Britain not only has been, but must be, our best friend in the world.[15]

Why was Eden's action "such a sad blow"? Eisenhower firmly believed that America's destiny on the international stage was inextricably linked to that of Great Britain. Although political considerations forced him to chastise George Patton for his remarks at Knutsford in 1944

14. Eisenhower, *Waging Peace*, 83.
15. Copies of both letters are in DDE Diary Series, November 2, 1956, Box 19, Ann Whitman File, EP, EL.

for stating that it was the evident destiny of the British and Americans and, (following a pause) of course, the Russians, to rule the world, Eisenhower firmly believed that the United States and Great Britain shared common goals of fostering democracy and world order in the post-World War II era. To be deceived by an enemy was understandable and possibly grounds for retribution, but to be deceived by a friend, one's most trusted and valuable ally at that, was quite another matter. The British had indeed "made a mess of it," and the president fully intended to keep the pressure on the prime minister until Eden returned Great Britain to the fold. In the following weeks, Eisenhower directed his efforts toward ensuring that the United States and Great Britain would again share a common destiny, but Eden's deceit destroyed the warm personal friendship that once existed between the American president and the British prime minister.

The majority by which the General Assembly passed the American-sponsored resolution left Britain and France in an awkward and embarrassing position. The debate had revealed the hypocrisy of their cause; there was obviously no justification for the Anglo-French "peace action" to separate the combatants by introducing their own forces along the Suez Canal. Within the United Nations, Lodge reported to Dulles that the British and French were in a very emotional condition and worried that there would be a bad impression at home if the United States was in a hurry to condemn them, while the U.S. procrastinated on the Hungarian issue. Consequently, the European ambassadors approached Lodge with a proposal that the Western nations act in concert to condemn the Soviet Union, but Dulles instructed Lodge to have no part of the scheme, replying that it "was mockery for them to come in with bombs falling over Egypt and denounce the Soviet Union for perhaps doing something that was not quite as bad."[16] By the president's direction, Lodge continued to pressure Britain and France to accept the cease-fire and keep the issues of Suez and Hungary separate.

On November 2, Eisenhower met with Dulles and Under Secretary Hoover to discuss measures intended to arbitrate the Arab-Israeli dispute and to establish an international commission to assume responsibility for reopening the Suez Canal. During the course of the meeting, Assistant Secretary Rountree called Dulles to discuss a cable from Paris, in which Pineau had disclosed the whole unmitigated story of the col-

16. Memorandum of a Telephone Conversation Between the Secretary of State and the Representative at the United Nations (Lodge), November 2, 1956, in Telephone Conversations Series, Box 5, Dulles Papers, Mudd Library, Princeton.

lusion. When Dulles asked whether the British were involved, Rountree replied, "Oh yes."[17] Dillon's previous cable, outlining Mollet's intent to initiate hostilities if Eisenhower failed to find an acceptable solution to the crisis, did not mention Eden's role in the conspiracy. Although Dillon's second cable was the first positive information the administration had regarding the actual extent of Eden's role in the conspiracy, its receipt did not seriously affect American policy toward the conflict, it only increased Eisenhower's determination.

Intent on getting Eden and Mollet to respond, Eisenhower utilized diplomatic and economic pressure to force the European governments to accept the cease-fire. In spite of Eisenhower's efforts and their ostracism in the United Nations, the British and French heads of state refused to cancel their proposed amphibious and airborne invasion, now scheduled for November 5. The burden of alienation, however, was affecting Eden, who had encountered an extremely hostile reception in the House of Commons when he announced that he intended to reject the cease-fire proposed by the General Assembly. In sharp contrast to the wavering prime minister, Mollet remained adamant in his conviction that the invasion must proceed on schedule. Mollet and Ben Gurion both foresaw the weakening of British resolve, and Mollet and Pineau flew to London to obtain assurances that Eden would uphold his commitment to the invasion. Although they were successful in obtaining the guarantees, Pineau stated that Eden was no Churchill in time of crisis. The prime minister had neither the tenacity nor the nerves, and the test was beginning to exhaust him. Summarizing Eden's deteriorating health, Pineau said, "It is not yet a 'breakdown', but we are not far from it."[18]

By November 3, the escalation of hostilities in the Middle East, which Eisenhower predicted and had so consciously sought to avoid, gained momentum. Syria severed diplomatic relations with Great Britain and France, and saboteurs destroyed three pumping stations along the Iraqi Petroleum Company pipeline. The ARAMCO pipeline across Saudi Arabia was still operable, but no one knew how long it would remain so. In Britain, Eden formally rejected the United Nations' cease-fire proposal, but agreed that the British and the French would stop firing as soon as (1) both Egypt and Israel agreed to accept a United Nations force to maintain peace, (2) the United Nations constituted and maintained such a force until the Arab-Israeli peace settlement could be achieved and until the international forum guaranteed "satisfactory arrangements"

17. Dillon's telegram is quoted in full in Department of State, *Suez Crisis*, 919–22. See also Eisenhower, *Waging Peace*, 84.
18. As quoted in Neff, *Warriors at Suez*, 397.

with respect to the Suez Canal, and (3) Israel and Egypt agreed to accept limited detachments of Anglo-French troops until the United Nations force arrived.[19]

To complicate matters in the Middle East, the Soviet Union prepared to launch a full scale assault to crush the Hungarian uprising the first week in November. In the United Nations, the Soviets vetoed an American resolution calling on the Russians to withdraw from Hungarian territory. Eisenhower now found himself in a peculiar situation. In Eastern Europe, he was aligned with Great Britain and France against the Soviet invasion of Hungary, while in the Middle East, he opposed the entry of British and French ground troops into Egypt. Upon careful reflection, he decided to direct his efforts toward halting the Anglo-French expeditionary force assembling at Cyprus before it reached Egypt and mending the Atlantic alliance with the utmost speed. The president's critics immediately chastised him for not taking a more aggressive stand against the Soviets, but Eisenhower correctly analyzed the logistical nightmare involved in attempting to move American troops across Eastern Europe. Not only would the United States have to act alone, it would also violate the territorial sovereignty of several nations if it acted independently. Moreover, U.S. intervention in Hungary would result in a direct confrontation with Soviet forces, thus precipitating a far more serious crisis than Suez. There were clearly limits to U.S. military power, and Eisenhower realized that Hungary was beyond those limits. Though not a popular stance in an election year, Eisenhower reluctantly accepted the reality that aside from vocal condemnation of the Soviet Union's aggression, there was little the United States could do to influence the action in Budapest. The president clearly recognized the interest and power of his adversary in the Soviet Union's own backyard. He might not like it, but there was virtually nothing he could do to halt the slaughter in the Hungarian capital. Because Hungary "was as inaccessible to American forces as Tibet," he wrote in his memoirs, "the United States did the only thing it could: We readied ourselves . . . to help the refugees fleeing from the criminal action of the Soviets, and did everything possible to condemn the aggression."[20]

Unfortunately, at the height of the dual crises, Eisenhower lost the able services of Dulles, who entered Walter Reed Hospital the morning of November 3 because of abdominal pains, which the physicians sub-

19. Statement by Prime Minister Eden, November 3, 1956, as quoted in Department of State, *Suez Crisis*, 946, and in Eden, *Full Circle*, 606–607.
20. Eisenhower, *Waging Peace*, 88–89. See also Ambrose, *Eisenhower: The President*, 367.

sequently diagnosed as intestinal cancer. Dulles remained at Walter Reed until November 18 and did not return to the Department of State until January. In the interim, Under Secretary Hoover assumed control of the Department of State. That there was no noticeable change in American policy was testament that Eisenhower, not the secretary of state, directed foreign policy in times of crisis. To ensure that Hoover understood the intricacies of the administration's policy, Eisenhower held another conference at the White House with Department of State officials, Press Secretary Hagerty, and Goodpaster.[21] Confusion reigned among the State Department personnel concerning a number of resolutions in the General Assembly until Eisenhower intervened. "We should get in with our resolutions quickly, calling on all parties to open the Canal." He also urged Hoover and company "to bring out that there is no cause for the UK and the French to go into the Canal area—that the UN can put in the force" to separate the combatants and to remove any need or basis for their [British and French] landings. The president did ask for a recommendation as to when he should next communicate with Eden, and there was universal agreement that he wait until after the resolutions had been submitted to the secretary general. Eisenhower's swift action in bringing Hoover on board ensured there was no disruption in his policy to force Eden and Mollet to abide by the U.N. resolutions.

On Saturday, November 3, the General Assembly met in emergency session at the request of the Egyptian government to consider the twin crises of Suez and Hungary. Although the forum postponed a debate on the Hungarian question at the request of the Soviet Ambassador, Eisenhower and Lodge were successful in convincing Lester Pierson, the Canadian Minister for External Affairs, to sponsor a resolution requesting the secretary general to develop a plan to introduce a United Nations police force into the Middle East within forty-eight hours. Under ordinary circumstances, the United States would have sponsored the resolution, but Lodge convinced the president that the United States should avoid the embarrassment of condemning its allies. Additionally, Lodge felt that the Canadian resolution would give the smaller countries a share of responsibility in obtaining a lasting peace.[22] The General Assembly subsequently passed the resolution on November 4 by a vote of

21. Memorandum of a Conference with the President, November 3, 1956, in folder marked "November 1956 Staff Memoranda," Box 19, DDE Diary Series, Ann Whitman File, EP, EL.

22. Lodge interview with the author, July 6, 1981; Lodge, *The Storm Has Many Eyes,* 136; Lodge, *As It Was* (New York, 1976), 93–97; Memorandum for the Record by the Representative at the United Nations, November 3, 1956, Department of State, USUN Files, quoted in Department of State, *Suez Crisis,* 956–57.

55–0, with nineteen abstentions. The resolution, which the United States supported, established a United Nations command for an emergency international force to secure and supervise the cessation of hostilities, and appointed Canadian General Eedson Burns as chief of command, authorizing him to recruit a force from nations other than the permanent members of the Security Council. An Indian resolution, calling on the secretary general to report in twelve hours whether or not the belligerents were complying with the cease-fire, also passed by a vote of 59–6, seven nations abstaining.

By November 4, Eisenhower realized he was waging a losing battle in his attempt to convince Eden to halt the Anglo-French armada moving toward Egypt. Eden had met with his cabinet twice during the day to consider the United Nations resolutions and the next stage in military operations. With respect to the Indian-sponsored resolution, Eden had to reply within twelve hours to Secretary General Dag Hammarskjold. It was Eisenhower who had insisted that Hammarskjold play a more active role in resolving the crisis, because the secretary general could move more freely than the committee of five nations that was originally envisioned in the General Assembly resolution. The military issue was more complex, but following a lengthy discussion with his advisers, Eden decided to proceed with the invasion and shoulder the political risks inherent in unilateral aggression. The next day, November 5, he explained his rationale to Eisenhower:

> It is a great grief to me that the events of the last few days have placed such a strain on the relations between our two countries. . . . I have always felt . . . that the Middle East was an issue over which, in the last resort, we [Great Britain] would have to fight.
>
> I am sure that this is the moment to curb Nasser's ambitions. If we let it pass, all of us will bitterly regret. . . . If we draw aback now, chaos will not be avoided. Everything will go up in flames in the Middle East. You will realize, with all your experience, that we cannot have a military vacuum while a United Nations force is being constituted and is being transported to the spot. That is why we feel we must go on to hold the position until we can hand over responsibility to the United Nations.[23]

Earlier that morning, at 0715 hours, November 5, the invasion that Eisenhower had feared since the Israeli assault on October 29, occurred as British and French paratroopers landed in the vicinity of Port Said. The crisis had entered a new and more dangerous stage.

---

23. Eden to Eisenhower, November 5, 1956, in Box 19, International Series, Ann Whitman File, EP, EL.

As the president's secretary noted in her personal dairy, "The day before the day [Election Day] for which we have worked so hard, was not at all a campaign day; it was a day of one crisis after another in the international field." According to Eisenhower's biographer, the news over the weekend had been quite disheartening and "all hell broke loose" on Monday, November 5.[24] Yet, it was also a day that typified the president's ability as a crisis manager. Picture Eisenhower on the eve of his bid for reelection. Dulles had entered the hospital for surgery for a disease that would eventually cost him his life. He was obviously lost for the duration of the crisis and possibly for several months. Eden and Mollet, the president's most trusted and valued allies, had rejected the U.N.'s call for a cease-fire and launched an invasion of Egypt. British and French troops were landing in Egypt in direct violation of the Tripartite Declaration and General Assembly resolution. On Sunday, November 4, the Soviet Union had vetoed a Security Council resolution calling upon Russian troops to withdraw from Hungary. That same morning Soviet troops launched a major assault on Hungary and brutally slaughtered thousands of freedom fighters in the streets of Budapest. Meanwhile, U-2 flights and reports from the United States 6th Fleet reported that the Anglo-French armada was approaching Egypt's shores and would soon land amphibious forces to augment the airborne contingent that had landed early on the morning of November 5. The day had to have been one of the busiest of his entire presidency. What else could go wrong? Despite the personal and political tragedies occurring on almost every front, speech-writer Emmet Hughes remembered the president as being calm and relaxed.[25] What was needed was a crisis manager who could apply rational leadership to a chaotic situation. Because crises by their nature breed chaos, Eisenhower's task was to prevent the chaos from becoming any more disorganized than it was. The president's calm and steady leadership on November 5 and 6 reinforced his image as the man around whom Americans could rally in time of crisis.

Eisenhower began the morning of November 5 with a meeting with Vice-President Nixon and Acting Secretary Hoover. Hoover seemed particularly concerned about the possibility that the Soviets would send "volunteers" to Syria. Aware that Syrian airfields were poor and could not support the receipt of a number of Soviet forces, Eisenhower preferred to concentrate on the oil shortage that Great Britain and France would soon be facing. Hoover informed him that oil supplies from the

24. Folder marked "Nov '56 Diary-acw," Box 8, Ann Whitman Diary Series, Ann Whitman File, EP, EL; Ambrose, *Eisenhower: The President*, 367.

25. Hughes, *Ordeal of Power*, 223.

Middle East were virtually nonexistent, with the exception of the Saudi Arabian tapline. Concerned that the oil supply of NATO military forces in Western Europe might soon be endangered, the president suggested, "We should put heavy tankers and oilers into use immediately, including all fleet oilers." With regard to the oil problem faced by the French and the British, Eisenhower felt that the purpose of peace and stability would be better served by not being too quick in attempting to render extraordinary assistance. Preferring to keep the economic pressure on his erstwhile allies, he then asked Hoover to coordinate with the Office of Defense Mobilization to work out arrangements for the Navy to assist if the situation further deteriorated.[26]

The only good news that reached Eisenhower on November 5 was a telegram from Ambassador Hare in Egypt. Hare reported, [The] "U.S. has suddenly emerged as a real champion of right . . . the crisis came and the Russians did nothing. The effect is one of general disillusionment with the Soviets."[27] It was a small triumph in an otherwise hectic day.

Meanwhile, the Soviet Union broke its silence on the Suez crisis and vehemently condemned the British and French for their unprovoked attack on Port Said. Soviet Premier Nikolai Bulganin sent sharply worded warnings to Eden, Mollet, and Ben Gurion. Condemning the "bandit-like aggression," Bulganin warned that the conflict in Egypt might spread to other countries and lead to the Third World War. Unless the recipients of the correspondence came to their senses, Bulganin warned, "I believe it is my duty to inform you that the Soviet Government [is prepared] to use the Naval and Air Forces to stop the war in Egypt and to curb aggression. The Soviet Government is fully determined to apply force in order to crush the aggression and to restore peace in the Middle East."[28] Simultaneously, Bulganin wrote Eisenhower and proposed that the United States and the Soviet Union combine forces and march into Egypt to end the fighting.[29]

Meeting with Hoover and the White House staff later that afternoon to consider a reply to Bulganin's cable, Eisenhower dismissed the invitation as "unthinkable," but he worried about the Russians and the pos-

26. Memorandum of a Conference with the President, November 5, 1956, in folder marked "November 1956 Staff Memoranda," Box 19, DDE Diary Series, Ann Whitman File, EP, EL.

27. As quoted in folder marked "Department of State (Nov 56) Suez Crisis," Box 72, Confidential File (Subject Series), White House Central Files, EP, EL.

28. Copies of all correspondence from Bulganin to Eden, Mollet, and Ben Gurion are in folder marked "Suez Canal Crisis (1–5)," Box 82, Confidential File (Subject Series), White House Central Files, EP, EL.

29. Copy of letter is in folder marked "Egypt (1)," Box 8, International Series, Ann Whitman File, EP, EL. See also Department of State, *Suez Crisis,* 993–94.

sibility of armed intervention. Referring to Hitler's last days in power, the president said the Soviets are "scared and furious, and there is nothing more dangerous than a dictatorship in this state of mind." Sensing an opportunity to bring pressure from the nonaligned world to bear on the side of peace and to limit the hostilities, Eisenhower then approved the text of a message to India's Prime Minister Nehru, which affirmed the need "to exert the greatest possible restraint lest this situation radically deteriorate."[30] Meanwhile, Eisenhower delayed sending a formal reply to Bulganin until he increased the size of American military forces in the region. In the interim, the White House released a statement informing Bulganin that the United States opposed the introduction of new forces into Egypt, as such a course was in contravention to the United Nations resolution calling for the withdrawal of foreign forces from the region.[31] The statement recommended that the Soviet Union take the first and most important step to ensure peace and stability by observing the United Nations' resolution calling for the withdrawal of Soviet troops from Hungary and the curtailment of Soviet repression of the Hungarian people. Eisenhower was clearly buying time, hoping that the huge financial burden of waging war would compel Eden to accept a cease-fire.

Not far from the Anglo-French armada sailing toward Suez was the powerful American 6th Fleet that had recently evacuated American citizens so successfully. On full combat alert, Admiral Brown stood prepared to intercept the amphibious force before it reached Egypt. Brown's orders from Burke were to stand by for any contingency. In the event of submarine attack, Burke, with the approval of Eisenhower, authorized immediate counterattack utilizing every available means to destroy the submarine. In the case of aerial attack by planes identified as Egyptian, Israeli, British, or French, he authorized only immediate and aggressive defensive action. Only if Soviet warplanes attacked the 6th Fleet did Burke authorize aggressive pursuit into enemy air space, but he forbade prolonged pursuit or the deliberate and systematic organization of a pursuing force. Additionally, the Chief of Naval Operations instructed Brown to make all preparations for retaliatory attacks in the event of a Soviet attack on British and French units, but to take no further action without orders from Washington.[32] Burke's directives signaled no shift in

30. Memorandum of a Conference with the President, November 5, 1956, in folder marked "November 1956 Staff Memoranda," Box 19, DDE Diary Series, Ann Whitman File, EP, EL.

31. Text of press release is in Department of State *Bulletin* (November 19, 1956), 795–96.

32. In an interview with the author, Burke emphatically declared that he personally

American policy; he was merely preparing for various contingencies. Because Brown received no instructions from Burke to intercept the Anglo-French armada, he permitted the European force to proceed to its destination.

At exactly 1430 hours, November 6, the first wave of the main assault force landed at Port Said and Port Fuad. The operation was totally successful, with the British and French seizing their initial objectives within a few hours. In terms of casualties, the cost to the allies during all phases of Operation "Musketeer" was light. British casualties numbered 22 killed, 97 wounded; French losses totaled 10 killed, 22 wounded. Egyptian losses were proportionately greater.[33] From a military standpoint, Musketeer was an unqualified success; from the political perspective it was an unmitigated disaster. Even before his forces consolidated their gains, General Kneightly, the expedition's commander-in-chief, received word from Eden that a cease-fire was to take effect at midnight, November 6, London time. The operation was over almost before it began.

Tuesday, November 6, was Election Day, and Eisenhower planned to spend a few hours at his Gettysburg farm. The preceding evening, he had prepared a cable to Eden, expressing both his concern that events were happening too quickly and his anxiety about the temporary, but admittedly deep, rift that had occurred between the two nations with respect to the situation in the Middle East. The president cautioned the prime minister about sending British troops into heavy concentrations of civilian population. Avoiding urban centers would prohibit the need for an increased police function that the British might not be able to relinquish easily. Turning his attention to the dangerous fiscal problems confronting Eden as a result of financing the war, Eisenhower agreed that it was indeed serious and ought to be an incentive for terminating

exercised direct command of American naval forces in the Middle East during this critical stage. For general orders to the American forces in the event of foreign aggression, see JCS 1887/299 in 381 EMMEA (11-19-47) Sec. 47, Records of the Joint Chiefs of Staff, RG 218. After the invasion, there were reports that Brown had interfered with the armada by maneuvering submarines under the task force. Both Burke and Brown categorically denied these allegations. See "When Trouble Came in the Mediterranean," *U.S. News & World Report,* XLI (December 14, 1956), 30–32.

33. Both Robert Jackson, *Suez 1956: Operation Musketeer* (London, 1980), 66–74, and Andre Beaufre, *The Suez Expedition, 1956* (New York, 1969), 101–107, carry accounts of the airborne assault. Neff, *Warriors at Suez,* 414, lists British casualties at 16 killed, 96 wounded.

the hostilities as soon as possible.[34] British gold reserves had already fallen by one-eighth of their remaining total. Extending the olive branch, he closed the letter by adding, "In the meantime, no matter what our differences in the approach of this problem, please remember that my personal regard and friendship for you, Harold [Macmillan], Winston [Churchill], and so many others is unaffected. On top of this, I assure you I shall do all in my power to restore to their full strength our accustomed practices of cooperation just as quickly as it can be done."[35]

Prior to leaving Washington for Gettysburg, Eisenhower again met with Allen Dulles, Hoover, and Goodpaster to discuss the latest developments in the Middle East. Dulles and the president reviewed the latest intelligence reports indicating that the Soviets told the Egyptians that they intended "to do something" in the Middle East hostilities. Maintaining his characteristic calm, Eisenhower directed Dulles to conduct U-2 reconnaissance flights over Israel and Syria, "avoiding, however, any flights into Russia." In the event that the Soviets attacked the British and French, Eisenhower said, "We would be in war, and we would be justified in taking military action even if Congress were not in session." He then added that if reconnaissance disclosed Soviet Air Forces on Syrian bases, "there would be reason for the British and French to destroy them."[36] Content that he was abreast of the situation, Eisenhower departed the White House and drove to Gettysburg.

Without the president at the helm, anxiety gripped the White House. Radford and Goodpaster conferred twice on reports of Soviet aircraft flying over Turkey. With the Middle East in a state of turmoil and the Anglo-French expeditionary force on the beaches, Goodpaster contemplated asking the president to turn around and return to Washington.[37] Radford's calmer approach prevailed, but Goodpaster sent a plane to Gettysburg so Eisenhower could return sooner. At the president's direc-

34. In order to contain the serious loss of British financial reserves, Macmillan had requested the International Monetary Fund to repay the British quota. According to Macmillan's memoirs, his call was referred to Washington, where the United States Government refused to support the loan until Britain agreed to a ceasefire. See Harold Macmillan, *Riding the Storm, 1956–1959* (New York, 1971),163–64; Horne, *Harold Macmillan,* I, 440; and Department of State, *Suez Crisis,* 1012–13.

35. Eisenhower to Eden, November 6, 1956, International Series, Box 19, Ann Whitman File, EP, EL. A marginal notation on the text by Ann Whitman reads: "Pres. said events had gone too swiftly. Letter was outdated, not to be sent."

36. Memorandum of a Conference with the President, November 6, 1956, 8:37 A.M., in folder marked "November 1956 Staff Memoranda," Box 19, DDE Diary Series, Ann Whitman File, EP, EL.

37. See Whitman's journal entry for November 6, in folder marked "Nov 56 Diary-acw (2)," Box 8, Ann Whitman Diary Series, Ann Whitman File, EP, EL.

tion, the staff secretary also scheduled an emergency meeting of Eisenhower's advisers in the cabinet room at 1230, when the president was due to return.

Meeting Eisenhower at the airport, Goodpaster informed the president that intelligence did not reveal any Soviet aircraft in Syria. Eisenhower reasoned that the immediate crisis was over. Shortly after noon, he met with Hoover, Allen Dulles, Deputy Secretary of Defense A. Willis Robertson, and the Joint Chiefs of Staff. Military preparedness was the principal topic of discussion, and the president concurred with Radford's recommendation to upgrade the military state of readiness in the region.[38] To avoid creating a stir, however, he disapproved the recommendation to recall all servicemen from regular leave, restricting his approval to alerting regional forces and increasing the number of ships and aircraft on ready status. Radford acquiesced and noted that it was difficult to decipher Bulganin's intentions in connection with the premier's proposal for a joint American-Soviet force to police the Middle East. Reflecting on the intelligence at hand, he surmised that it was virtually impossible for the Russians to intervene unless they did so with long-range nuclear weapons, which seemed totally improbable. The chairman's reasoning proved sound, but his naval colleague, Admiral Burke, remained skeptical. By his own admission, Burke had never seen the world situation so confused. He particularly hoped that the Soviet Union did not believe it could take unilateral action against Great Britain and France without a severe and violent retaliation from the United States.[39] In any event, he intended to keep the 6th Fleet on combat alert.

During the meeting, Eisenhower received the long awaited word that Eden had agreed to the cease-fire. The French violently disagreed with Eden's surrender to American pressure, but without British support, Mollet and Pineau had no recourse but to accept the cease-fire too. The extent of French disgust for Eden's acquiescence was best told by Ambassador Dillon, whom Mollet summoned to his office on the evening of November 5. When Dillon arrived, an emergency meeting of the French Cabinet was in progress, so Dillon waited in the anteroom. Shortly after midnight (November 6), Mollet entered and handed Dillon a ticker-tape quotation from TASS, which implied a very clear threat that the Soviet Union would use rockets against the expeditionary force unless the invasion of Egypt stopped. Obviously concerned with the TASS

38. For specific recommendations, see CJCS, 091 Palestine (June '56–December '56), Records of the Joint Chiefs of Staff, RG 218.

39. See Arleigh A. Burke's letter to Vice Admiral Friedrich Ruge, Federal Republic of Germany, November 14, 1956, in Admiral Arleigh A. Burke Personal File, Operational Archives Branch, Washington Navy Yard.

statement, Mollet inquired what the United States' reaction would be if the Soviets entered the conflict. Dillon simply replied that the language of the NATO treaty dictated that the United States would support its European allies even though Eisenhower currently disagreed with what the British and French were doing. Somewhat mollified, Mollet returned to the cabinet meeting, but within a few minutes, he returned to the anteroom to take a telephone call from Eden. Eden discussed the Soviet threat and informed Mollet that the British government had decided to order a cease-fire. Clearly agitated, the French prime minister protested vehemently, but the British were in command of the operation, and there was little he could do to sway Eden. Aghast, Mollet returned to his meeting and informed the cabinet of Eden's decision.[40]

To Mollet, Eden had simply lost his nerve, but the British prime minister's political predicament was far worse than Mollet appreciated. In an attempt to put the best face forward on a deteriorating political situation, Eden claimed that he had ordered the cease-fire because the British had achieved all their objectives. Economic and political pressures were actually the determining factors. Unlike France, which had borrowed sufficiently prior to the crisis to be able to withstand American economic pressure, Britain was simply running out of financial reserves. Moreover, Eden realized that domestic support for his policy of aggression had virtually disintegrated. The *Economist* raised the question whether the prime minister should "go or stay." The *Times* criticized Eden for sabotaging the three principles on which Great Britain had based its foreign policy since World War II: solidarity within the Commonwealth, the Anglo-American alliance, and the Charter of the United Nations. Additionally, the *Observer* and the Manchester *Guardian* were calling Suez "Eden's war."[41]

Not only had Eden lost his public support, but Parliament and his own cabinet were in revolt. Opposition leader Gaitskell chastised the prime minister for his veto of the initial Security Council resolution demanding an immediate cease-fire. Gaitskell also assailed Eden for abstaining from the Canadian resolution that established the peace-keep-

40. Dillon interview with the author, June 29, 1982, EL. Dillon also noted an interesting sidelight concerning French military intelligence. The actual battle scene depicted on the French situation map was totally erroneous. Mollet thought his forces were in Ismailia, but they were actually twenty miles short of their objective. Had the diplomatic leaders been aware of the actual military situation, Dillon stated that they would have been even more adamant about protesting Eden's cease-fire order.

41. *Economist,* November 3, November 10, 1956; *Times* (London), November 1, 1956. Neff, *Warriors at Suez,* 409, carries accounts of the *Observer* (London) and the Manchester *Guardian.*

ing force. It was increasingly obvious to the opposition that Eden's actual purpose was not the separation of the combatants, but the conquest of the Suez Canal. At one point, James Griffith, a Laborite who opposed Eden's Suez policy, stated, "I say to the Prime Minister that he forfeited the trust of millions of our people. For the first time in the history of this House, it has been left to the leader of the Opposition to speak for Britain."[42] By November 6, the entire Labor contingent of the House of Commons demanded the termination of hostilities. Confronted with the greatest potential defeat of his political career unless he reversed his policy, Eden finally addressed the new session of the House to announce the cease-fire. Gaitskell praised Eden for finally coming to his senses. After the session, Gaitskell addressed an audience organized by the National Council of Labor. In extolling the virtues of his party, Gaitskell said that the announcement of the cease-fire marked the greatest triumph of democracy the world had ever seen and attributed the cessation of hostilities to the "passionate, determined protests of the British people against the policy of the Eden Government."[43]

Gaitskell's opposition was only one nail in the prime minister's political coffin. Early on November 6, Chancellor of the Exchequer Macmillan informed Eden that the run on the British sterling that had begun in September had reached critical proportions. British gold and dollar reserves had already dropped $141 million in October; by November these losses doubled to $279 million. When Macmillan telephoned Secretary of the Treasury Humphrey seeking assistance, he was notified by Humphrey that he would be available only if Britain accepted the cease-fire. According to newly appointed British Ambassador Sir Harold Caccia, "We meet a brick wall at every turn with the administration."[44] Macmillan was the first cabinet member to bolt from Eden's policy toward the Middle East. In order to keep British industry from collapsing, Macmillan told Lloyd that it was necessary to import aid from abroad until the Suez Canal was clear and the oil pipelines operational. With dwindling financial reserves, Great Britain did not have enough hard currency to pay for the oil unless the United States agreed

42. The *Times* (London), November 6, 1956, carried the full text of the debate. See also *Hansard's Parliamentary Debates,* Vol. 558, pp. 1631–38.

43. *Times* (London), November 7, 1956. For primary accounts of the reasons behind Eden's decision to proclaim a ceasefire, see Eden, *Full Circle,* 620–25; Lloyd, *Suez 1956,* 210–11; Macmillan, *Riding the Storm,* 163–67; and Nutting, *No End of a Lesson,* 145–47. Nutting also cited lack of support from the members of the Baghdad Pact nations as playing an instrumental role in Eden's decision.

44. As quoted in Steven Freiberger, *Dawn over Suez: The Rise of American Power in the Middle East, 1953–1957* (Chicago, 1992), 194–95.

to furnish credit, and both Eden and Lloyd realized that Eisenhower had no intention of rescuing his European allies while the fighting continued.

Now that the fighting was over, Eisenhower called Eden and expressed his satisfaction that the prime minister had seen fit to order the cease-fire. Calling the prime minister's attention to the United Nations resolution establishing a peace-keeping force, the president hoped Eden would tell Hammarskjold that the cease-fire arrangement was "without condition." Eden asked Eisenhower whether the United States intended to provide any troops to the force, but the president declined. "What I want to do is this. I would like to see none of the great nations in it. I am afraid the Red boy is going to demand the lion's share. I would rather make it no troops from the big five [permanent members of the Security Council]." Eden reluctantly agreed, adding, "If I survive here tonight [Parliamentary vote of confidence], I will call you tomorrow." The prime minister then asked how things were going with the president, to which Eisenhower replied, "We have given our whole thought to Hungary and the Middle East. I don't give a damn how the election goes. I guess it will be all right."[45] Eisenhower then took the afternoon off to relax and await the electoral returns.

Election Day, however, was hardly a relaxing experience. Canceling a scheduled round of golf, Eisenhower remained in the White House until around 10 P.M. when he left to go to Republican headquarters. Reasonably assured of victory by recent polls, Eisenhower monitored the votes carefully, noting popular margins and congressional races, as well as national returns. Discussing the election with speech-writer Hughes in the late evening, Eisenhower reminded Hughes of a soldier surveying the electoral battlefield with clinical concern and passion. "There's Michigan and Minnesota still to see. You remember that story of Nelson [British victor at Trafalgar]—dying, he looked around and asked, 'Are there any of them still left?' I guess that's me. When I get in a battle, I just want to win the whole thing . . . six or seven states we can't help. But I don't want to lose any more. Don't want any of them 'left'—like Nelson. That's the way I feel." Like Nelson, Eisenhower wanted not only total victory, but unconditional surrender. Clearly frustrated that Stevenson refused to concede the election, the president retired for the evening, leaving his aides "to receive the surrender."[46]

45. Transcript of a Telephone Conversation Between President Eisenhower in Washington and Prime Minister Eden in London, November 6, 1956, 12:55 P.M., in folder marked "November 1956, Phone Calls," Box 19, DDE Diary Series, Ann Whitman File, EP, EL.

46. Hughes, *Ordeal of Power*, 228; and Ambrose, *Eisenhower: The President*, 369–70.

By midnight, it was all over. The president received the endorsement he sought. Eisenhower's popular vote of 35,581,003 topped Stevenson's 25,738,765 by nearly ten million votes. The electoral margin was even more impressive, 457 for Eisenhower versus 73 for Stevenson. His reelection was by no means a referendum on his Suez policy, but rather on his calm leadership and the general prosperity that the majority of Americans enjoyed. The president's triumph was even greater in scope than his 1952 victory over the same Democratic challenger. Even in heavily populated Jewish areas, Eisenhower did not fare badly despite his firm opposition to Israel. Although the loss of both houses of Congress tempered his personal victory, Eisenhower was ecstatic at his margin of victory over Stevenson.

The president's reference to Nelson was hardly accidental, and it was indicative of Eisenhower's leadership during the Suez crisis. The "Nelson touch" consisted of carefully analyzing an opponent's capabilities and intentions and then marshaling one's own strength against the enemy's weakness at the decisive point on the battlefield. Under the personal leadership of an audacious commander, who was willing to take risks to achieve total victory, the Nelson touch produced repeated successes for the British Navy during the Napoleonic wars, most notably at Aboukir Bay in 1798 and at Trafalgar in October 1805. In a sense, Eisenhower had engineered his own Trafalgar. Early in the crisis, he analyzed Eden's and Nasser's strengths and weaknesses, as well as the intentions of French and Soviet leaders. When some of his personal advisers urged military and diplomatic support for Great Britain and France, the president remained fixed on his objective of preventing a disastrous turn of events that might facilitate Soviet access to the Middle East. At the critical moment, Eisenhower had applied his greatest strengths—marshaling world opinion against the nations involved in the collusion and denying Eden the economic assistance the British so desperately needed—against the aggressor states' principal weakness, their declining financial reserves. Just as Nelson personally directed the naval action off the Iberian coast in 1805, Eisenhower himself devised the strategy that ultimately achieved his political objective of forcing Eden to accept the cease-fire. Where Nelson employed superior seamanship to defeat his opponents, Eisenhower used economic and diplomatic pressure, supported by America's financial and military might, as his instruments of coercion. The president's decisive involvement in formulating foreign policy and ensuring that his policy goals were clearly defined and understood had averted the need to commit American military forces into what was perhaps the world's most troubled region.

7

THE CRISIS RESOLVED

Above all, we should keep in mind that the real enemy of the United States is in the Kremlin, not Cairo or Tel Aviv.

—Dwight D. Eisenhower

With the acceptance of the cease-fire by Eden and Mollet, the crisis in the Middle East rapidly dissipated. From an American perspective, the president's management of the crisis was a major foreign policy success. To Eisenhower, and Eisenhower alone, belonged the credit for forcing the British and French, and ultimately the Israelis, to accept the terms of the United Nations. Having accomplished his immediate goal of ending the fighting, he now directed his attention toward the following goals: (1) preventing a recurrence of hostilities, (2) upholding the prestige of the United Nations, (3) removing any pretext for Soviet military intervention, (4) facilitating the withdrawal of Anglo-French forces from Egypt, and (5) reducing the friction within the Atlantic alliance.[1] Although he could afford to take a more relaxed approach to the crisis since the belligerents had ceased fighting, Eisenhower pursued all his policy objectives. He demanded the immediate withdrawal of British, French, and Israeli forces from Egypt in order to achieve his longer-term objectives of regional stability and the exclusion of Soviet influence from the Middle East. These objectives dominated the president's agenda in the last two months of 1956. In achieving them, Eisenhower was only partially successful, but his personal influence in the decision-making process was readily apparent. Crisis management, however, was more suited to achieving short-term objectives than long-term goals.

Eisenhower's greatest frustration centered on countering the expansion of Soviet influence in the moderate Arab states. The overwhelming defeat suffered by the Egyptian military forces had caused consider-

---

1. For a synopsis of the administration's policy objectives, see Acting Secretary of State Hoover's testimony to the Senate Foreign Relations Committee, November 12, 1956, in *Executive Sessions of the Senate Foreign Relations Committee,* Vol. VIII, 84th Cong., Second Sess., 605–17 (hereinafter cited as *Senate Foreign Relations Committee*).

able depression within the Arab world, and the Soviet Union seized the opportunity to inject itself into the region by its dramatic threat of intervention to repel the Anglo-French invasion of Egypt. From the time of his initial proclamation on the subject, Bulganin had done everything within his power to create the impression that the cease-fire and the demand to withdraw foreign troops from Egypt were due to Soviet diplomatic pressure on the European states. Regrettably, the unprovoked attack on Egypt by Great Britain and France had forced Eisenhower to unite with the Soviet Union in condemning the Anglo-French aggression. Still uncomfortable over the obvious differences with respect to the policies of Eden and Mollet, Eisenhower never wavered with regard to his attitude toward the Soviet Union or his determination to rebuild the cohesion of the Atlantic alliance. Accordingly, Eisenhower continued to flex American muscle to prevent the introduction of Soviet military forces into the region, and he devoted his greatest efforts to restoring cordial relations with his NATO partners. The restoration of the alliance received Eisenhower's complete attention, but he still refused to give Eden and Mollet unqualified support. Only when the evacuation was complete would diplomatic relations return to the *status quo ante bellum*.

At 8:43 A.M. on the morning of November 7, Eisenhower received a telephone call from Eden, in which the prime minister requested an immediate summit conference in Washington between himself, Eisenhower, and Mollet.[2] Eden had previously consulted with Mollet, who strongly endorsed his effort for a Washington summit. Such a meeting, the prime minister maintained, would demonstrate Western solidarity against the threat of possible Soviet military thrusts in support of Arab nations. Apparently in accordance with a previous suggestion, Eisenhower stated he would be delighted to have Eden and Mollet come to the United States. No sooner did he hang up than Eisenhower began to wonder if Eden had some hidden agenda and was perhaps trying to back out of the cease-fire or compliance with the U.N. plan for the proposed withdrawal of the expeditionary force. An hour later, he called Eden to ensure there was no misunderstanding about the purpose of the visit. "If the purpose of the visit would be to concert ourselves in NATO and what we are going to do in the future, then we have nothing to fear," said the president. Eisenhower then told Eden to ensure Mollet understood that and

2. Memorandum of a Telephone Conversation Between President Eisenhower in Washington and Prime Minister Eden in London, November 7, 1956, 8:43 A.M. in folder marked "November 56 Phone Calls," Box 19, DDE Diary Series, Ann Whitman File, EP, EL. See also Transcript of a Telephone Conversation Between President Eisenhower in Washington and Prime Minister Eden in London, November 7, 1956, 9:55 A.M., *ibid.*

again stressed a meeting was okay, but only if "we are going to talk about the future and about the Bear [Soviet Union]."

Eisenhower next met with Adams and Goodpaster, whom Hoover had called as soon as the president mentioned plans for the upcoming summit. Both members of Eisenhower's inner council disapproved of the proposed meeting, as it might give the "possible appearance that we were now concerting action in the Middle East independently of the U.N. action."[3] Their opposition prompted Eisenhower to call Eden and indicate that he [the president] considered the meeting's purpose to be to solidify their support of NATO, and under no circumstances did it signify a deviation from his position on the cease-fire. While this call was in progress, Hoover entered the president's office. Hoover immediately informed the president that Secretary Dulles, with whom he had just conferred, opposed the summit because it would give the impression that the United States was "teaming with the British and French." Additionally, Hoover reported that the Soviets had offered Egypt 250,000 volunteers and were "making great efforts to put themselves in the position of liberators." Eisenhower directed Goodpaster to check the report of Soviet troop movements with Allen Dulles. As Eisenhower expected, the report was groundless; no massive movement of Soviet troops had taken place. Secretary Humphrey then joined the conference and agreed with Hoover and Goodpaster's recommendation against holding the summit at the present time. Stating "he appreciated how hard it was for the President to tell a man [Eden] that he wouldn't talk to him, but the timing question was overriding," Humphrey recommended that the meeting be postponed to a more opportune time.

After further discussion, Eisenhower accepted the prudent advice of his associates and telephoned Eden at 10:27 A.M. to say that the timing of the proposed visit was bad and, regrettably, the leaders would have to visit the United States at a later time.[4] In the interim, Eisenhower would send Gruenther to London to discuss the military situation and proposed reactions to any Soviet military involvement. Eden was obviously disappointed with the president's decision and attempted to have Eisenhower make an about face on the subject. Growing somewhat irritated with the prime minister, Eisenhower said, "I am not talking about not meeting and talking with our friends. But I have had opposition about

3. Memorandum for the Record by the President's Staff Secretary, November 7, 1956, in folder marked "November 1956 Staff Memoranda," Box 19, DDE Diary Series, Ann Whitman File, EP, EL. See also White House Memoranda Series, Meetings with the President, in Box 4, Dulles Papers, Mudd Library, Princeton.

4. Transcript of the telephone conversation is in folder marked "Nov. 56 Phone Calls," Box 19, DDE Diary Series, Ann Whitman File, EP, EL.

the timing." Eden again asked for a specific time, but Eisenhower put him off, claiming he had to confer with Dulles, the cabinet, Departments of State and Defense, ODM, and others. Realizing he wasn't getting anywhere, Eden asked Eisenhower to call Mollet with the message of the postponement, but Eisenhower told him to call and to call right away. That ended the conversation.

In retrospect, Eisenhower's handling of Eden seemed almost callous. Whether the president was now intent on working behind the scenes to pressure Eden's removal as British prime minister, as one recent author claimed,[5] or whether he was content to work with his British counterpart to salvage his own Middle Eastern policy, it was evident that the warm relationship that had existed between Eisenhower and Eden since World War II had cooled. Indeed, Eden's biographer recorded that the prime minister found Eisenhower's veto of their meeting the most traumatic event of the crisis.[6]

The president then took time from his normal duties to visit Dulles at Walter Reed Hospital. Accompanying him was Hoover and William B. Macomber, special assistant to the secretary of state. Following the exchange of a few pleasantries, Eisenhower said he thought "there was no point now in indulging in recriminations with the British, but rather that we should jointly consider what should be done in the face of the Russian threat."[7] As outlined in notes prepared by Macomber, Eisenhower clearly set the agenda during the discussions, outlining the need to coordinate an intelligence estimate with the British concerning the Russian threat and the necessity of applying pressure on Israel to withdraw to the 1949 armistice lines. Concerning the Soviet Union, the president made the point that the important thing to remember in the present situation was that "the Bear is still the central enemy." Dulles, of course, agreed and the conversation moved to Eisenhower's concern that without Dulles, there was no one to coordinate the activities between the Departments of State and Defense as related to the Suez crisis. Could Dulles recommend someone to coordinate the two agencies? The secretary suggested Robert Anderson (special emissary for the president to the Middle East) or Douglas MacArthur II (counselor of the Department of State, not his uncle, the famous general). Eisenhower concurred and said he would look into it later that evening.

5. Freiberger, *Dawn over Suez*, 212.

6. Robert R. James, *Anthony Eden* (London, 1986), 576–77. See also Kunz, "The Economic Diplomacy of the Suez Crisis," 135.

7. Memorandum of a Conversation, Secretary Dulles' Room, Walter Reed Hospital, November 7, 1956, 11:10 A.M., as quoted in Department of State, *Suez Crisis*, 1049–53.

Later that afternoon, Eisenhower conferred with Hoover about what to do with Ben Gurion. Israel had already rejected the General Assembly resolution calling for the immediate withdrawal of all foreign troops from Egypt. The vote in the United Nations was 65–1, Israel being the lone dissenter. Earlier that day, Ben Gurion had addressed the Knesset and declared that the Israeli-Egyptian Armistice Agreement of 1949 was "dead and buried." The president thought Ben Gurion's statement was absolutely "terrible." Since Israeli Chargé d'Affaires Reuven Shiloah was scheduled to see Hoover at 6 P.M., the acting secretary needed presidential guidance. Eisenhower then outlined a hard line that included the threat of economic sanctions. When Shiloah later met with Hoover, the acting secretary informed him, "I consider this to be the most important meeting ever held with Israeli representatives. Israel's attitude will inevitably lead to most serious measures, such as the termination of all United States governmental and private aid, United Nations sanctions, and eventual expulsion from the United Nations. I speak with utmost seriousness and gravity."[8] No doubt about it, Eisenhower was playing hard ball.

To bolster Hoover's tough language, the president then cabled Ben Gurion and informed him that the United Nations intended to dispatch its forces to Egypt in accordance with pertinent resolutions of the General Assembly. Then, getting to the heart of the matter, Eisenhower said, "Statements attributed to your [Israeli] Government to the effect that Israel does not intend to withdraw from Egyptian territory have been called to my attention." If true, Eisenhower continued, "I must say frankly, Mr. Prime Minister, that the United States views these reports with deep concern." Urging immediate compliance with the General Assembly resolution, the president requested Ben Gurion to make his "decision known immediately." And he added, "It would be a matter of the greatest regret to all my countrymen if Israeli policy on a matter of such grave concern to the world should in any way impair the friendly cooperation between our two countries."[9] Eisenhower was hardly being subtle. Although cloaked in diplomatic language, his message was clear: comply with the United Nations resolutions or face immediate economic sanctions. Ben Gurion got the message.

Now that all the partners in the coalition against Egypt had succumbed

8. As quoted in Neff, *Warriors at Suez,* 416. A transcript of the president's conversation with Hoover is located in folder marked "Nov. 56 Phone Calls," Box 19, DDE Diary Series, Ann Whitman File, EP, EL.

9. Eisenhower, *Waging Peace,* 94. See also Message from President Eisenhower to Prime Minister Ben Gurion, November 7, 1956, in Department of State, *Suez Crisis,* 1063–64.

to Eisenhower's demands, the president met with the National Security Council on November 8 to pick up the pieces in the Middle East.[10]
Taking his place at the center of the table, the president informed the
council that the first item on the agenda was a discussion of the European oil situation. Robert Anderson, who had been working with the oil
companies by the direction of the president, stated there was approximately two weeks' supply of crude in Europe at the present time and one
month to six weeks' supply of refined products on hand. Moreover, saboteurs had cut the Iraqi pipeline and destroyed three pumping stations.
The ARAMCO tapline was still intact, but it "was touch and go as to
how long it would remain in operation." American oil companies estimated it would take six months to a year to rehabilitate the Iraqi Petroleum Company's pipeline. Anderson then addressed Europe's dilemma
in generating enough dollars to purchase Western Hemisphere petroleum and gave a report on the Office of Defense Mobilization's efforts
to plan for the control of the shipment of oil from the Gulf Coast to Europe. Throughout Anderson's presentation, Eisenhower interrupted repeatedly, asking pointed questions concerning the availability of oil from
East Asian resources, whether Anderson could increase U.S. oil production, and how to increase American production without giving the
Arab world the impression that the United States was bailing out the
British. Having stated his concerns, the president asked if any of the other
members of the NSC had different views to contribute. After lengthy discussion, the NSC noted the president's approval of the authorization of
the movement of Gulf coast oil to the U.S. east coast in foreign flag tankers
for possible shipment to European markets.

Turning to the situation in the Middle East, Allen Dulles commented
that Nasser's prestige had grown immensely as a result of the Soviet
Union's promise of support. In spite of the efforts of the three aggressor
nations, internal security in Egypt remained tightly under Nasser's control, and Egyptian disillusionment with Nasser was not likely to be strong
enough to bring him down. The net result of the fighting seemed to have
made the Egyptian president an international hero, particularly among
the nonaligned nations and the Arab states. Dulles next addressed the
Soviet position, stating that the real question was how far the Soviet
Union was prepared to go in this situation. Fully cognizant of the limitations imposed by their actions in Hungary, he concluded that he was

10. Memorandum of Discussion at the 303d Meeting of the National Security Council, Washington, November 8, 1956, in folder marked "NSC Summaries of Discussion,"
Box 8, National Security Council Series, Ann Whitman File, EP, EL. In *Eisenhower: The
President*, 371, Ambrose cites the NSC meeting as occurring on November 9. The meeting was actually held on the morning of November 8.

inclined to think that for the time being, the main Soviet thrust would be on "keeping the pot boiling." Radford then interjected his analysis of the Soviet military presence in the region and expressed his opinion that "the situation in the Near East as a whole was even worse than Dulles had suggested."

As was his fashion in NSC meetings, Eisenhower patiently listened to all the participants, most of whom echoed rather gloomy forecasts of what the Soviet Union was or wasn't going to do. Summarizing this portion of the discussion, he calmly enumerated American priorities at this stage of the crisis. First priority was obviously "to get the UN police force into Egypt and the British and French forces out of Egypt." This action would pull the rug from under the Soviet psychological offensive. Second priority was to give "the moving pictures of Soviet atrocities in Budapest the fullest possible exploitation." Correctly gauging the Soviet threat, Eisenhower concluded that he "just couldn't help believing that the Russians would play their game short of anything which would induce the United States to declare war on them." Furthermore, it remained "wholly inexplicable to him that any state in the world would play with the Russians after witnessing what had happened in Hungary."

Following his policy guidance, Eisenhower sought the council's advice on the best manner to deal with the briefing of congressional leaders, which he had scheduled for the following day. After some deliberation, Eisenhower decided to have Dulles conduct an intelligence briefing, followed by Radford's synopsis of the military situation. Hoover would address the legislators on United Nations activities and future policies of the administration. Last, Eisenhower directed Flemming to update the congressmen on the oil crisis and proposed solutions to address potential petroleum shortfalls. Before adjourning, the president instructed the key members of the NSC to be careful when briefing the congressional leaders that "we not place all the blame for what had happened on Great Britain and France," since "the Russians had jumped rapidly into the Near East situation not simply because the British and French had given them an opportunity, but because they have long hoped that somehow or other they could reach into the Middle East."

Following the NSC meeting, Eisenhower returned to the Oval Office to collect his thoughts and consider the policy options available to him in pursuit of U.S. diplomatic objectives. In a private memorandum,[11] he carefully laid out his options and contingencies. The result was highly

11. Memorandum by the President, November 8, 1956, in folder marked "November 1956 Misc.," Box 25, DDE Diary Series, Ann Whitman File, EP, EL; also quoted in Department of State, *Suez Crisis*, 1088–89.

indicative of the president's managerial style. Reminiscent of a military commander's war gaming an upcoming operation, Eisenhower listed his objectives, analyzed opposing courses of action, compared his own strategic alternatives to achieve political ends, and then decided on what action, he as president, would undertake. In military jargon, Eisenhower had conducted a commander's estimate, a logical process of reasoning by which a commander considered all the circumstances affecting a military situation, and arrived at a decision as to the course of action to be taken to accomplish the mission. Included in any commander's estimate was also a realistic appraisal of one's own strengths and weaknesses, as well as the power and limitations of one's adversaries. As supreme commander in 1944, he had followed a similar process on the eve of the invasion of Europe. What Eisenhower's memorandum illustrated was not only the president's mastery of the complete range of policy options, but also his ability to state succinctly American political objectives from which his subordinates could devise appropriate strategies. This memorandum also formed the basis for a White House briefing of congressional leaders on November 9.

With respect to the Suez crisis, Eisenhower noted that "information indicates that both Israel and Egypt have now fully accepted the terms of the UN cease-fire plan." If that report was borne out by events, the U.S. needed to "take any kind of action that would minimize the effects of the recent difficulties and exclude from the area Soviet influence." Eisenhower then enumerated measures to be taken to accomplish these objectives. First, the U.S. should "make certain that none of these governments [Middle East states] fails to understand all the details and the full implications of the Soviet suppression of the Hungarian revolt." He also wanted to ensure "that every weak country understands what can be in store for it once it falls under the domination of the Soviets." Next, Eisenhower outlined a "carrot and stick" approach to woo regional states from Soviet influence. For example, "We can provide Egypt with an agreed-upon amount of arms . . . in return for an agreement that it will never accept any Soviet offer." In Israel, "We could renew an economic compact and take up again the $75 million economic loan that Ben Gurion desired." Eisenhower also considered translating the Tripartite Declaration of 1950 into a bilateral treaty with each of the countries in the Middle East and exploring other means of assisting the Arab States of Iraq, Jordan, Saudi Arabia, and Lebanon as a means of strengthening American economic and diplomatic ties.

If the president's assessment was faulty in any way, it was in Eisenhower's inability to view the crisis in any terms other than a cold war scenario. He designed his entire program to bar Soviet influence into the region. Such an approach failed to consider the full impact of pan-Arabism and emerging nationalism within the Arab community. Still, Eisenhower's assessment of Soviet capabilities was fairly accurate. In the days following the cease-fire, he remained convinced that the Soviet capabilities did not match Bulganin's rhetoric. To ensure that the Department of Defense was on board, Eisenhower received daily briefings from Radford with respect to American military readiness. On November 7, as a result of JCS recommendations, the president approved orders that augmented the Defense Early Warning Line (DEW-LINE), increased ocean reconnaissance and the number of hunter-killer antisubmarine groups, prepared to sail carrier task forces to the Middle East, and placed heavy troop carrier wings on twelve-hour alert status.[12] Eisenhower also approved a Chief of Naval Operations memorandum for shipping a Marine battalion landing team from the Far East to the Middle East. The Joint Chiefs decided to take no further action regarding deploying a Marine amphibious force from the eastern United States until the situation in the Middle East clarified. Upon presidential approval, the units mentioned in the JCS recommendation proceeded to their duty stations.

Having flexed his military muscle, Eisenhower next wrote a formal reply to Bulganin's letter that suggested Soviet-American intervention in Egypt. In a stern cable,[13] Eisenhower wrote on November 11 that with respect to Bulganin's suggestion, it was his view "that neither Soviet nor any other military forces should now enter the Middle East area except under United Nations mandate." The employment of any Soviet-American military force, reasoned Eisenhower, would "be directly contrary to resolutions of the General Assembly." Unable to reconcile Bulganin's expressed concern for the principles of morality and the objectives of the United Nations with action taken by the Soviet government in Hungary, Eisenhower threatened that in the event of the introduction of Soviet forces into the region, "it would be the duty of all United Nations members, including the United States, to oppose any such effort." Perhaps the Soviet Union could make a great and notable contribution to the cause of peace by complying with the General Assembly's resolutions on the subject of Hungary. As he expected, the president

12. Military options are listed in the Chronology of Naval Activities, Operational Archives Branch, Washington Navy Yard. See also Memorandum for Colonel Goodpaster, November 7, 1956, in CJCS 091 Palestine (June, 1956–December, 1956), Records of the Joint Chiefs of Staff, RG 218.

13. Copy of Message from President Eisenhower to Prime Minister Bulganin, November 11, 1956, is in folder marked "Egypt (1)," Box 8, International Series, Ann Whitman File, EP, EL.

did not receive a reply. Again, he had correctly gauged Bulganin's reaction.

Eisenhower backed his warning two days later in General Gruenther's final press conference at SHAPE headquarters. Gruenther, who frequently spoke for the president in NATO, issued a communiqué that lacked the diplomatic rhetoric that characterized Eisenhower's telegram, but the message was identical. If the Soviets attacked the West [Great Britain and France], the Soviet Union and the Soviet bloc "would be destroyed . . . as sure as day follows night."[14] Keeping pressure on Bulganin, Acting Secretary Hoover then addressed the General Assembly on November 16 and declared that any Soviet military action would be "clearly contrary" to the United Nations resolution of November 2, and that it was the duty of all members to refrain from introducing national forces into the area, except those of the U.N. emergency force. The arrival of Soviet forces, he continued, would present a threat to the United Nations forces then entering the area and would compel the international body "to take appropriate action." President Eisenhower, Hoover concluded, had already announced that the United States would fully support any U.N. action.[15]

To ensure Soviet compliance with his warning, Eisenhower increased the intelligence coverage of arms shipments via Soviet bloc merchant ships to the Middle East. Brigadier General Richard Collins, Deputy Director of Intelligence for the Joint Chiefs of Staff, and the Office of Naval Intelligence began monitoring all commercial shipping in the eastern Mediterranean and the Black Sea. By November 15, however, the threat of Soviet intervention had subsided to the point that Radford instructed Burke to deactivate the various task forces that had been formed to augment the 6th Fleet.[16] On December 13, Admiral Boone, the commander in chief, Naval Forces, Eastern Atlantic and Mediterranean (CINCNELM), returned to London from his flagship, USS *Pocono*. Four days later, the 6th Fleet resumed normal operations. The Soviet promise to send volunteers, as Eisenhower predicted, was a hollow threat and served merely as a propaganda ploy.

As he faced down the Soviets, Eisenhower turned his attention to mustering congressional approval for his Suez policy. Briefing the bipartisan leadership of Congress remained an important component of Eisenhower's management of international crises. He took extraordinary measures to ensure that executive briefings received the full attention of his

14. As quoted in Eisenhower, *Waging Peace*, 97.
15. Department of State *Bulletin*, No. 908 (November 19, 1956), 795–96.
16. CCSS 381 EMMEA (11-19-47) Sec. 53, Records of the Joint Chiefs of Staff, RG 218.

aides. Because Congress would not reconvene until January, he considered it essential to inform the leaders of both parties of the administration's policies in the event the situation deteriorated and he had to summon the legislative branch into emergency session. As his briefing of congressional leaders on November 9 demonstrated, however, Eisenhower intended to inform Congress, not consult legislative leaders with respect to formation of national policy.

If Eisenhower sought to obtain congressional approval for his actions by submitting proposals that would increase executive authority to deal with the Middle East fiasco, he was entirely successful. Following the White House briefing, Senator Lyndon Johnson found the president's remarks "very fruitful and helpful," and promised the administration that the Democrats would not play politics with foreign policy. Additionally, the senate majority leader said that the Senate would give responsible consideration to Eisenhower's proposals for a comprehensive revision of Middle Eastern policy. Senator John F. Kennedy joined Johnson in urging a bipartisan approach to foreign policy to provide "dissent without disunity." Not only had Eisenhower secured congressional support for what he considered his visionary proposals but he also allayed Democratic fears that the crisis was beyond the administration's ability to control it. Senator George, chairman of the Senate Foreign Relations Committee, departed the White House that morning, stating there was no need "to be unduly alarmed," nor was it necessary to reconvene Congress for a special session.[17]

Eisenhower did not confine his efforts to secure congressional approval to the bipartisan gathering of legislators on November 9. Three days later, he dispatched his principal advisers, including Hoover, Allen Dulles, Radford, Flemming, and Phleger, to an emergency hearing by the Senate Foreign Relations Committee to discuss Suez and Hungary. Following introductory remarks by George, Hoover reviewed the major developments in the Middle East since the committee had last met on July 28. Radford then discussed the current military situation, but his remarks were off the record. The members of the Foreign Relations Committee questioned the administration's team, and all but Senator William Fulbright seemed reasonably satisfied. The Arkansas senator repeatedly sought to have Hoover outline Eisenhower's specific policies for bringing stability to the Middle East, but Hoover remained evasive— probably because he didn't know—and merely summarized the on-going debate in the United Nations and the contingency plans for increasing oil shipments to Europe if the Arabs severed all the pipelines to the West.

17. *CQ Weekly Report,* No. 46 (November 16, 1956), 333–34.

George adjourned the meeting two and one-half hours after it began, promising to issue a short statement, in which he said that representatives of the Department of State, the Joint Chiefs of Staff, and other executive department agencies had given his committee substantially all the information that the president had briefed to legislative leaders three days earlier.[18]

For the remainder of November, Eisenhower directed his efforts toward securing a lasting peace in the Middle East and repairing the damage to the Atlantic alliance. On November 10, he approved a joint State-Defense memorandum, under which the United States would provide the initial air and surface lift of the United Nations Emergency Force (UNEF) to Egypt on a nonreimbursable basis. The United Nations, however, would pay the United States for any subsequent logistical support the country provided. There were to be no American military personnel or supporting facilities in the area under supervision of the U.N. force. The plan further provided that nations having bilateral military assistance agreements with the United States were to be granted authority to use equipment acquired through the Mutual Defense Assistance Program.[19] Advance parties of the United Nations Emergency Force under command of Canadian General Eedson Burns began arriving in Egypt on November 15. Although Nasser's objections regarding the composition of the force delayed its full deployment, the most serious obstacle to stability in the region was overcome.

Now that the multinational force was in Egypt, Eisenhower kept economic and diplomatic pressure on Great Britain, France, and Israel to expedite the withdrawal of their forces from Egyptian soil. It took another United Nations vote on an Afro-Asian resolution condemning the continued presence of the Anglo-French expeditionary force and Eisenhower's refusal to bolster the faltering British sterling and demand for oil before the initial contingent of British forces departed Egypt on December 3.[20] As usual, the French were reluctant to go along, but lack of British support and economic hardship convinced Mollet to withdraw all French forces. According to Dillon, the oil shortage had begun affecting the people of Paris, and several deaths had already occurred by early December due to lack of heat in Parisian homes. Consequently,

18. For a transcript of these hearings, see *Senate Foreign Relations Committee,* 605–60.

19. See Memorandum of Conference Between Representatives of the Department of Defense (Gordon Gray, Arthur Radford, *et al.*) and Department of State (Robert Murphy *et al.*), November 10, 1956, in Department of State, *Suez Crisis,* 1102–1103.

20. See Department of State Press Release 606, December 3, 1956, in Department of State *Bulletin* (December 17, 1956), 951–52, for a description of the evacuation of British forces.

French forces debarked from Egypt in mid-December, and by December 22 Egypt was once again free of Anglo-French troops. Nor did Ben Gurion escape Eisenhower's economic pressure. Once Eisenhower threatened to impose economic sanctions against Israel and once the British and French consented to withdrawal, there was little Ben Gurion could do other than go along. The last Israeli troops departed Egypt on March 7, 1957.

In the interim between the General Assembly vote of November 20 and the debarkation of British forces from the Suez region, Eisenhower approved a "Middle East Plan of Action" that the Departments of the Interior and Justice and the Office of Defense Mobilization had prepared during the preceding summer. The plan added 200,000 barrels of oil a day to the quota of 300,000 barrels then being shipped to Europe. On November 30, the president authorized the director, ODM, to request the Secretary of the Interior to permit the United States petroleum industry to coordinate their efforts to assist in handling the oil supply problem. Private industry cooperated fully with the administration to make the effort a success. In addition, Eisenhower began financial aid to the British,[21] but not before the British were well on their way out of Suez.

The president's seemingly belated economic assistance to Great Britain did not signal a new direction for his foreign policy. He was still perplexed as to how Eden could have made such a catastrophic diplomatic blunder in Suez. Yet, he had no intention of abandoning Great Britain once Eden had agreed to his terms and signaled his intention of withdrawing British forces from Egypt. When newly appointed British Ambassador Sir Anthony Caccia called on Eisenhower to present his credentials on November 9, Eisenhower said just because Britain and the United States had had a sharp difference over the attack on Egypt, "there was no thought that we would not keep our friendship over the long term."[22] Referring to the need for Anglo-American cooperation in the post-Suez world, Eisenhower expressed his own bewilderment that "the Russians, as cruel and brutal as they are, can get away with murder, domination, etc. However, if we breach the smallest courtesy, the whole world is aflame." To bring stability to the region, Eisenhower told Caccia, "It was necessary to think beyond a single battle such as the Suez seizure,

21. See Actions by the President, November, 1956, Office of the Staff Secretary, L. Arthur Minnich Series, White House Office Files, EP, EL.

22. See Memorandum of a Conference with the President, White House, Washington, November 9, 1956, 8:45 A.M. in folder marked "November 1956 Staff Memoranda," Box 19, DDE Diary Series, Ann Whitman File, EP, EL.

to the campaign as a whole." In closing, the president said he looked forward to a productive association with Caccia.

By this time, Eisenhower was not only looking beyond the immediate crisis, he also was exploring a post-Eden Great Britain. Meeting with Hoover, Humphrey, and Goodpaster on the afternoon of November 20,[23] Eisenhower discussed a possible successor to Eden. Ambassador Aldrich had called Eisenhower directly the day before to inform the president that Eden was emotionally and physically drained and on the verge of a physical breakdown.[24] Aldrich also had met secretly with Macmillan, who seemed all too willing to outline Eden's planned vacation to recoup his health. Once the prime minister departed Great Britain, Macmillan stated that the first order of business would be the withdrawal of British forces from Egypt. Macmillan continued that if Eisenhower "can give us a fig leaf to cover our nakedness, I believe we can get a majority of the Cabinet to vote for immediate withdrawal." Moreover, Aldrich reported that Macmillan was desperately anxious to see the president at the earliest possible opportunity to discuss the situation.

To some observers, it appeared that Eisenhower, and certainly Macmillan, were attempting to ease Eden from power. Eisenhower's opinion of the prime minister certainly deteriorated as the crisis evolved. Speaking to Dulles in the secretary's hospital room on November 17, the president confessed that he had started "with an exceedingly high opinion of [Eden] . . . and then [had] continually to downgrade this estimate [after] succeeding contacts with him."[25] Eisenhower certainly preferred to work with Macmillan, who was far more receptive to his own policies. Macmillan, he told his advisers, was "a straight, fine man, and so far as he was concerned the outstanding one of the British he served with during the war." Consequently, Eisenhower told Aldrich to pass to Macmillan that "as soon as things happen that we anticipate, we can furnish 'a lot of fig leaves.'"[26]

In approving informal and secret contacts with individual members of Eden's cabinet, the president was playing a dangerous diplomatic game, but a game nevertheless. Moreover, it was a game in which Eisenhower was a willing participant. In discussing options with Humphrey

23. Memorandum of a Conference with the President, White House, Washington, November 20, 1956, 5:30 P.M., in folder marked "November 1956 Staff Memoranda," Box 19, DDE Diary Series, Ann Whitman File, EP, EL.

24. See Telegram from the Embassy in the United Kingdom to the Department of State, November 19, 1956, as quoted in Department of State, *Suez Crisis*, 1163.

25. As quoted in Freiberger, *Dawn over Suez*, 199.

26. As quoted in Chester J. Pach and Elmo Richardson, *The Presidency of Dwight D. Eisenhower* (Lawrence, Kans., 1991), 135.

and Hoover at the White House meeting on November 20, Eisenhower outlined the sequence of events as he saw it. First, "we are ready to talk about help as soon as the precondition (French and British withdrawal) is established." Next, "we will talk to the Arabs to obtain the removal of any objections they may have regarding the provision of oil to Western Europe." Then and only then, "we will talk the details of money assistance with the British." Eisenhower's program was a cold-blooded game of power politics, pure and simple. He could be ruthless when he had to be.

The promise of economic assistance was the first step toward the reconstruction of friendly relations between the chief partners of the Atlantic alliance. In late November, Eisenhower and Churchill exchanged letters, in which both statesmen expressed their conviction that it was time to restore the traditional friendship that existed between the United States and Great Britain. In replying to Churchill's letter, Eisenhower hoped "that this one [Suez] may be washed off the slate as soon as possible and that we can then together adopt other means of achieving our legitimate objectives in the Middle East. Nothing saddens me more than the thought that I and my old friends of years have met a problem concerning which we do not see eye to eye. I shall never be happy until our old time closeness has been restored."[27]

Placing the Suez crisis in perspective, Vice-President Nixon reiterated Eisenhower's remarks in a December speech, in which he stated:

Now that our allies have subordinated what they considered to be their national interests to the verdict of the United Nations, it is essential that we recognize that neither we nor our allies were without fault in our handling of the events which led to the crisis. Now is the time for us all to recognize that recrimination and fault-finding will serve no purpose whatever.

We are proud of our association with Britain and France and of our common dedication to the principles of freedom and justice which joined us together as allies in both World War I and World War II. Together, the United States, Great Britain, and France have a solemn obligation to give leadership and support to the United Nations program which will assure the solution by peaceful means of the problems which brought about the armed conflict in that area.[28]

Although Eisenhower differed with the vice-president as to the responsibility the United States bore for the crisis, he recognized the necessity to mend political fences as rapidly as possible.

---

27. Eisenhower to Churchill, November 27, 1956, as quoted in Eisenhower, *Waging Peace,* 680–81.

28. As quoted in Department of State *Bulletin,* No. 912 (December 17, 1956), 947.

It is difficult to determine if any one nation emerged victorious from the long and debilitating Suez crisis. There were certainly no clear-cut victors. Nasser, the victim of the aggression, clearly lost the war from the military standpoint, but his conduct of the war greatly enhanced his prestige in Egypt, the Arab world, and the Afro-Asian nations. From 1956 until his death in 1970, the Egyptian president exerted a charismatic hold over the Egyptian masses. His staunch opposition to the imperial European powers transformed him into a pan-Arab hero. "It was," quoted one biographer, "not he who took possession of Arabism, but Arabism which took possession of him. It was Arabism that invested him and established him as its hero."[29]

Of the conspirators, Israel seemingly benefited the most from the conflict. The war forced Egypt to open the Gulf of Aqaba to Israeli shipping and led to the presence of an international force on the Israeli-Egyptian border to prevent guerrilla raids. The rapid conquest of the Sinai also contributed to the myth of Israeli military invincibility, which the Six-Day War of June 1967 certainly reinforced. It was not until the opening days of the War of Ramadan in 1973 that the first blemish appeared on the image of Israeli military superiority.

The two countries that suffered the greatest loss of prestige were Great Britain and France. The Suez affair was the harbinger of the collapse of their colonial empires in the Middle East. Eden's Conservative government was the first casualty of the post-Suez world. Frustrated by the weight of adverse national and international public condemnation of his policies and gravely ill from the months of unbelievable tension—to say nothing of Eisenhower's diplomatic slap in the face at postponing a tripartite conference in November—Eden vacationed for three weeks in Jamaica beginning November 23. Unknown to most outside his own inner circle of advisers, Eden was still suffering the effects of a gallstone operation in 1953. A subsequent operation had brought minimal relief, and his workaholic habits during the crisis only exacerbated an increasingly dangerous medical condition. Although Eden returned to London on December 14, the end was obviously near. The *Times, Economist,* Manchester *Guardian,* and the *Daily Telegraph* all warned Eden that unless he could provide leadership in time of crisis, he ought to resign.[30] On January 9, 1957, the prime minister summoned Macmillan to 10 Downing Street and informed him that because of deteriorating health, he had decided to resign.

29. Jean Lacouture, *Nasser: A Political Biography* (New York, 1973), 188. See Michael Hudson, *Arab Politics: The Search for Legitimacy* (New Haven, 1977), 242–43, for an elaboration of the theme of charismatic personality as a source of political legitimacy.

30. As quoted in New York *Times,* December 15, 1956.

Until his death, Eden denied charges that his government had colluded with France and Israel to overthrow Nasser. Speaking to the House of Commons on December 20, 1956, he emphatically stated, "I wish to make it clear that there was not foreknowledge that Israel would attack Egypt, there was not."[31] Before submitting his resignation, he affirmed the righteousness of his cause. "I am convinced, more convinced than I have been about anything in all my public life that we were right, my colleagues and I, in the judgments and decisions we took, and that history will prove it."[32] When Eden died in 1977, the *Times* obituary succinctly summarized his tragic career. "He was the last Prime Minister to believe Britain was a great power, and the first to confront a crisis which proved she was not."[33]

Guy Mollet's government quickly followed the fate of Anthony Eden's. Mollet fell in May 1957, to be replaced by a coalition headed by his former defense minister, Bourges-Maunoury. Unlike his British counterpart, Mollet made no secret of the collusion. Christian Pineau, disgusted with the British for having ordered the cease-fire, washed his hands of the entire affair and was quite frank about the details of the conspiracy in the months following the debacle.[34] The political humiliation of Suez proved to be the last straw to a nation that had experienced defeat by the Germans in World War II, the loss of Indo-China, and the disintegration of Algeria within the span of two decades. Until Charles De Gaulle established the Fifth Republic in 1958, no French government was able to extract the country from the malaise that engulfed it. As General Beaufre stated, the Suez affair was "largely responsible for the events of May 13, 1958 [De Gaulle's return to power]."[35] If that were true, the Suez crisis brought to the forefront the only Frenchman capable of restoring French pride and grandeur.

Of the Atlantic partners, only the United States emerged from the crisis with increased prestige within the international community, but Anglo-French bitterness tempered the friendly relations that had once existed among the three most powerful NATO members. The most obvious result of the crisis was the termination of European colonialism in the Middle East and the introduction of the United States as a major

31. *Times* (London), December 21, 1956. See also *Hansard's Parliamentary Debates*, Vol. 562, p. 1457. Selwyn Lloyd also denied the conspiracy. On December 6, Lloyd stated, "It is quite wrong to state that Israel was incited by this action by Her Majesty's Government." As quoted in New York *Times*, December 6, 1956.

32. New York *Times*, December 15, 1956.

33. Neff, *Warriors at Suez*, 435.

34. Dillon interview with the author, June 29, 1982.

35. As quoted in Cooper, *The Lion's Last Roar*, 272–75.

power broker in that troubled region. Although the crisis alone did not substitute the United States for Great Britain and France, it certainly was a contributing factor. Within the Arab world, the United States earned enhanced prestige. Ambassador Hare cabled from Cairo to inform Eisenhower that the United States had suddenly emerged as the "champion of the right." King Saud of Saudi Arabia commended the president for the American position in the General Assembly against his traditional allies. Even Nasser lauded Eisenhower for the president's firm stand against aggression in spite of the personal and political risks involved during the election. "By taking that position," said Nasser, "you put your principles before your friends."[36]

Unfortunately, Eisenhower's misconception of the Soviet threat to the Middle East, and his failure to comprehend the realities of Arab nationalism and pan-Arabism, forfeited many gains the United States achieved as a result of his moral stand against aggression in the fall of 1956. On January 5, 1957, Eisenhower addressed Congress and outlined his concept for joint executive-legislative action to confront the increased danger from international communism. When passed in March, the "Eisenhower Doctrine" authorized the employment of American military forces in the Middle East "against overt aggression from any nation controlled by International Communism," to be used only "at the desire of the nation attacked."[37] It was a laudable goal for a cold war chief executive, but like many presidents who succeeded him, Eisenhower failed to comprehend the realities of Middle Eastern politics and the limits of American military power on anything but a temporary basis.

Reaction to the doctrine within the Arab community was mixed. Syria insisted that the maintenance of stability was strictly a regional affair. In Beirut, the Lebanese foreign minister hailed Eisenhower's initiative as a "good and timely move by the United States."[38] Nasser, of course, viewed the Eisenhower Doctrine for what it was, a blatant attempt to replace Anglo-French colonialism with an American presence. Put more precisely, the Eisenhower Doctrine was a declaration of American intentions to step into the shoes that Great Britain was vacating.[39] The doc-

36. See Hare's oral history transcript at the Eisenhower Library. See also Eisenhower's letter to King Saud on November 17, 1956, on file in Office of the Staff Secretary, L. Arthur Minnich Series, White House Office Files, EP, EL. Nasser's remarks are found in Heikal, *Cairo Documents*, 189.

37. Parmet, *Eisenhower and the American Crusades*, 494. See also Eisenhower, *Waging Peace*, 180–82.

38. Cooper, *The Lion's Last Roar*, 247.

39. Heikal was exeptionally critical of American intentions in the post-Suez world in *Cutting the Lion's Tail*, 216.

trine did little to convince Nasser that the United States was not ultimately malevolent. Relations between Egypt and the United States deteriorated until Nasser severed diplomatic ties with the United States
in 1967.

Far more important to Eisenhower than American-Arab relations was
the strain the Suez affair placed on the Atlantic alliance. Both the Eden
and Mollet governments were distraught over the lack of support from
their American allies during the latter quarter of 1956, and both European leaders were predictably vocal in their criticism of Eisenhower and
Dulles. Mollet was particularly incensed with the Americans, telling a
domestic audience, "If I had been the American Secretary of State, I
should have tried to understand better the real problems that faced the
British and the French. I think the present situation is attributable
principally to lack of mutual comprehension."[40] Pineau, always prone
to exaggeration, said Suez had made the French forget the Normandy
landing and the Marshall Plan.[41]

The official British position was no less critical than the French, but
the British press was much more supportive of the Americans generally and Eisenhower particularly for his role in mending the frayed alliance. Officially, Eden lamented the misunderstanding that had made
Eisenhower so obstinate and intractable. Repeatedly misreading Washington's intentions, both Eden and Lloyd attributed the blame for the
lack of American support directly to Eisenhower.[42] The hardening of the
American position against Great Britain in the immediate aftermath of
the cease-fire also disturbed Macmillan, but the Chancellor of the Exchequer was not so foolish as to refuse the offer of American financial
aid on November 30, even though it was "a little wounding to feel that
we were to be given a 'reward' for our submission to American pressure."[43] The only British public official who actively sought to reconcile
the differences between the two allies was Churchill, who wrote Eisenhower on November 23 to prevent the misunderstanding from creating
a permanent gulf in the Anglo-American alliance.

Britain's conservative press revealed the extent of ill will and bitterness caused by the crisis. Nevertheless, the tabloids recognized that Great
Britain's interest could best be protected within the context of the
Anglo-American alliance. The *Economist* praised Eisenhower: "No man
was more shocked by what the British and French did in Egypt, yet no

40. As quoted in New York *Times*, December 10, 1956.
41. Christian Pineau, *1956/Suez* (Paris, 1976), 191.
42. Eden, *Full Circle*, 640; Lloyd, *Suez, 1956*, 259.
43. Macmillan, *Riding the Storm*, 177

man, after the first anger, was more intent upon rescuing the partnership." The Manchester *Guardian* urged the British government to make every effort to restore the atmosphere of political trust. The great task of statesmanship was the reconstruction of the alliance, and the *Economist* ventured to report that the British needed to realize that they "are not the Americans nor can they be; hence, Great Britain must play a junior role in any Anglo-American alliance."[44] The net result of this good will manifested itself in the Bermuda Conference, beginning March 20, 1957, in which Eisenhower and Prime Minister Macmillan reaffirmed their cooperative partnership.

Ironically, the pressures of Suez did not seriously disrupt NATO, although the advent of De Gaulle on the French political scene in 1958 significantly altered the solidarity of the pact. Dulles met with Pineau and Lloyd in December in an attempt to smooth over differences among the three leading NATO members. Neither Army Chief of Staff Maxwell Taylor nor NATO commander General Lauris Norstad felt that the alliance was in jeopardy as a result of tensions among the major governments in the crisis.[45] Frederick Nolting, U.S. ambassador to NATO, viewed the situation as an incredible breakdown in allied communications, but he foresaw the birth of a new impetus to form a consultative process within and among NATO countries that would prevent any future Suez-type fiasco. Eisenhower concurred, telling Republican leaders on New Year's Eve, "Underneath, the governments [Great Britain and France] are thankful we did what we did. But publicly, we have to be the whipping boy."[46] Perhaps, but European animosity with Eisenhower's policy lingered for many years.

Last, the Suez crisis reflected the increasing tension between the United States and the Soviet Union during the cold war. Despite the threat that "rockets would fly" if the British and French did not halt their aggression, the Eisenhower team viewed these statements as nothing more than appeals for favor in the Arab community. Staff Secretary Goodpaster felt that the strong American military posture in the Mediterranean had successfully deterred the Soviet Union from executing their promise of sending volunteers to assist Nasser against the European conspirators.[47] Perhaps it did, but the Soviet Union had its own hands full

44. *Economist,* November 10, 1956; Manchester *Guardian,* November 15, 1956; *Economist,* November 17, 1956.

45. Taylor interview with the author, June 17, 1981. Norstad succeeded Gruenther as NATO commander in November, 1956. His remarks are on file in his oral history at Mudd Library, Princeton.

46. As quoted in Ambrose, *Eisenhower: The President,* 373.

47. Andrew Goodpaster, *For the Common Defense* (Lexington, 1977), 59.

with internal problems in its satellite states. Strong public rejoinders by the United States and the early United Nations cease-fire, however, may have prevented a direct American-Soviet confrontation.

In summary, the Suez crisis was one of the most important crises of the post–World War II era. From the international perspective, the crisis revealed the extent of European colonial decline. The crisis also drew the United States further into the Middle East and altered America's relationships with both the Arab community and its European allies. Although the crisis strained the Atlantic alliance, it did not break it. NATO survived the crisis. If Suez accomplished anything for American policymakers, it demonstrated the necessity of reevaluating American national interests outside the traditional limits of the continental United States and Western Europe.

For Eisenhower, the crisis dominated one of the most anxious periods of his presidency. Once again, he had proved to be the man of the hour, able to exert calm and reasoned leadership in times of international crisis. In the process, he accomplished most of his short-term objectives—ending the fighting; preventing the introduction of Soviet forces into the region; forcing Eden, Mollet, and Ben Gurion to withdraw their forces; and enhancing the prestige of the United States and the United Nations. He was not as successful in accomplishing his longer-term objectives. Never fully understanding Nasser and his nationalist movement, Eisenhower confused anticolonial sentiment against Great Britain and France with the Egyptian president's willingness to court favor from any government, including the Soviet Union, that would support his nationalist and pan-Arab policies. As a result, regional stability and the establishment of cordial relations between Nasser and the United States eluded Eisenhower's grasp. Moreover, with Nasser's increased prestige as a result of the crisis, Eisenhower was unsuccessful in creating an acceptable alternative to Nasser as the leader of the Arab world.

And yet, Eisenhower achieved many of his goals. If one equated success as the implementation of a strategy that achieved Eisenhower's political objectives, then the president was successful in that the United States was now an active participant in Middle Eastern affairs—albeit at the expense of Britain and France—the Soviet Union had demonstrated its inability to challenge the West, and regional stability returned, if only for a brief period. On the whole, Eisenhower's credits outweighed his debits.

8

CONCLUSION

How effectively a president manages crises often determines the relative success of his presidency. Detractors might point out that a policy that eventually alienated Egypt, led to secret unilateral actions by America's closest allies, and strained the bonds of the NATO alliance could hardly be considered successful; however, the president considered his management of the Suez crisis a remarkable achievement. Throughout the crisis, Eisenhower refused to overreact, maintaining his stand against resorting to force in response to an issue that he felt could be resolved by peaceful negotiations. He always insisted that a solution could be found and then found one that not only achieved his own policy objectives but enhanced the prestige of the United States and the United Nations. Moreover, he remained unflappable in the face of dissenting allies, contentious military chiefs, and political opposition in a presidential election year. Though he failed to keep the crisis from escalating, he, more than any other statesman, restored peace to the troubled region. It was a splendid performance.

This examination of the critical junctures of the Suez crisis clearly reveals the scope of Eisenhower's involvement in the direction of foreign policy and his ability to dominate the decision-making process during a major international crisis. In managing crises, Eisenhower employed a methodology drawn from three decades of military experience. In planning military operations, Eisenhower had followed a planning process reminiscent of a military commander's estimate of a situation. Such a process included situation development, crisis assessment, development of courses of action, selection of a course of action, operational planning, and ultimately, the execution of a specific course of action. He followed the identical sequential planning process during the Suez crisis. From the outset, the president employed a variety of leadership techniques and bureaucratic skills to ensure that his judgments prevailed and his decisions were executed. Through adept personal diplomacy, he mobilized public and congressional support for his policy of renouncing armed aggression to settle the international dispute. The president also used personal contacts and supervised an elaborate staff system that aided him in gathering information, making decisions, and implementing presidential directives. His efforts were largely responsible for bringing the crisis to a satisfactory conclusion.

During the initial stage of the crisis, the *ad hoc* meeting with his inner circle of advisers was the forum through which Eisenhower shaped his strategy and policy in response to Nasser's nationalization of the Suez Canal. On the surface, it seemed ironic that Eisenhower, with all his emphasis on staff training and planning and with his stated desire to turn the National Security Council into a policy formulation body, held his most critical discussions and made his most important decisions with a small group of advisers in informal meetings in the Oval Office. Yet Eisenhower established clearly defined lines between policy development on the one hand and operations on the other. He expected most operations to be carried out at departmental level within the guidelines of policy (developed through the NSC process), with coordination at the interagency level (executed by the NSC's Operations Coordinating Board). Those operations that required his direct participation were handled by *ad hoc* meetings in the Oval Office. Use of the *ad hoc* meetings for crisis management evolved from the president's belief that combining operations with policy would result in short-range operations taking over the prejudice of more comprehensively examined, longer-range policy formulation and planning.

This division between policy development and crisis management was particularly true during the Suez crisis, when the president met frequently with Goodpaster, Dulles, Hoover, Radford, and other administration officials to determine the American response. Without formal consultation with either the National Security Council or the legislative branch, the president correctly assessed the impact of Nasser's action and determined that Western survivability was not in jeopardy and that peaceful negotiations between Nasser and America's European allies were the more productive path to resolve the crisis. After considering a number of courses of diplomatic action, Eisenhower acted with singleness of purpose in forming a clear policy line against resorting to arms. His decision to oppose the military option was particularly striking since Eisenhower took a stand his principal military advisers and European allies strongly opposed. Indeed, throughout the Suez dispute, Eisenhower risked disrupting the solidarity of the Atlantic alliance by opposing the policy of force that Great Britain and France had adopted as early as July 1956.

Only after he explored a wide range of policy options and then decided on the American response, did Eisenhower consult with other executive and legislative institutions in the federal government. Confident that the series of diplomatic conferences he had initiated would purchase time and possibly defuse the volatile situation, the president then expanded the decision-making process by including the National Security Council, the Joint Chiefs of Staff, Congress, and the cabinet. In combining the formal and informal advisory process, Eisenhower established an organizational system that he used with great skill, partly explained by the immense contribution that was made by Goodpaster in convening the *ad hoc* advisory team. In other words, the president profited not only from well-tested organizational patterns, but also from loyal and talented assistants.

During the first four months of the crisis (August–November 1956), Eisenhower initiated specific measures to reconcile Anglo-French interests with the vigorous nationalistic policies of Nasser. These diplomatic endeavors included the tripartite discussions (August 1–3), the first London Conference (August 16–23), and the second London Conference (September 19–21), which established the framework for the Suez Canal Users Association. During the same period, the National Security Council convened seventeen times, with the Middle East a principal topic of discussion. With two exceptions, the discussion focused more on economic issues than political actions. Except for one November session, Eisenhower presided over all the NSC proceedings, setting the tone of discussion and directing the internal debate in order to gather advice and recommendations from the diverse body. When the debate strayed from the issue on which Eisenhower wanted to focus, as during the November 1 meeting when NSC members started discussing the military situation, the president immediately interrupted to remind the council that he wanted to concentrate on policy actions, not military matters. Beginning in November, he also authorized additional attendance at the council meetings to hear for himself the pros and cons of the debate so he could make the best decisions and ensure that his military and economic advisers received the full benefit of his direct guidance. In short, while Eisenhower recognized the benefit of the NSC serving as an advisory body and a forum for coordinating policy development, including long-range planning, the president still felt that the onus and responsibility for crisis management lay with him. During the Suez crisis the National Security Council was merely the vehicle that Eisenhower used to ensure consensus and coordination. It was not the premier decision-making forum.

In addition to his adept employment of the National Security Council, the president demonstrated his comprehension of the military aspects of foreign policy by his relationship with the Joint Chiefs of Staff. Of course, his former professional experience significantly contributed to his understanding of the military facets of complicated international issues and to his ability to control an assertive military staff. Early in the crisis, Taylor and Burke expressed their dissent with Eisenhower's decision to oppose logistical assistance to Great Britain and France. Both dissident Chiefs felt the United States could best protect its national interests by supporting its European allies during the planned invasion of Egypt. Just as he had rejected the recommendations of his military advisers during the Quemoy-Matsu crisis, Eisenhower vetoed this proposal and said that the United States would honor its commitment on nonintervention, as stated in the Tripartite Declaration of 1950. The principal reason for his objection to Taylor's and Burke's suggestions was Eisenhower's conviction that a military expedition would result in no lasting solution and American support of aggression would seriously jeopardize the moral reputation of the United States. Most important, the introduction of United States troops might invite Soviet intervention into the region, thus negating Eisenhower's principal regional objective.

With respect to the perceived Soviet threat to the region, the Joint Chiefs strongly supported the president's directive to increase the strength and readiness of American forces in the Middle East. This was particularly true of Burke, whose 6th Fleet was the principal United States military force in the eastern Mediterranean. Yet it was Eisenhower, not the Joint Chiefs, who made the decision to upgrade the readiness of American military forces in the region to forestall the Soviet Union from injecting its own forces into the troubled area. Accepting the Joint Chiefs' recommendations on upgrading readiness had its limits, however, and the president rejected Radford's proposal to recall military servicemen from leave at the height of the crisis. There was no need to frighten the American people or to overreact to Soviet incursions that Eisenhower reasoned were beyond the capabilities of the Soviet military. The net result of the president's interaction with his military advisers during the crisis was that Eisenhower's own military expertise enabled him to reject or accept the recommendations of the Joint Chiefs on both political and military grounds.

Eisenhower also proved himself an adroit politician in dealing with the legislative branch. Fully aware of the value of "consensus-building," particularly in a national election year, the president sought to involve Congress—or at least give the impression that he was involving the legislative branch—in the formation of foreign policy. In dealing with Congress, Eisenhower returned presidential primacy to the formulation of foreign policy. Not since Franklin Roosevelt had a president so dominated the decision-making process. He informed rather than consulted.

By refusing to convene Congress for a special session to debate the Suez crisis, the president, in effect, excluded the legislative branch from the policymaking process. Nevertheless, he was scrupulous about informing key leaders of his decisions and soliciting their recommendations for future political decisions.

The two most publicized conferences with the bipartisan congressional leadership were the sessions on August 12 to discuss the American position at the upcoming London Conference and the session on November 9 to explore possibilities for creating a new Middle East policy from the shambles of the Suez War. The latter meeting was particularly significant because Eisenhower used the forum to inform the legislators of the administration's policy and to submit new proposals that would greatly increase the power of the executive branch. Before each meeting with the legislators, Eisenhower met with close advisers to outline the proposed agenda. He was an extremely active participant in the quest for bipartisan support of his own policies. The president's succinct policy memorandum of November 8 actually served as the format for the following day's meeting and became the foundation for future Middle East policy during Eisenhower's second term. How effective Eisenhower was in obtaining congressional support during the Suez crisis was evidenced in the wide approval rating he received from congressional Democrats following his reelection on November 6. His methods also were indicative of his skill as a political manipulator. By avoiding confrontational rhetoric and emphasizing the need for political unity in the shadow of possible Soviet incursions into the Middle East, Eisenhower was successful in obtaining full bipartisan support for his actions.

The president's careful cultivation of congressional support revealed a skilled political practitioner who was able to convince legislative leaders that they shared fully in the decision-making process. During the Suez crisis, the president followed his practice, which had proven so successful in previous crises, of explaining essential foreign policy decisions to congressional leaders during an atmosphere of crisis and requesting their support. The Suez crisis was reminiscent of the Indo-China crisis of 1954 and the Quemoy-Matsu crisis the following year. In both instances, Eisenhower refused to commit American ground forces without prior approval of Congress because he believed that the American people would never approve direct military intervention unless the provocations against the United States were clear and serious.

The president was less successful in persuading European allies of the merits of his course of action. In dealing with British and French leaders, Eisenhower focused principally on Eden, since he reasoned that Mollet was not strong enough to act against Nasser on his own. Mollet, in fact, seemed better prepared, both politically and economically, for the Suez crisis than Eden. Though Secretary Dulles might have misled British and French leaders as to the extent to which Eisenhower opposed the use of force to resolve the crisis, Eden's and Mollet's claims that Eisenhower himself vacillated between opposition to and support for intervention were unfounded. In every correspondence between the Atlantic partners, Eisenhower stated emphatically that the United States was opposed to the use of military force to settle the dispute. In personal messages, letters, and within the United Nations, Eisenhower remained steadfast in his belief that armed intervention against Egypt was self-defeating. That Eden and Mollet concealed the specifics of their collusion with Israel from the American president was evidence that both European leaders fully understood Eisenhower's opposition to their own policies.

If Eisenhower failed to convince his European allies of the prudence that governed his own policy, it was hardly his fault. The prime minister's perfidy hardly contributed to cordial relations, but the president could have done more and possibly avoided much of the later bitterness that existed between himself and the European leaders. What the president should have done was state his policy against intervention—which he did on numerous occasions—and also reveal the extent to which he would oppose military intervention. That Eisenhower would impose economic sanctions, oppose monetary loans from the World Bank, and threaten to devalue the British pound sterling unless he abandoned his militant policies never dawned on Eden until the situation was hopelessly lost and his own political career lay in ruins. It was left to Eisenhower and Macmillan, Eden's successor, to pick up the pieces. To their credit, they did so, but mutual distrust lingered between the chiefs of state.

Finally, the popular view of a chief executive who relegated major foreign policy decisions to Secretary of State Dulles does not bear up under a close examination of the facts. Dulles was merely the most visible figure in an elaborate staff system in which all aspects of operations and policy coalesced at the Oval Office. Though Eisenhower gave Dulles some latitude in executing his decisions on Suez, Eisenhower alone decided what the American response to the nationalization of the Suez Canal would be. The president made the initial commitment against the use of force without prior consultation with the secretary of state. Dulles merely worked within the parameters established by the president. Although Eisenhower and Dulles were men of strong conviction, the latter deferred to the former on issues of great political importance. It was Eisenhower, rather than Dulles, who reacted so violently when he received word of the Anglo-French invasion of Egypt. It was Eisenhower who dictated to Dulles what the general lines of American policy would be in the United Nations debate. The decision to take the matter to the Security Council in order to bring world opinion to bear against Great Britain, France, and Israel was the president's alone. Extended telephone conversations between Eisenhower and Lodge at the United Nations, together with the president's numerous missives to Eden, Mollet, and Ben Gurion, revealed the true extent of Eisenhower's impact on foreign policy and crisis management. When cancer removed Dulles from the scene at the height of the crisis, there was no discernible alteration in the content of the American response to the European aggression. Indeed, the president increased his efforts to terminate the fighting by applying strong economic pressure and threatening sanctions against his European allies. It was the combination of American political and economic pressure that eventually led to the cessation of hostilities and the withdrawal of foreign troops from Egypt.

In conclusion, the extent and complexity of the Suez crisis engaged the president in a full test of his ability to manage crises and direct foreign policy. The evidence casts serious doubt on the traditional view of Eisenhower as a weak chief executive who was content to allow Dulles a free hand in handling all crucial foreign policy decisions. On the contrary, the image that emerges from this analysis reinforces the current revisionist trend that Eisenhower was an extraordinarily active president whose effectiveness depended on his personal administrative and leadership abilities. By ensuring that it was *only* at the presidential level that the political, economic, and military dimensions of crisis management coalesced, Eisenhower was able to deal actively with department chiefs, legislative leaders, erstwhile allies, and dissenting military advisers to achieve his major policy objectives. The Eisenhower who emerged from the Suez crisis was a chief executive who was flexible and experimental in his decision making, not one tied to a rigid military model from which he seldom departed. By clearly articulating the difference between daily operations that demanded his personal attention and those decisions more conducive to formal and longer-range policymaking bodies, Eisenhower remained in charge throughout the crisis by reserving the right to adapt his methods for managing crises to the problems he faced. He was successful due to the force of his own personality, his bureaucratic skill, and his personal direction of an elaborate staff network that deferred all major decisions to the president before coordinating their execution. During the Suez crisis, Eisenhower proved himself to be a skilled and competent chief executive who dominated the decision-making process and placed the indelible imprint of his forceful leadership on United States foreign policy.

BIBLIOGRAPHY

PRIMARY SOURCES

MANUSCRIPTS

Eisenhower Library, Abilene, Kansas

(NOTE: There is a printed guide to the holdings of the library—*Historical Materials in the Dwight D. Eisenhower Library.*)

Eisenhower, Dwight D. Papers as President of the United States, 1953–61
    Ann Whitman File
    Administration Series
    Ann Whitman Diary Series
    Ann Whitman Name Series
    Cabinet Series
    DDE Diary Series
    Dulles-Herter Series
    International Series
    International Meetings Series
    Legislative Meetings Series
    National Security Council Series
    White House Central Files
    Confidential File
    General File
    Official File
    President's Personal File
Dulles, John Foster. Papers
Gruenther, Alfred M. Papers
    White House Office Files
        National Security Council Staff Papers
            Executive Secretary's Subject File Series
            Operations Coordinating Board Central File Series
            Operations Coordinating Board Secretariat Series
        Office of Staff Secretary
        Minnich, L. Arthur Series

Oral Histories
  Aldrich, Winthrop. OH 250
  Allen, George V. OH 279
  Anderson, Dillon. OH 165
  Black, Eugene. OH 341
  Burgess, W. Randolph. OH 407
  Dillon, C. Douglas. OH 211
  Eisenhower, Dwight D. OH 11, OH 14
  Goodpaster, Andrew. OH 37
  Gray, Gordon. OH 73, OH 342
  Hare, Raymond. OH 189
  Henderson, Loy. OH 191
  Murphy, Robert. OH 224
  Norstad, Lauris. OH 385
  Patterson, Bradley. OH 225
  Rabb, Maxwell M. OH 479
  Twining, Nathan. OH 274

Oral History Interviews Conducted by the Author

Burke, Arleigh A.
Dillon, C. Douglas
Eisenhower, Milton
Goodpaster, Andrew J.
Taylor, Maxwell D.

Library of Congress, Washington, D.C.

Twining, Nathan F. Papers

National Archives of the United States, Washington, D.C.

Records of the United States Joint Chiefs of Staff, Record Group 218

*Naval Historical Center, Operational Archives Branch,
Washington Navy Yard, Washington, D.C.*

Burke, Admiral Arleigh A. Personal Files
Radford, Admiral Arthur. Personal Files. October 1, 1956–February 22, 1957
Radford, Admiral Arthur. Personal Log. April 1, 1956–February 22, 1957
Chronology of Naval Activities, Suez Incident
Chronology of Significant Events Relating to the Current World Crisis
      October 2–22, 1956
      October 23–31, 1956
      November 1, 1956–December 3, 1956
      December 4–31, 1956

Seeley G. Mudd Manuscript Library, Princeton, New Jersey

Dulles, John Foster. Papers, 1888–1959
    General Correspondence and Memoranda Series
        Memoranda of Conversations Subseries
    Selected Correspondence and Related Material, 1956
        Hoover, Herbert, Jr.
        Middle East, 1956
        Sue Canal, 1956
    Telephone Conversations Memoranda, 1956
    White House Memoranda Series, Meetings with the President, 1956

U.S. Army Military History Institute, Carlisle Barracks, Pennsylvania

Goodpaster, Andrew. Papers, Recollections, and Reflections: Oral History

U.S. Department of State, Washington, D.C.

Retired Office Files, 61D47
    Memorandum of Conversation. Subject: Nationalization of the Suez Canal
        Company, August 1, 1956.
    Memorandum of Conversation. Subject: Suez Crisis, September 24, 1956.
    Suez Crisis of 1956
    Talking Paper for NSC Meeting, October 12, 1956
Retired Office Files, 71D411

U.S. Marine Corps Historical Center,
Washington Navy Yard, Washington, D.C.

Pate, Randolph D. Folder
Suez Situation Reports (1–15)

GOVERNMENT PUBLICATIONS

Congressional Record. 84th Cong., 2nd Sess., 1956.
Executive Session of the Senate Foreign Relations Committee. Volumes VIII–IX.
    84th Cong., 2nd Sess., 1956; 85th Cong., 1st Sess., 1957.
Parliamentary Debates (Hansards). 5th Series. Volumes 558–62. House of
    Commons.
Public Papers of the President of the United States, 1956.
U.S. Department of State. *Foreign Relations of the United States 1952–1954.*
    Volume II: *National Security Affairs.*
U.S. Department of State. *Foreign Relations of the United States, 1955–1957:*
    Suez Crisis, July 26–December 31, 1956.
U.S. Department of State *Bulletins.* December 26, 1955–December 17, 1956.

MEMOIRS

Adams, Sherman. *Firsthand Report: The Story of the Eisenhower Administration.* New York, 1961.

Beaufre, Andre. *The Suez Expedition, 1956.* New York, 1969.

Ben Gurion, David. *Israel: Years of Challenge.* New York, 1963.

Cutler, Robert. *No Time for Rest.* Boston, 1965.

Dayan, Moshe. *Moshe Dayan: Story of My Life.* New York, 1976.

Eban, Abba. *Abba Eban: An Autobiography.* New York, 1977.

Eden, Anthony. *Full Circle.* Boston, 1960.

Eisenhower, Dwight D. *Mandate for Change, 1953–1956.* New York, 1963.

——. *Waging Peace, 1956–1961.* New York, 1965.

Eisenhower, Milton. *The President Is Calling.* New York, 1974.

Heikal, Mohammed. *Cutting the Lion's Tail: Suez Through Egyptian Eyes.* New York, 1987.

——. *The Cairo Documents.* New York, 1973.

Hughes, Emmet John. *The Ordeal of Power: A Political Memoir of the Eisenhower Years.* New York, 1973.

Lloyd, Selwyn. *Suez 1956.* New York, 1978.

Lodge, Henry Cabot. *As It Was.* New York, 1976.

——. *The Storm Has Many Eyes.* New York, 1973.

Macmillan, Harold. *Riding the Storm, 1956–1959.* New York, 1971.

Murphy, Robert. *Diplomat Among Warriors.* New York, 1964.

Nutting, Anthony. *No End of a Lesson.* New York, 1967.

Pineau, Christian. *1956/Suez.* Paris, 1976.

Sadat, Anwar. *In Search of Identity.* New York, 1977.

Taylor, Maxwell. *Swords and Plowshares.* New York, 1972.

NEWSPAPERS

Atlanta *Constitution,* April, 1956.

London *Economist,* July–November, 1956.

London *Observer,* July–December, 1956.

London *Spectator,* September, 1956.

London *Times,* July–December, 1956.

Louisville *Courier Journal,* August 30, 1956.

Manchester *Guardian,* July–November, 1956.

New York *Herald Tribune,* June–November, 1956.

New York *Times,* December, 1956–January, 1957.

San Francisco *Chronicle,* February 28, 1956.

Washington *Post,* January–November, 1956.

SECONDARY SOURCES

BOOKS

Adams, Michael. *Suez and After.* Boston, 1958.

Ambrose, Stephen. *Eisenhower: The President.* New York, 1984.

―――. *Ike's Spies.* Garden City, 1981.

―――. *The Wisdom of Dwight D. Eisenhower: Quotations from Ike's Speeches and Writings, 1939–1969.* New Orleans, 1990.

Anderson, Roy R. *Politics and Change in the Middle East.* Englewood Cliffs, 1982.

Baker, Raymond. *Egypt's Uncertain Revolution.* Cambridge, 1978.

Betts, Richard K. *Soldiers, Statesmen, and Cold War Crisis.* Cambridge, 1977.

Blechman, Barry, and Stephen Kaplan. *Force Without War.* Washington, D.C., 1978.

Branyon, Robert, and Lawrence Larsen. *The Eisenhower Administration, 1953–1961: A Documentary History.* New York, 1971.

Brendon, Piers. *Ike: His Life and Times.* New York, 1986.

Carlton, David. *Anthony Eden: A Biography.* London, 1981.

―――. *Britain and the Suez Crisis.* Oxford, 1988.

Childs, Marquis. *Eisenhower: Captive Hero.* New York, 1958.

Condit, Kenneth. *The History of the Joint Chiefs of Staff: The Joint Chiefs of Staff and National Policy, 1955–1956.* Wilmington, 1981.

Cooper, Chester L. *The Lion's Last Roar: Suez, 1956.* New York, 1978.

Cottam, Richard. *Nationalism in Iran.* Pittsburgh, 1979.

Crosswell, D. K. R. *The Chief of Staff: The Military Career of General Walter Bedell Smith.* Westport, 1991.

Dekmejian, R. Hrair. *Egypt Under Nasser.* Albany, 1971.

Divine, Robert. *Eisenhower and the Cold War.* London, 1981.

Drummond, Roscoe. *Duel at the Brink.* New York, 1960.

Ferrell, Robert H. *American Diplomacy: The Twentieth Century.* New York, 1988.

―――, ed., *The Eisenhower Diaries.* New York, 1981.

Freiberger, Steven Z. *Dawn Over Suez: The Rise of American Power in the Middle East 1953–1957.* Chicago, 1992.

Gaddis, John Lewis. *Strategies of Containment.* Oxford, 1982.

Gallup, George. *The Gallup Poll: Public Opinion 1935–1971.* Vol. II of 5 vols. New York, 1972.

Geelhoed, E. Bruce. *Charles E. Wilson and Controversy at the Pentagon, 1953 to 1957.* Detroit, 1979.

Goodpaster, Andrew J. *For the Common Defense.* Lexington, 1977.

Gould-Adams, Richard. *John Foster Dulles: A Reappraisal.* New York, 1962.

Graebner, Norman. *The New Isolationism: A Study in Politics and Foreign Policy Since 1950.* New York, 1956.

Greenstein, Fred I. *The Hidden-Hand Presidency: Eisenhower as Leader.* New York, 1982.

Griffith, Robert W., ed. *Ike's Letters to a Friend, 1941–1958*. Lawrence, Kans., 1984.

Guhin, Michael. *John Foster Dulles: A Statesman and His Times*. New York, 1972.

Halperin, Morton H. *Bureaucratic Politics and Foreign Policy*. Washington, D.C., 1974.

Hahn, Peter L. *The United States, Great Britain, and Egypt, 1945–1956: Strategy and Diplomacy in the Early Cold War*. Chapel Hill, 1991.

Henderson, Phillip G. *Managing the Presidency: The Eisenhower Legacy—From Kennedy to Reagan*. Boulder, 1988.

Hill, Jim M. *Suez Crisis, 1956*. Washington, D.C., 1974.

Holbo, Paul S., and Robert W. Sellen, eds. *The Eisenhower Era*. Hinsdale, 1974.

Hoopes, Townsend. *The Devil and John Foster Dulles*. Toronto, 1973.

Horne, Alistair. *Harold Macmillan, 1894–1956*. Vol. I of 2 vols. New York, 1989.

Hudson, Michael. *Arab Politics: The Search for Legitimacy*. New Haven, 1977.

Isaacson, Walter, and Evan Thomas. *The Wise Men: Six Friends and the World They Made*. New York, 1986.

Jackson, Henry M., ed. *The National Security Council: Jackson Subcommittee Papers on Policy-Making at the Presidential Level*. New York, 1965.

Jackson, Robert. *Suez 1956: Operation Musketeer*. London, 1980.

James, Robert R. *Anthony Eden*. 1986.

Jurika, Stephen, ed. *From Pearl Harbor to Vietnam: The Memoirs of Admiral Arthur R. Radford*. Stanford, 1980.

Kaufman, Burton I. *Trade and Aid: Eisenhower's Foreign Economic Policy, 1953–1961*. Baltimore, 1982.

Kinnard, Douglas. *President Eisenhower and Strategy Management*. Lexington, 1977.

———. *The Secretary of Defense*. Lexington, 1980.

Korb, Lawrence. *The Joint Chiefs of Staff*. Bloomington, 1976.

Lacouture, Jean. *Nasser: A Political Biography*. New York, 1973.

Louis, William Roger, and Roger Owen, eds. *Suez 1956: The Crisis and Its Consequences*. Oxford, 1989.

Love, Kennett. *Suez: The Twice Fought War*. New York, 1969.

Love, Robert. *The Chiefs of Naval Operations*. Annapolis, 1980.

Magnus, Ralph H., ed. *Documents on the Middle East*. Washington, D.C., 1969.

Miller, William J. *Henry Cabot Lodge*. New York, 1967.

Millett, Allan R. *Semper Fidelis*. New York, 1980.

Moskin, J. Robert. *The U.S. Marine Corps Story*. New York, 1977.

Mosley, Leonard. *Dulles*. New York, 1978.

Neal, Steve. *The Eisenhowers: Reluctant Dynasty*. New York, 1978.

Neff, Donald. *Warriors at Suez*. New York, 1981.

Neustadt, Richard E. *Presidential Power and the Modern Presidents*. New York, 1990.

Pach, Chester J., Jr., and Elmo Richardson. *The Presidency of Dwight D. Eisenhower*. Lawrence, Kans., 1991.

Parmet, Herbert S. *Eisenhower and the American Crusades.* New York, 1972.

Patterson, Thomas G., ed. *Major Problems In American Foreign Policy Since 1914.* Vol. II of 2 vols. Lexington, Massachusetts, 1989.

Pineau, Christian. *1956 / Suez.* Paris, 1976.

Reichard, Gary W. *The Reaffirmation of Republicanism.* Knoxville, 1975.

Robertson, Terrence. *Crisis: The Inside Story of the Suez Conspiracy.* New York, 1965.

Rubin, Barry. *Paved with Good Intentions: The American Experience in Iran.* New York, 1980.

Rubinstein, Alvin. *Red Star over the Nile.* Princeton, 1977.

Schlesinger, Arthur M., Jr. *The Cycles of American History.* Boston, 1986.

———. *The Imperial Presidency.* Boston, 1973.

Schonfield, Hugh. *The Suez Canal in Peace and War, 1869–1969.* Coral Gables, 1969.

Sherwood, Elizabeth D. *Allies in Crisis.* New Haven, 1990.

Taylor, Maxwell D. *The Uncertain Trumpet.* New York, 1959.

Thomas, Hugh. *Suez.* New York, 1967.

Troen, Selwyn Ilan, and Moshe Shemesh, eds. *The Suez-Sinai Crisis, 1956.* New York, 1990.

Twining, Nathan. *Neither Liberty nor Safety.* New York, 1966.

Vatikiotis, P. *Nasser and His Generation.* New York, 1978.

Watt, Donald C., ed. *Documents on the Suez Crisis.* London, 1957.

Zahniser, Marvin. *Uncertain Friendship.* New York, 1975.

PERIODICALS

Accinelli, Robert. "Eisenhower, Congress, and the 1954–55 Offshore Island Crisis." *Presidential Studies Quarterly,* II (Spring, 1990), 329–48.

Aldrich, Winthrop W. "The Suez Crisis: A Footnote to History." *Foreign Affairs,* XLVI (April, 1967), 541.

Ambrose, Stephen. "The Presidency and Foreign Policy." *Foreign Affairs,* LXX (Winter, 1991/92), 120–37.

Feis, Herbert. "Suez Scenario: A Lamentable Tale." *Foreign Affairs,* XXX (July, 1960), 598–612.

Garrett, William B. "The U.S. Navy's Role in the 1956 Suez Crisis." *Naval War College Review,* XXII (March, 1970), 66–78.

George, Alexander L. "Crisis Management: The Interaction of Political and Military Considerations." *Survival* (September–October, 1984), 225.

Graebner, Norman A. "Eisenhower's Popular Leadership." *Current History,* XXXIX (October, 1960), 230–36, 244.

Greenstein, Fred I. "Eisenhower as an Activist President: A Look at New Evidence." *Political Science Quarterly,* XCIV (Winter, 1979–80), 575–99.

Griffith, Robert. "Dwight D. Eisenhower and the Corporate Commonwealth." *American Historical Review,* LXXXVII (February, 1982), 87–122.

Harlech, Lord. "Suez Snafu, Skybolt Saber." *Foreign Policy,* II (Spring, 1971), 38–50.

Hoxie, R. Gordon. "Eisenhower and Presidential Leadership," *Presidential Studies Quarterly,* XIII (Fall, 1983), 589–612.

———. "The National Security Council." *Presidental Studies Quarterly,* XII (Winter, 1982).

Immerman, Richard H. "Eisenhower and Dulles: Who Made the Decisions." *Political Psychology,* I (Autumn, 1979), 5–19.

McMahon, Robert J. "Eisenhower and Third World Nationalism: A Critique of the Revisionists." *Political Science Quarterly,* CI (1986), 453–73.

Mueller, John E. "Presidential Popularity from Truman to Johnson." *American Political Science Review,* LXIV (March, 1970), 18–34.

Neal, Steve. "Why We Were Right To Like Ike." *American Heritage,* XXXVII (December, 1985), 49–64.

Perlman, M. "Between the Devil and the Deep Red Sea." *Middle Eastern Affairs,* VII (December, 1956), 432–57.

———. "Egypt Versus the Baghdad Pact." *Middle Eastern Affairs,* VII (March, 1956), 95–101.

Reichard, Gary. "Divisions and Dissent: Democrats and Foreign Policy." *Political Science Quarterly,* XCIII (Spring, 1978), 51–72.

Rushkoff, Bennett C. "Eisenhower, Dulles and the Quemoy-Matsu Crisis, 1954–1955." *Political Science Quarterly,* XCVI (Fall, 1981), 465–80.

Sloan, John W. "The Management and Decision-Making Style of President Eisenhower." *Presidential Studies Quarterly,* II (Spring, 1990), 295–313.

Thornton, A. P. "The Trouble with Cousins." *International Journal,* November 2, 1979, pp. 281–86.

"When Trouble Came in the Mediterranean." *U.S. News and World Report,* December 14, 1956, pp. 30–32.

SYMPOSIA

Gettysburg College. The Eisenhower Legacy: A Centennial Symposium. October 10–13, 1990. Gettysburg, Pennsylvania.

U. S. Military Academy Lecture Series and Symposium on the Theory and Practice of American National Security, 1945–1960. Presented in cooperation with the Association of Graduates, USMA, April 21–23, 1982. West Point, N.Y.

DISSERTATIONS

Klingaman, William. "Congress and American Foreign Policy for the Middle East." Ph.D. dissertation, University of Virginia, 1978.

Kunz, Diane B. "The Economic Diplomacy of the Suez Crisis." Ph.D. dissertation, University of North Carolina at Chapel Hill, 1991.

INDEX